面向旅游管理专业英语教材

旅游交际
英语通 第四版

The Way to Communicative Ability in Tourism

初丽岩◎主编

华东师范大学出版社
·上海·

图书在版编目（CIP）数据

旅游交际英语通/初丽岩主编.—4版.—上海:
华东师范大学出版社，2018

　　ISBN 978-7-5675-7753-4

　　Ⅰ.①旅… Ⅱ.①初… Ⅲ.①旅游–英语–口语–自
学参考资料 Ⅳ.①F59

　　中国版本图书馆CIP数据核字（2018）第101831号

旅游交际英语通（第四版）

主　　编　初丽岩
项目编辑　何　晶
特约审读　王　利
责任校对　曹　勇
装帧设计　俞　越

出版发行　华东师范大学出版社
社　　址　上海市中山北路3663号　邮编 200062
网　　址　www.ecnupress.com.cn
电　　话　021-60821666　　行政传真 021-62572105
客服电话　021-62865537　　门市（邮购）电话 021-62869887
地　　址　上海市中山北路3663号华东师范大学校内先锋路口
网　　店　http://hdsdcbs.tmall.com/

印 刷 者　上海华顿书刊印刷有限公司
开　　本　787×1092　16开
印　　张　21.75
字　　数　375千字
版　　次　2020年3月第4版
印　　次　2021年6月第2次
书　　号　ISBN 978-7-5675-7753-4
定　　价　45.00元

出 版 人　王　焰

（如发现本版图书有印订质量问题,请寄回本社客服中心调换或电话021-62865537联系）

FOREWORD 前言（第四版）

当一本书仍在持续重印的时候，修订它是一个很大的挑战，要突破旧版的窠臼有所创新，才能赢得读者的喜爱，才能适应使用者不断发展变化的需求。

本教材第三版修订时，编者们有意识地从文化介绍的角度选择材料、编写教材。贯穿全书的强烈的文化意识是本教材最大的特点。除了旅游预订和入境（Tour Reservation and Arrival）、宾馆住宿（Accommodation）、饮食文化（Food Culture）、观光（Tourist Attractions）、购物（Shopping）以及离境（Departure）外，增加了中国文化瑰宝（Gems of Chinese Culture）一个单元，集中介绍中国文化的精华，涵盖戏剧、武术、中药、风俗礼仪以及传统节日等。

单元按照主题分类，每课则是各单元主题的细分。每课均分为 Part A Conversation、Part B Reading 和 Part C Exercises 三部分。Part A 一般有一到两个对话。对话的内容同主题密切联系，结合语言的灵活性和知识性，旨在以口语形式表现主题，学习者可以拿来即用。Part B 主题阅读，进一步丰富主题，为读者提供覆盖面广泛的素材。Part C 为练习，除了帮助读者内化课文知识外，还补充了 Part A 和 Part B 所未能涵盖的知识和信息，进一步扩展读者的知识面和信息量。全书的最后附有练习答案。

本书第四版在听取广大使用者的建议和意见基础上，将旅游景点介绍部分按照东北、华北、西北、华东、中南、西南六区的区划分布，精简所用的材料，充实了前三版疏漏及一些新开发景点的介绍。

本教材适合做旅游管理专业的英语教材。本教材中的对话由具有十几次旅华经历的 Sherrie Love 女士审读，确保语言真实地道，有效培养学生的会话能力；每课提供的阅读素材可以提高学生的词汇量，培养学生的阅读能力，同时也提供了一定的旅游专业知识以及丰富的文化知识。练习方面也做了相应调整，确保每个单元都有五个以上练习题型，兼顾从口语到语法到信息积累各个方面，力求做到对使用者说、读、译能力的全面操练。

一名导游就是一个文化窗口，一名称职的导游不但要在语言上能够与外国游客进行有效沟通，还应该能够满足游客对中国文化的求知欲。虽然本书编者们尽量做到面面俱到，但鉴于中国文化的博大精深，本书所能提供的材料也只是沧海一粟，期望我们的努力能起到抛砖引玉的作用，激发读者的兴趣，学会查找并利用更多、更新的语料。

编　者
2020年3月

CONTENTS 目录

CONTENTS 目录

CONTENTS 目录

UNIT

UNIT 1
Tour Reservation and Arrival

UNIT 1 — Lesson 1
At the Travel Agency

Part A Conversation

Dialogue — What about a Yangtze Cruise?

(T: Travel Agent   C: Customer)

C: My husband and I are trying to decide where to go for a vacation.

T: There are many choices. Is there anything that interests you?

C: We'd like something romantic.

T: How about a cruise along the Yangtze River in China?

C: That sounds perfect. I'd like to know more about your Yangtze Cruise.

T: Sure. It's really a great deal. Eight days and seven nights for only $3,200 for each couple. It includes all your meals and round-trip air.

C: Indeed, it is a great deal, but my husband always says there's nothing to do on ships.

T: Well, you can tell him about the Royal Star. This ship has a swimming pool, a badminton court and even a gym.

C: Which brochure tells about that?

T: This one right here. And the ship makes several stops.

C: Where?

T: Well, it begins in Wuhan, Hubei Province and then it goes to Wanxian County where you can visit the Minor Three Gorges. Then it takes you to Chongqing, passing through the famous Three Gorges along the way.

C: Sounds great. I will talk it over with my husband.

T: And here is a VCD that you can show him as well.

C: Thanks.

Words and Expressions to Learn

agency / 'eɪdʒənsɪ / *n.* 代理公司,中介

cruise / kruːz / *n.* 乘船游览

vacation / veɪ'keɪʃən / *n.* 假期

royal / 'rɔɪəl / *a.* 皇家的,皇室的

badminton / 'bædmɪntən / *n.* 羽毛球

gym / dʒɪm / *n.* 健身房

brochure / brou'ʃʊr / *n.* 小册子

***　　***　　***　　***　　***　　***

a great deal 很划算

round-trip air 来回机票

tell about 讲述

the Minor Three Gorges 小三峡

talk over 详尽地讨论,商量

Part B　Reading

Passage 1　China Travel Service Overview

Preparation is the key to a successful trip. By planning your visit before you leave, you can greatly reduce the chances of things going wrong.

Before you board a plane, take some time to learn about the political, cultural and economic environment of the country you are traveling to. Try to learn at least a few key phrases in the country's language. When you are traveling, the laws of the country you are visiting apply to you too. Never assume that because you are a foreigner, you are immune to the laws there. In fact as soon as you land in the country you are visiting, you are subject to the country's laws and rules.

One of the best and easiest ways to handle your trip to China is to book it through a China travel service. There can be a lot less trouble than trying to do it alone.

Regardless of whether you book your trip through a China travel service or plan to handle it by yourself, there are a few facts that you should keep in mind about visiting China when planning your trip.

First, be aware that there are many dialects in China. Mandarin (Putonghua) is the official language of China and most of the population of China speaks Mandarin, but if you're planning to go with a China travel service to the southern regions of China you will most likely hear Cantonese.

The currency of China is known as the People's Money or Renminbi. Bank of China is the most common and safest place to make your currency exchanges. Some hotels also have money exchange service. Unlike in some countries, you will receive a better exchange rate for traveler's checks than cash.

When you are traveling in China, it's a good idea to remember that prices can be very different throughout the country. By and large goods are much cheaper in the western than in the eastern regions.

China is full of natural and man-made wonders. Its great rivers include the Yellow River and the Yangtze River. There are also many mountain ranges including the Himalayas and the Kunlun Mountains. Part of the Gobi Desert is located in China's Inner Mongolia. China's most popular man-made wonder is the Great Wall. The Great Wall was built in the 3rd century B.C. (completed in 204 B.C.). It extends for about 1,500 miles from Gansu Province to the Bohai Gulf. The wall averages 20 to 50 feet high and 15 to 25 feet thick. The actual length, including branches, is more than 2,000 miles.

Hong Kong SAR is highly developed, and a popular destination. Macao SAR has well developed tourism. Gambling and tourism are some of the major factors in Macao's economy.

Visitors to China should be aware that Chinese regulations strictly prohibit travel in "closed" areas without special permission. However, over 1,200 cities and areas in China are open to visitors, including most major scenic and historical sites. If you need to know whether an area is open to travel, get advice from the nearest Chinese embassy or consulate, or, if you are already in China, from the U.S. Embassy in Beijing, the nearest U.S. consulate, or the local Chinese public security bureau.

 Words and Expressions to Learn ·······················

board / bɔːd / v. 登上
assume / ə'sjuːm / v. （主观）认为
dialect / 'daɪəlekt / n. 方言
Cantonese / ˌkæntə'niːz / n. 粤语
currency / 'kʌrənsɪ / n. 货币
exchange / ɪks'tʃeɪndʒ / v. n. 兑换

average / 'ævərɪdʒ / v. 平均为
destination / destɪ'neɪʃən / n. 目的地
gambling / 'gæmblɪŋ / n. 赌博
regulation / regjʊ'leɪʃən / n. 规章制度,规定
embassy / 'embəsɪ / n. 大使馆
consulate / 'kɒnsjʊlɪt / n. 领事馆

be the key to 是……的关键   the Himalayas 喜马拉雅山

apply to 适用于   the Gobi Desert 戈壁滩

be immune to 对……有免疫力,不受影响   Inner Mongolia 内蒙古自治区

be subject to 受……支配   Hong Kong SAR 香港特别行政区

regardless of 不管,不顾,不考虑   Macao SAR 澳门特别行政区

keep in mind 记住,牢记   public security bureau 公安局

by and large 大致,总的来说

Passage 2   What to Bring Along

"Lightweight" and "Compact" are two words you should remember when you are deciding what to bring along. China today is well stocked with most daily items. You will have many chances to buy whatever you may need. It would be much better to buy them when you need along the way, than to end up throwing them away because you have too much to carry!

However, there are some things we suggest that you bring from home.

Buy a good backpack and you will never regret. A strong backpack is much easier to carry than a suitcase.

A small shoulder bag is necessary for carrying your camera and other daily items around after you have left your backpack at the hotel or railway station. But do not place valuables in them.

Clothing is inexpensive and one of the best buys in China, so we do not suggest you bring too much from home. Basically you need only two sets of clothes, one to wear while the other set is being washed. Take with you just a couple of shirts, sweaters, and a jacket (depending on the season). These can be worn in layers in case of climatic changes. Dark colored clothing is a better choice because it does not show the dirt.

If you are traveling in north China during winter, prepare yourself for extreme cold. A good down jacket, a hat, mittens and boots are necessary. Besides underwear and rainwear, comfortable socks and hiking boots are also needed.

Bring a good pair of sunglasses, a hat, sunscreen lotion and a water bottle especially when you are traveling in the desert areas or at high altitudes.

Tooth-brush, towel, wet tissue, cold and indigestion medications, lip balm and any other first-aid items you may generally need should be included. If you have to take regular prescription medicines, be sure to bring enough supplies for your trip.

Remember to pack your camera, charger or batteries as well. Note that while print film can be found in most places, slide film may be difficult to find.

Electrical multi adaptor is a must if you plan on bringing electrical appliances. An alarm clock would also be useful.

A China guidebook, a pen and a notebook to keep track of all the exciting things happening on the trip are also "must-brings" on your trip.

Last but not least, DO NOT FORGET your passport, visa, traveler's checks, ATM cards and airline tickets!!

 Words and Expressions to Learn

compact / kəm'pækt / *a.* 紧凑的
item / 'aɪtəm / *n.* 一件（东西）
backpack / 'bækpæk / *n.* 背包
mitten / 'mɪtən / *n.* 手套
altitude / 'æltɪtjuːd / *n.* 高度，海拔
tissue / 'tɪʃuː / *n.* 薄纸，绵纸

indigestion / ˌɪndɪ'dʒestʃən / *n.* 消化不良
medication / medɪ'keɪʃən / *n.* 药物，药剂
first-aid / 'fɜːst'eɪd / *n.* 急救
prescription / prɪ'skrɪpʃən / *n.* 处方
battery / 'bætərɪ / *n.* 电池
appliance / ə'plaɪəns / *n.* 器具，设备

***   ***   ***   ***   ***   ***

be stocked with 供应，提供
end up (doing) 结果，以……而告终
in case of 在……的时候；以防
down jacket 羽绒服
hiking boots 旅游靴
sunscreen lotion 防晒霜

lip balm 润唇膏
print film 负片，胶卷
slide film 幻灯胶卷，彩色反转胶片
electrical multi adaptor 多用电源插头
keep track of 记录
last but not least 最后但并非最不重要的（一点）

Part C Exercises

I. *Make up a brief dialogue according to the given situation.*

You and five other students in your class are planning to book a package tour to somewhere for the National Day holidays. The travel agent suggests Suzhou, but you don't

fancy man-made scenery like gardens. Then he suggests going to Mt. Xiangshan (Mt. Fragrance) in Beijing to enjoy the red maple leaves. All of you think it a good idea and agree to book the tour.

II. *Translate the following dialogue into English.*

—小姐，下午好。

—下午好。我想为父母订一趟包价旅游。

—好的。我们这儿有许多适合中老年人的包价旅游计划。你可以看一下我们的目录（catalogue），看看你对哪个计划比较感兴趣？

—好像大多数团队都是去名山大川的。我父母年纪大了。有没有离上海不远又不必翻山越岭的线路？

—去苏州怎么样？他们可以参观园林。

—他们去那儿好几次了。他们的确对历史和古建筑感兴趣。

—有了。那就去安徽宏村吧。那儿离上海六个半小时的车程，又有徽商古建筑可看。这是今年最热门的线路之一。

—听起来不错。就订它吧。

—好。请填一下这张表格。

III. *Fill in the blanks with the phrases in the list. Change the form where necessary.*

be immune to	regardless of	by and large	be subject to
be stocked with	end up	in case of	keep in mind

1. They made up their minds to go on with the plan _____ all possible difficulties.

2. You'd better take an umbrella _____ rain.

3. _____, the people there are very friendly to foreigners.

4. He was always late for work and _____ losing his job.

5. Every piece of luggage _____ X-ray screening at the airport.

6. Though very small, the store _____ almost anything we might need.

7. _____ the suggestions I have just made, and you will surely have a nice trip.

8. He seems to _____ the influence of modern fashion and always wears old-fashioned clothes.

IV. Choose the best answer for each of the following.

1. If you want a smooth trip to China, the best way is to _____.
   A. book a package tour with a Chinese travel agency
   B. learn the Chinese language though it is a very difficult task
   C. study the laws of China and obey them when you are there
   D. plan it carefully before setting off

2. What can we learn from the statement "Unlike in some countries, you will receive a better exchange rate for traveler's checks than cash"?
   A. You can get the best exchange rate for traveler's checks in China throughout the world.
   B. There is a higher exchange rate for traveler's checks in China than in other countries.
   C. In China, your traveler's checks are worth more than the cash of the same face value.
   D. China is more willing to accept foreign currencies in cash than to take traveler's checks.

3. Which of the following is NOT TRUE according to Reading Passage 1?
   A. The Yellow River, the Yangtze River, the Great Wall, the Himalayas, the Gobi Desert are all among China's world famous natural wonders.
   B. The economy of Macao SAR heavily depends on gambling and tourism.
   C. Tourists are not allowed to go everywhere they want to visit in China.
   D. The best place for a traveler to exchange his money is in Bank of China.

4. When travelers break a certain law of China, they will be _____.
   A. sent back to their home country immediately
   B. on trial and sentenced according to the Chinese laws
   C. judged by their home country's embassy or consulate in China
   D. forgiven and released as free people since they don't know the Chinese laws

5. Which of the following statements can best summarize Reading Passage 2?
   A. Packing is an art because not everyone knows what he should pack before traveling.
   B. Traveling to China, you needn't pack clothes because clothes are cheaper and better there.
   C. The best way is to pack as much as possible with some items necessary but not found in China.
   D. Pack as lightly as possible and pack differently according to the seasons and the regions you are traveling to in China.

V. Topics for discussion.

1. Which is your favorite way of traveling, package tour or independent traveling? Why?
2. Comment on the packing tips listed in Reading Passage 2. What other tips can you provide?

UNIT 1 Lesson 2
Ticket Reservation and in Flight

Part A Conversation

Dialogue 1   Flying Out of Hongqiao or Pudong?

(A: Reservation Agent   C: Customer)

C: Hello. I need to get to Beijing the day after tomorrow by noon. And I'd like to book a ticket on the 8:15 flight from Hongqiao International Airport.

A: I'm afraid that our flights from Hongqiao International Airport are all full.

C: Oh, no. Do you fly out of Pudong International Airport?

A: Yes, we do. Just a moment, please.

There is a 9:00 flight out of Pudong. It flies about one and a half hours and gets to the Capital Airport at 10:30.

C: I'll have to take it. The last name is Howard. H—O—W—A—R—D. The first name, Fred.

A: All right, Mr. Howard. You are confirmed on China Eastern Flight MU1234 departing from Pudong International Airport at 9:00 March 18. We will send the ticket to your place within 12 hours. What is your address, please?

C: No. 3663 North Zhongshan Road.

A: No. 3663 North Zhongshan Road. Good. Anything else I can do for you, Sir?

C: No, that is all. Thank you.

A: Thank you for flying China Eastern.

Dialogue 2   What Can I Do for You?

(A: Flight Attendant   P: Passenger)

(A passenger pushed the overhead call button asking for help.)

A: Yes, Sir. What can I do for you?

P: Can I have a cup of hot water?

A: Sure. (Leaves and soon returns with a cup of hot water.) Here you are, Sir.

Oh, you look rather pale. Are you feeling OK?

P: Not really. I am feeling dizzy and sick.

A: It must be airsickness. Is this your first time to fly?

P: Yes.

A: We have some pills to make you feel better. Do you want one?

P: Hmm, no, thank you. I will be fine in a minute.

A: Are you sure?

P: Yes. Thank you.

A: OK. By the way, there is a waterproof paper bag you can use in the pocket in front of you, and if you do need our help, just push the button again.

P: OK. Thank you very much.

 Words and Expressions to Learn ···

reservation / ˌrezəˈveɪʃən / *n.* 预订   dizzy / ˈdɪzɪ / *a.* 头晕目眩的
confirm / kənˈfɜːm / *v.* 确定，核实   airsickness / ˈeəsɪknəs / *n.* 晕机
depart / dɪˈpɑːt / *v.* 离开   pill / pɪl / *n.* 药丸

***　　***　　***　　***　　***　　***

in a minute 片刻，一会儿   by the way 顺便说一句

Part **B** Reading

 Passage 1 | Safety Tips for Air Travel

A safe flight can begin as early as booking your flight. Facts have shown that non-stop flights if possible are the way to go; 79.9% of all airline accidents occur during the takeoff and landing of a flight.

Allow extra time for special situations. During busy periods, or when traveling with young children, babies, elderly or disabled passengers, you'd better build in more time.

Keep your photo identification ready. If you don't have a photo ID, make sure you have two pieces of identification, one of which must be issued by the government. Children under 18 are not required to have identification. Failure to have proper identification may result in additional security check. Some airlines may forbid you from boarding without proper ID. For international flight, airlines are required to collect your full name and ask you for a contact name and phone number.

Beware of unattended packages. If you see an unattended package or bag at the airport, report it to the airport security people.

Know what you are carrying. Watch your bags while you are at the airport and don't accept packages from strangers. Be prepared to answer questions about who packed your bags and whether you might have left them unattended at any time. Think carefully and answer honestly — history has shown that criminals and terrorists use passengers to carry bombs or other dangerous items on board, either by tricking passengers into carrying packages or by simply putting items into unwatched bags. If you have doubts, say so.

Humor is not always good. Don't joke about having a bomb or guns. Security staff are trained to react when they hear these words. Punishment can be harsh, and can include the possibility of time in prison and/or fines.

Expect to have your bags searched. Both carry-on and checked bags are subject to being hand-searched, especially when airline security staff cannot decide what is in a package by X-ray. Don't wrap up your gifts until after you arrive at your destination. Airline security staff will open it if X-rays are unable to make out its contents.

Leave your dangerous goods at home. There are many dangerous goods that are not allowed on the aircraft. Don't pack nor carry guns, fireworks, flammable materials, household cleansers. Breaking the dangerous materials regulations can lead to harsh punishment.

After boarding the plane, follow the suggestions listed below.

Pay attention as you enter the aircraft, and know where your exits are. Count the rows of seats to the nearest exits. Your closest exit could be right behind you.

Read the safety card and pay attention as you follow along with the flight attendant's safety demonstration. As you listen, imagine yourself going through the motion. Remember the information in the safety cards can save your life.

Know your responsibilities. If you are seated next to an emergency exit, you may have to open it after you have decided that it is safe to do so. You need both physical power and a cool head.

Do not self medicate. Many people will use tranquilizer or drink heavily before the take-off; this slows down thinking and won't help anything. If you have motion sickness problems, take your medicine in time so it will have the greatest effect during the flight.

During a flight, keep your seat belt fastened and keep movement around the plane to a minimum.

Dress properly. What you wear can also affect your chance of survival in an emergency. Do not wear shorts and try not to wear short sleeves. Also wear hard-soled shoes, not sandals. Do not wear synthetic material; it will melt under high heat. Women should not wear pantyhose.

 Words and Expressions to Learn ·

identification / aɪˌdentɪfɪˈkeɪʃən / n. 身份证明
unattended / ˌʌnəˈtendɪd / a. 无人照管的
criminal / ˈkrɪmɪnəl / n. 罪犯
terrorist / ˈterərɪst / n. 恐怖分子
wrap / ræp / v. 包装
flammable / ˈflæməbl / a. 易燃的
cleanser / ˈklenzə / n. 清洁剂
demonstration / demənˈstreɪʃən / n. 演示

medicate / ˈmedɪkeɪt / v. 用药
tranquilizer / ˈtrænkwɪlaɪzə / n. 镇静剂
survival / səˈvaɪvəl / n. 存活
hard-soled / ˈhɑːdsəuld / a. 硬底的
sandal / ˈsændəl / n. 凉鞋，拖鞋
synthetic / sɪnˈθetɪk / a. 合成的，人造的
pantyhose / ˈpæntɪhəuz / n. 连裤袜

***　　***　　***　　***　　***　　***

build in 使……成为组成部分
result in 导致，引起
beware of 当心，谨防
trick sb. into doing 骗某人做某事
carry-on and checked bags 携带行李和托

运行李
make out 辨认出
emergency exit 紧急出口
motion sickness problems 晕动症
keep ... to a minimum 使……保持在最低量

Passage 2   Safety Demonstration

Ladies and gentlemen:

Welcome aboard XXX Airlines Flight YYY.

Now we request your full attention as the flight attendants demonstrate the safety features of this aircraft.

When the seat belt sign is on, you must fasten your seat belt. Put the metal pieces one into the other, and tighten by pulling on the loose end of the strap. To loosen your seat belt, lift the upper part of the buckle. We suggest that you keep your seat belt fastened throughout the flight, as we may experience turbulence.

There are several emergency exits on this aircraft: two forward, two aft, and one over each wing. Please take a few moments now to find the nearest exit. During evacuation, don't carry any of your belongings with you. The floor and the exits are clearly marked.

The oxygen mask is in the compartment above your seat. In the event of emergency, the mask will drop in front of you automatically. Pull the mask towards you to start the flow of oxygen, and place it firmly over your nose and mouth, secure the elastic band behind your head, and breathe normally. If you are traveling with a child or someone who requires assistance, please attend to yourself first, and then the other person.

The following electronic devices: calculators, CD players, laptop computers, may be used when the seat belt sign is off. Any electronic device operating with an antenna must be turned off at all times.

We remind you that this is a non-smoking flight. Tampering with, disabling, or destroying the smoke detectors located in the WCs is forbidden by law.

The safety information card in the seat pocket in front of you contains additional information. Please read it carefully before take-off.

Thank you and wish you an enjoyable flight.

 Words and Expressions to Learn ·

strap / stræp / n. 带子，皮带   buckle / ˈbʌkl / n. 扣环，搭扣

turbulence / 'tɜːbjʊləns / *n.* 湍流，气流

aft / ɑːft / *ad.* 在机尾

evacuation / ɪˌvækjʊˈeɪʃən / *n.* 撤离

compartment / kəmˈpɑːtmənt / *n.* 小间，车厢

elastic / ɪˈlæstɪk / *a.* 有弹力的

device / dɪˈvaɪs / *n.* 设备，仪器

antenna / ænˈtenə / *n.* 天线

*** *** *** *** *** ***

in the event of 如果，在……情况下

attend to 照顾，照料

tamper with 擅自乱动，捣弄

smoke detector 烟雾探测器

(be) located in 位于

Part  Exercises

I. *Make up a brief dialogue between a customer and a ticket agent according to the given situation.*

You and your parents plan to fly to Kunming for the May Day holidays. You phone a ticket agent to book three round-trip tickets from Shanghai for April 30. The agent tells you all the flights for that day are full and suggests reservation for May 4. The fare is much lower then. But you don't want it since it will be a too short stay in Kunming.

II. *Complete the dialogue by translating the Chinese sentences into English.*

— Hello. Shanghai Airlines. Can I help you?

— Hello. 1. _____ (我想订十五张去青岛的机票).

— For what day?

— Next Friday, May 26.

— OK. Round-trip or one way?

— 2. _____ (十张往返，五张单程票). And we'd like to fly out of Hongqiao International Airport because we are a big group and we also have a child with us.

— A child? How old is it? 3. _____ (如果是十二岁以下只需付儿童折扣票价就行了).

— It's eighteen months old. How about that?

— Oh, it's an infant. 4. _____ (你只要支付成人票价的10%就可以了).

— Wow, that's really cheap. 5. _____ (那么我们买这么多张机票，成人票有折

扣吗)?

— Er, let me see. 6. _____ (我可以给你七折,可以吗)?

— 7. _____ (可以再低一点吗)?

— I'm afraid that is the lowest I can offer.

— 8. _____ (那好吧。你们什么时候能把票送来)?

— Within 24 hours. 9. _____ (我需要你们所有人的姓名和身份证号码).

— Oh, that's a lot of work. 10. _____ (我用传真发给你好吗)?

— Fine. Good-bye.

— Bye-bye.

III. *Decide whether the following statements are true or false according to the Reading Passages.*

1. Non-stop flight is the only safe way of air travel because air crashes happen at the takeoff and landing of the plane.

2. When you find an unattended package at the airport, you should look after it until its owner returns to it.

3. You'd better take good care of your bags all the time because someone may steal them.

4. Passengers don't have to fasten their seat belts when the sign is off.

5. Passengers should leave their luggage behind when evacuating the plane in an emergency.

6. You must know where the oxygen mask is kept so that you can pull it down when needed.

7. When in an emergency, a passenger should take care of himself and then try to help the other people including his own children.

8. No electronic devices are allowed to be used during the flight.

9. It's against the law to smoke on a non-smoking flight.

10. What kind of clothes you wear can sometimes decide whether or not you will stay alive in an air accident.

IV. *Answer the following questions about the Reading Passages.*

1. What will happen if I don't have proper identification at the check-in counter?

2. When will the security personnel hand search the passengers' bags?

3. Why should the passengers not wrap their gifts before arriving at the destination?

4. Why is it better to keep your seat belt fastened throughout the flight?

5. Where can passengers find more safety information on a plane?

6. Retell the safety suggestions for passengers on a plane.

V. *Topics for discussion.*

1. Most airlines now sell electronic tickets. What are their advantages and disadvantages?
2. Do you think it right to severely punish a passenger joking about having a bomb? Why?
3. Why should a passenger take a few moments to locate the nearest emergency exit?
4. What do you think of the suggestion given in the safety demonstration that a passenger should look after himself/herself and then help the others including children in an emergency on a flight?

UNIT **1** Lesson 3
Customs Inspection

Part **A** *Conversation*

Dialogue **No Food, Please.**

(O: Customs Officer   T: Traveler)

O: May I see your passport, please?

T: Here is my passport. And this is the customs declaration form.

O: What is the purpose of your visit to China?

T: Business. I have a meeting to attend in Guangzhou.

O: This visa is good for two weeks. Do you plan to stay longer than that?

T: No. I will fly back twelve days from now.

O: And you will do some traveling while you are here?

T: Yes. I want to spend a couple of days in Kunming. I have some friends there to visit.

O: What do you have in that bag, Sir?

T: Just my cameras, my clothes and some books.

O: You're not carrying any food with you today?

T: No.

O: Okay, Mr. Johnson. This is just a routine check. Would you mind opening the bag for me?

T: All right.

O: Hmm. You have three cameras. Are you a photographer?

T: My company makes cameras. I'm also a photographer, but two of these are for display.

O: I see. And what's in this bag?

T: Egg tarts.

O: I thought you said you didn't bring any food today.

T: When you asked me, I thought you meant vegetables and meat and things like that.

O: I'm sorry, Mr. Johnson. Egg tarts are food, too. We will have to confiscate them.

T: Confiscate?

O: Yes. We will have to get rid of them.

T: That's too bad. They are very delicious.

O: I know. But I'm sorry, we can't allow them in.

T: Oh, well. That's OK.

O: Enjoy your visit to China, Mr. Johnson.

T: Thank you.

 Words and Expressions to Learn

routine / ruːˈtiːn / *a.* 例行的   confiscate / ˈkɒnfɪskeɪt / *v.* 没收
photographer / fəˈtɒɡrəfə / *n.* 摄影师

***   ***   ***   ***   ***   ***

egg tart 蛋挞   customs declaration form 报关表

Part B Reading

 Passage 1 | Passport and Visa

A valid passport is required to enter China. China does not allow entrance if the holder's passport expires in less than six months; returning home with an expired passport is against the law, and may result in a fine.

The passport will contain the following personal information: passport number, surname, first name(s), date of birth, place of birth, gender, validity, photograph, signature. The personal information, photograph and signature are all on a certain page of the passport. The page is in two parts. The lower part has two lines of print which can be read by special passport reading equipment. All the information on the page can also be read by the human eye. There is no hidden information and there will be no way of adding information to the page after the passport has been issued.

Passports are also needed as it will be the most important means of identification. You will have to show them when you cash traveler's checks, make plane or train reservations, exchange money or prove your identity.

There must be at least one totally blank page in the passport to be used as a visa page. Single or double entry visa requires a passport valid for at least 6 months. For multiple entry visas, a passport should be valid for at least 9 months.

Traveling in China requires a tourism visa (L). L Visa is divided into two kinds: group visa and individual visa. If you are a part of a group, the tour operator will often help to get it. Group visas will usually be issued for groups with at least 5 members, and the guide of your group will keep the visas.

An individual traveler can apply for one at any Chinese embassy or consulate, and the procedure is usually simple.

Foreigners who want to stay in China longer than what their visa allows need to apply for an extension to their visa with proper reasons.

The extension application should be made at the public security bureau seven days before the visa expires. Multiple entry visas cannot be extended.

 Words and Expressions to Learn ·

valid / ˈvælɪd / *a.* 有效的，在有效期内的

identity / aɪˈdentɪtɪ / *n.* 身份

expire / ɪkˈspaɪə / *v.* 到期，期满

entry / ˈentrɪ / *n.* 进入

surname / ˈsɜːneɪm / *n.* 姓氏

multiple / ˈmʌltɪpl / *a.* 多次的

gender / ˈdʒendə / *n.* 性别

procedure / prəˈsiːdʒə / *n.* 手续，步骤

signature / ˈsɪgnətʃə / *n.* 签名

extension / ɪkˈstenʃən / *n.* 延期

issue / ˈɪsjuː / *v.* 颁发，发给

***   ***   ***   ***   ***   ***

apply for 申请

Passage 2   Customs Regulations

Chinese border crossings are generally very easy. All visitors entering China must fill out customs declaration forms upon arrival. The departure copy will be put in your passport and you must show it as you leave China.

Each passenger is allowed to carry a camera, a tape recorder, a small movie camera, a video camera, and a word processor. If a passenger carries more than these, he or she should make declaration to the customs. Passengers should bring what they have brought with them back on their departure with the permission of the customs.

Passengers with gold, silver, and articles made of these metals, each more than 50 grams, should make declaration to the customs, and should carry them out of China. Gold, silver, and their products bought from fixed shops shall be allowed out of China by the customs after examination of the Special Receipts issued by the People's Bank of China.

If passengers coming to China with cultural relics want to carry the relics out of the country, they should make a clear declaration to the customs. Passengers could carry out the relics bought in China with the appraisal by the Chinese Administrative Department for Cultural Relics. When cultural relics leave the country, the customs shall examine the export permit from these departments and the appraisal marks put on the relics. Passengers trying to carry cultural relics out of the country without declaring them to the customs may face criminal charge.

The following articles are not allowed to be brought into China:

1. Weapons, imitation weapons, ammunition, and explosives;

2. Fake money and securities;

3. Printed matter, records, films, audio and video recordings, laser discs, computer storage media and other articles containing materials regarded as harmful to China politically, economically, culturally, or ethically;

4. Deadly poisons and other narcotics;

5. Dangerous bacteria and harmful animals, plants, and their products;

6. Food, drugs, and other articles from epidemic-stricken areas if such articles may be harmful to human beings and animals.

Articles that may not be taken out of China:

1. All articles mentioned above;

2. Printed matter, photos, records, films, audio and video recordings, laser discs, computer storage media and similar articles if they contain state secrets;

3. Cultural relics and relics not allowed to exit;

4. Endangered and protected animals and plants (including specimens), their seeds and breeding materials.

 Words and Expressions to Learn

relic / 'relɪk / *n.* 古董，遗物
appraisal / ə'preɪzəl / *n.* 鉴定
imitation / ɪmɪ'teɪʃən / *n.* 仿真
ammunition / æmjʊ'nɪʃən / *n.* 弹药
explosive / ɪk'spləʊsɪv / *n.* 爆炸物
securities / sɪ'kjʊərɪtɪz / *n.* （复数）证券

ethically / 'eθɪklɪ / *ad.* 在伦理道德方面
narcotic / nɑː'kɒtɪk / *n.* 毒品
bacteria / bæk'tɪərɪə / *n.* （复数）细菌
endangered / ɪn'deɪndʒəd / *a.* 濒危的
specimen / 'spesəmən / *n.* 标本
breeding / 'briːdɪŋ / *n.* 繁殖

***   ***   ***   ***   ***   ***

word processor 文字处理器
the Chinese Administrative Department for
   Cultural Relics 中国文物管理局

the export permit 出口许可证
criminal charge 刑事诉讼
epidemic-stricken area 疫区

Part  Exercises

I. *Make up a brief dialogue according to the given situation.*

> Mr. Brown from Australia is going through the customs at Shanghai Pudong International Airport. He comes to visit his son who works in a big company in Shanghai. The customs officer checks his passport and visa and reminds him that the validity of the visa is only 3 months and if he wants to overstay, he should apply for extension in advance. The officer also asks him to open his bag for a routine check. The officer finds a box with a small lizard（蜥蜴）in it. Mr. Brown tells the officer it is a gift for his grandson Alex. The officer says that Mr. Brown has to say goodbye to it since it is not allowed into China.

II. *Translate into English the following dialogue between a customs officer and a traveler.*

> — 下午好。可以看一下你的护照吗？
> — 当然。给你。

— 你是到中国来旅游的吗?

— 是的。我要在上海等我们的旅行团。他们现在在北京。

— 哦。你的签证有效期为一个月。你们的旅行将持续多久呢?

— 大概二十天左右。

— 请把这个包打开一下,好吗?我们需要做一下例行检查。

— 好吧。只是些衣服和日用品。绝对没有武器和毒品。

— 有什么要报关的吗?

— 没有。

— 好的。你可以过境了。祝你在中国过得愉快。

— 谢谢。再见。

III. *Choose the best answer for each of the following.*

1. You will find all the information on a passport EXCEPT _____.
   A. the holder's family name and given name
   B. when and where the holder was born
   C. age of the passport owner
   D. how long the passport will remain valid

2. Passport is very important to anyone traveling in another country mainly because _____
   A. it shows the identity of the traveler
   B. it is needed when the holder exchanges money at the bank of another country
   C. the holder has to show it when checking in at a hotel
   D. it proves that the traveler is a foreigner and needs special treatment

3. Which of the following is NOT TRUE about visa extension?
   A. The person needs to have convincing reasons to apply.
   B. The traveler has to apply 7 days before the visa expires.
   C. The visa holder has to have a single or multiple entry visa.
   D. The public security bureau has the right to approve visa extension.

4. According to the customs regulations, visitors entering China should _____.
   A. fill out customs declaration forms for everything they carry along if they want to bring them back home after the visit
   B. get permission of the customs if they want to bring back whatever they have brought into China
   C. get special permit from China when carrying cultural relics into China or they will be heavily fined
   D. make declarations to the customs when they bring relics into China or they will have to leave them behind at departure

5. Which of the following is NOT among the items not allowed to be brought into China?

    A. Fireworks used for celebrations.

    B. Toy guns made like real ones.

    C. Music CDs and classic novels.

    D. Drugs used to kill mice and insects (昆虫).

IV. *Topics for discussion.*

1. Why are imitation weapons not allowed brought into our country?

2. Why should a foreign traveler have proper reasons to apply for visa extension?

3. Many Chinese people including many students have experienced refusal to their visa application. What do you think are the most common reasons?

UNIT 2
Accommodation

UNIT 2 Lesson 4
Room Reservation

Part A *Conversation*

Dialogue 1 Reserving a Room on the Phone

(R: Hotel Receptionist   G: Guest)

R: Hello. Shanghai Peace Hotel. Can I help you?

G: Yes. I am calling to book a room for the week of August 6.

R: OK. What kind of room do you want, Sir? We have singles, doubles, suites and deluxe suites in different styles.

G: I'm traveling alone, so a single room will do.

R: Fine. We still have Bund-view rooms available.

G: Are they the same price?

R: No. They are $110 a night, and other rooms are $80.

G: I'll take a room without the Bund-view then. Do you have a special price for this low season?

R: The prices I have just quoted are already the low season prices.

G: That's fine. Can I hold the reservation with a credit card?

R: Sure. Can I have the last name on the card, please?

G: It's Jackson. J—A—C—K—S—O—N. The visa card number is 9876–5432–1023–4567.

R: The expiration date, please?

G: October 20, 2020.

R: Thank you, Sir. You have successfully reserved a single room without the Bund-view at Peace Hotel for the week of August 6 at the price of $80 a night.

G: That's right. Thank you. Bye-bye.

R: Good-bye.

Dialogue 2   May I Suggest Another Hotel?

R: Good morning. Shangri-La Hotel Beijing. Can I help you?

G: Morning. I'd like to book five double rooms with twin beds and shower.

R: For which dates?

G: From October 1 all the way to the 15.

R: I am sorry, but our double rooms are fully booked for those days.

G: Are you sure?

R: Absolutely.

G: How come?

R: October 1 to the 7 is our National Day holiday, and October is a peak season for traveling in Beijing. But we still have single rooms available.

G: Oh, we don't want to live in separate rooms since we are five couples.

R: I see. May I suggest Beijing International Hotel?

G: Ah, you are really considerate. Could you please tell me their telephone number?

R: Sure. It is 12345678.

G: I'll have a try. Thank you very much.

R: You are always welcome. Good luck.

G: Good-bye.

 Words and Expressions to Learn

suite / swiːt / *n.* 套房

deluxe / dɪˈlʌks / *a.* 豪华的

quote / kwəʊt / *v.* 报价

expiration / ekspɪˈreɪʃən / *n.* 失效, 到期

considerate / kənˈsɪdərət / *a.* 周到的

***   ***   ***   ***   ***   ***

Bund-view room 可看到外滩的观景房

low season 淡季

double room with twin beds 有两张床的双人房间

Shangri-La Hotel Beijing 北京香格里拉大酒店

How come? 怎么会?/为什么？

peak season 旺季

Part B Reading

Hotels worldwide use the star rating system to describe the nature of their services. Generally this star rating is done by an external organization. But even when it is not the case, hotels have taken to describing their service in terms of this system.

One-star hotels meet a traveler's basic needs for comfort and convenience. They tend to be located near major attractions or main streets and provide clean guest rooms. Many hotels do not have a restaurant on site but are usually located within walking distance of restaurants.

Two-star hotels meet a traveler's basic needs for comfort and convenience while offering some aesthetic improvements in the grounds, room décor, and quality of furnishings. Some may offer limited restaurant service, however room service is usually not provided.

Three-star hotels are usually large enough to offer greater quality facilities and services than the lower star hotels. Reception and other public areas are larger and the restaurant will serve both hotel guests and non-guests. All bedrooms will have bathrooms and will offer a good standard of comfort and equipment, such as a hair dryer, direct dial telephone, toiletries, etc. There will most likely be some room service and some services for business travelers.

Four-star hotels include a degree of luxury and quality in the furnishings, décor and equipment in all areas of the hotel. Rooms will be larger than in the lower star hotels, and will have well designed furnishings and décor. The bathrooms will probably have both bath and shower. Services will include doorman, 24-hour room service, laundry and dry-cleaning, sports, etc. The restaurants will provide very good food.

Five-star hotels offer spacious and luxurious rooms with its quality and attention to detail. Interior design should be both comfortable and elegant. Furnishings should be perfect. Services should be formal, well organized and pay every attention to guests' needs. There will be a number of restaurants and they will display a high level of skill in producing dishes to the highest international standards. Facilities will be extensive and will include pool, gym, business center, banquet and conference rooms, shops, salons, etc.

 Words and Expressions to Learn

rating / ˈreɪtɪŋ / *n.* 排名，品级

external / ɪkˈstɜːnəl / *a.* 外部的，行业外的

convenience / kənˈviːnɪəns / *n.* 方便，便利

aesthetic / esˈθetɪk / *a.* 美学的，审美的

décor / ˈdeɪkɔːr / *n.* 室内装饰，布置

furnishings / ˈfɜːnɪʃɪŋz / *n.* 固定设备，家具

toiletries / ˈtɔɪlətrɪz / *n.* 盥洗用具

luxury / ˈlʌkʃərɪ / *n.* 豪华，奢侈

laundry / ˈlɔːndrɪ / *n.* 洗衣房，待洗的衣服

spacious / ˈspeɪʃəs / *a.* 宽敞的

luxurious / lʌgˈzjʊərɪəs / *a.* 豪华的，奢侈的

interior / ɪnˈtɪərɪə / *a.* 内部的

banquet / ˈbæŋkwɪt / *n.* 宴会

conference / ˈkɒnfərəns / *n.* 会议

salon / ˈsælɒn / *n.* 沙龙；美发厅

***   ***   ***   ***   ***   ***

take to 喜欢上

on site 在现场

Hotels work hard as a rule to earn and keep high ratings, but such classifications are based on many values, not all of which may necessarily be important to each and every guest. The classifications are the opinion of a classifier which may be the tourist office of a nation, a hotel association, an auto club, a guide book publisher, etc.

Hotels, for example, are rated on their amenities and recreational facilities, not just rooms. Among criteria used are size of rooms, décor/furnishings, public areas, hospitality services, staff attitudes, housekeeping, sanitary standards, etc. For example, a hotel with luxurious rooms can still receive a lower rating because its restaurants don't serve three meals a day, or the hotel doesn't have a restaurant open all year.

Hotel meals are often more expensive, and if you're going to be eating out most of the time, the hotel's restaurant may not be important to you. But they can play an important role in the hotel's classification. In the same vein, if you're not likely to use a golf course, tennis courts, or other hotel amenities, you might not want to take this factor into consideration when planning your accommodations. Similarly, why pay for

24-hour room service when you're not likely to use that service.

Internationally, classifications tend to be similar around the world, but different meanings may apply to the same words. The word "deluxe" generally means the best, but the characteristics that are included in the best may not be the same in different countries. First-class usually suggests top-grade, certainly including a bathroom. But travelers in other parts of the world may be more impressed with other aspects of a room, such as the charm and elegance of décor and furnishings than with such a functional quality as a bath fixture .

Your best course of action is to zero in on what you want from a hotel. It may well be that your desires are more easily satisfied than you realize, which can mean saving some money. If you use a travel agent, ask what the classification, if any, used for hotels in your itinerary really mean. Don't just accept the descriptions in brochures and ads.

You can also contact the tourist office of the city/state/country and try to learn more about the rating system and a certain hotel. Generally, there are three base terms: deluxe, first-class, and tourist/standard/economy/budget , with sub-categories in each section. It's quite possible, if you're aware of some of the finer points, not to find any great difference except when it's time to open your wallet/purse at check-out time.

 Words and Expressions to Learn ·

classification / klæsɪfɪˈkeɪʃən / *n.* 分类，划分
amenity / əˈmenətɪ / *n.* 便利设施
recreational / rekrɪˈeɪʃənəl / *a.* 娱乐的
criteria / kraɪˈtɪərɪə / *n.* 标准
hospitality / hɒspɪˈtælətɪ / *n.* 热情，好客
sanitary / ˈsænɪtərɪ / *a.* 卫生的

aspect / ˈæspekt / *a.* 方面
fixture / ˈfɪkstʃə / *n.* 固定装置
itinerary / aɪˈtɪnərərɪ / *n.* 行程安排
budget / ˈbʌdʒɪt / *a.* 经济的，节俭的
fine / faɪn / *a.* 细微的

***   ***   ***   ***   ***   ***

as a rule 通常，一般来说
in the same vein 与此相似，同样道理

take ... into consideration 把……考虑进去
zero in on 把注意力集中在……上

Part  Exercises

I. Make up a dialogue according to the given situation.

> You and five other students in your class are going to travel to Qingdao during the May Day holidays. Now you are calling a local hotel to reserve 6 single rooms. Because it is a peak season, all single rooms are fully booked. The receptionist offers 3 double rooms with twin beds. But you are 3 boys and 3 girls and it is not convenient to use double rooms. Then the receptionist suggests a nearby hotel and gives you a telephone number.

II. Complete the following dialogue.

— Holiday Inn Hotel. 1. _____ ?

— Yes. Do you have a room available for 5 nights from the 10th?

— Yes. 2. _____ ?

— I'd like a double room, please.

— 3. _____ ?

— I prefer shower.

— No problem.

— 4. _____ ?

— It's $80 a night.

— 5. _____ . Do you have anything less expensive?

— No, Sir. 6. _____ left for those days.

— All right. I guess I will have to take it.

— 7. _____ ?

— It's Stein, Edward Stein.

— OK, Mr. Stein. 8. _____ ?

— By credit card.

— 9. _____ ?

— Sure. It's 9876—5432—1098—76.

— Thank you, Mr. Stein. 10. _____ ?

— Nothing else. Good-bye.

III. *Translate the following sentences into English.*

1. 您要单人房还是双人房？
2. 您想要一间带浴缸的还是带淋浴的房间？
3. 我想要一间朝向花园的有两张床的双人房间。
4. 这是明天最便宜的豪华套房了。
5. 我明天什么时间可以登记入住？

IV. *Answer the following questions according to the passages.*

1. What is the most important difference between three-star hotels and lower star hotels?
2. Say something about the characteristics of five star hotels.
3. What are the criteria used in classifying hotels according to Reading Passage 2?
4. What is the most important factor to consider when I am looking for a hotel?
5. When you are booking a hotel in another country, what facts do you have to remember?
6. What does the last sentence in Reading Passage 2 imply?

V. *Topics for discussion.*

1. In the past twenty years or so, a large number of five star hotels have been built in China. Comment on this phenomenon.
2. When you go traveling, what kind of hotel would you prefer? Why?

UNIT 2 Lesson 5
Registration and Room Services

Part A *Conversation*

Dialogue 1   Can We Change Our Room?

(R: Hotel Receptionist   G: Guest)

R: What can I do for you, Sir?

G: I'd like to check in.

R: Do you have a reservation?

G: Yes. I made the reservation two weeks ago. The last name is Leonard.

R: Just a minute, please. Let me check. Yes, Mr. Leonard. You have reserved a double room for five nights. Is that right?

G: Yes. But we'd prefer a change to a suite if possible.

R: One moment, please. I think we can arrange that. But could I have a look at your passports, please?

G: Certainly. Here they are.

R: Good. Do you mind filling out the room change form?

G: Not at all. (Minutes later.) Here you are.

R: Thank you. Your suite is on the 10th floor, Room 1001. Here is your key.

G: Thank you. By the way, how much is the suite?

R: It's 720 *yuan* per night.

G: OK. Good-bye.

R: Bye-bye, and enjoy your stay.

(R: Hotel Receptionist　G: Guest)

R: Front desk. Can I help you?

G: Hello. I'd like to know how I can make local calls from my room.

R: Just dial 9 and wait for the dial tone, then dial the number you want.

G: OK. And what about an international call to New York?

R: Dial 9, then 001. That's the number for the United States. Then dial the area code for New York, which is 212, and finally dial the number you want.

G: That is very simple and convenient. Thank you.

R: It's my pleasure.

G: Oh, by the way, how am I supposed to pay for the calls I make?

R: Don't worry. They will be charged to your room.

G: Oh, there is another thing. My husband and I really want to get up early enough to take a walk along the Bund. So we need an early morning call tomorrow. Can you arrange that?

R: Certainly, Madam. What time would you like to get the call?

G: 5:30, please.

R: OK. Would you please leave your room number with us?

G: Of course. Nancy Webber, Room 1108.

R: Mrs. Webber in Room 1108. OK. We'll call you up at 5:30 tomorrow morning.

G: Thank you very much.

R: My pleasure.

Words and Expressions to Learn ·

arrange / ə'reɪndʒ / *v.* 安排, 办理

* * *　　* * *　　* * *　　* * *　　* * *　　* * *

the dial tone 电话接通信号音　　　　　　　be charged to 记到……账下
area code 地区代号, 区号

Part B Reading

Passage 1   Phone Answering Tips to Win Business

Do you know how you answer the phone says a great deal about your business?

Phone answering skills are extremely important for every business, and the way you answer your company's phone will form your customer's first impression of your business. The following phone answering tips will ensure that callers know they're dealing with a winning business:

1) Answer all phone calls before the third ring.

2) When you answer the phone, be warm and friendly. Your voice at the end of the telephone line is sometimes the only impression of your company a caller will get.

3) When answering the phone, welcome callers politely and identify yourself and your organization. Say, for example, "Ocean Hotel, Jennifer speaking. May I help you?" No one should ever have to ask if they've reached such and such a business.

4) Keep your voice volume moderate, and speak slowly and clearly when answering the phone, so your caller can understand you easily.

5) Don't use slang or jargon. If you're a person who uses fillers when you speak, such as "uh, huh", "um", or phrases such as "like" or "you know", train yourself carefully not to use these when you speak on the phone.

6) Train your voice and words to be positive when answering the phone, even on a "down" day. For example, rather than saying, "I don't know", say, "Let me find out about that for you."

7) Take telephone messages completely and correctly. If there's something you don't understand or can't spell, such as a person's name, ask the caller to repeat it or spell it for you. Then make sure the message gets to the correct recipient.

8) Return all your calls within one business day. I can't emphasize this point enough. Remember the early bird? The early caller can get the contract, the sale, the problem solved ... and reinforce the good impression of your business that you want the customers to have.

9) Always ask the caller if it's all right to put her on hold when answering the

phone, and don't leave people on hold. Provide callers on hold with progress reports every 30 to 45 seconds. Offer them choices if possible, such as "That line is still busy. Will you continue to hold or should I have xxx call you back?"

10) Don't use a speaker phone unless absolutely necessary. Speaker phones give the caller the impression that you're not fully concentrating on his call, and make him think that his call can be heard by everybody in your office. The only time to use a speaker phone is when you need more than one person to be in the conversation at your end.

11) If you use an answering machine to answer calls when you can't, make sure that it gives the callers the necessary information before it records their messages. Record the latest information in your answering machine. For instance, if your business is going to be closed for a holiday, make your recorded answering machine message say so and say when your business will reopen.

12) Train everyone else who answers the phone to do it the same way. Check on how your business' phone is being answered by calling in and seeing if the phone is being answered in a professional manner. If they don't pass the test, go over these telephone answering tips with them.

 Words and Expressions to Learn ·

identify / aɪˈdentɪfaɪ / v. 表明身份

volume / ˈvɒljuːm / n. 音量

moderate / ˈmɒdərət / a. 适度的，适度的

slang / slæŋ / n. 俚语

jargon / ˈdʒɑːgən / n. 行话

filler / ˈfɪlə / n. 说话时用的点缀词

positive / ˈpɒzətɪv / a. 积极的，肯定的

recipient / rɪˈsɪpɪənt / n. 收信人，收到消息
的人

emphasize / ˈemfəsaɪz / v. 强调

reinforce / riːɪnˈfɔːs / v. 加强，强化

professional / prəˈfeʃənəl / a. 专业的，内行的

***　　***　　***　　***　　***　　***

deal with 与……打交道

such and such a business 某某公司或单位

the early bird (catches the worm) 捷足先登
者，早起的鸟（有虫吃）

put sb. on hold 让某人等着

speaker phone 扬声电话

concentrate on 集中精力于

Passage 2 | Five Secrets of Good Customer Service

Good customer service is the bread and butter of your business. There are several business success secrets, and all of them relate to good customer service.

Secret Number One — Build Business to Customer Loyalty This is the number one customer service secret, and is by far the most important one. The following example can shed some light on this secret. A hotel insists that every one of its staff members who had contact with their customers know the customer by his full name and, when possible, other personal or business information about him. "Good evening, Mr. Smith. Welcome to our hotel." Then, after a bit of chit-chat "By the way, Mr. Smith, did you manage to sell at a profit those hundred shares that you thought were a bit risky?" or, "Was your daughter accepted at Harvard? Last time you were a guest with us, you expressed concern that Emily was having difficulty with her math, and wasn't sure if she had enough points to qualify for admission"

Now, here's a customer who knows that he's welcome at your hotel, and whenever he's back in town, you can count on him staying in your hotel! Is this spying on customers? Not at all! It's simply remembering a few concerns that your customer shared with you the last time he stayed in your hotel.

When you can show concern about what matters to your customer, that's Business to Customer Loyalty, and you've just gained a customer for life.

Secret Number Two — Provide True Customer Service. In today's market environment, service has become a cliché and it seems like "everyone's doing it." So, if everyone is doing it, why not jump ahead of the others by providing even more creative, personalized service to your customers?

One size shoe does not fit all feet. Nor is one type of customer service suitable for all your customers. Let's say your advertised customer service is home delivery. The first customer may welcome this home delivery because it's difficult for him to get out and shop in person. But your second customer may enjoy "window shopping" and carrying his purchases around with him as he goes from shop to shop. He is not the least interested in your home delivery service. So, with what you save by not needing home delivery for this customer, why not offer him a discount on a second cash purchase, or give him an in-store percentage-off coupon that he can use the next time he's in your store?

I repeat, be creative. Get to personally know your customers and recognize their individual needs. Above all, make certain that what you are offering really is something that your customer can value; that's the key to good customer service.

Secret Number Three — "The Customer Is Always Right." If a customer comes to you about a complaint, be very serious about how you handle it. Is the customer upset and angry? First, calm him with words and action and show that you are serious about doing something to solve the problem. Even if it is obvious that he's wrong, sometimes it's better for repeat business to take the loss and compensate the customer.

Then, when your customer is satisfied that his complaint has been properly addressed, thank him for bringing the problem to your attention. Remember, no amount of advertising can repair the damage done by failing to properly address a customer's concern. Even more damaging to a small business is the "silent complainer." That's the customer who simply walks out of your shop without saying a word, and you never see him again. These silent complainers have friends. And their friends have friends.

Secret Number Four — Be Honest with Your Customers. If your customer even suspects that you are trying to cheat him, you can kiss that customer goodbye — forever! Were you lucky enough to buy something from a wholesaler at a discount price? Instead of improving your bottom line, pass that saving on to your customer. This will strengthen your customers' trust in you so that, in the future, your customers will know where to come for real savings. Did you manage to pick up some out of date or reject item? Don't try to sell it to your customers at a regular price without at least telling them that it's a reject or of lower quality.

If your customer asks you for advice on a product, don't try to sell him the item that best enhances your bottom line. Sell him the item that's best for your customer. In the long run, your bottom line will thank you for having made this choice.

Secret Number Five — Educate your staff to be equally as concerned about your customers as you are. Suppose you walk into a hardware store and ask the young clerk for some rubber cement.

"You mean, a toy for babies?"

"No," You repeat. "I want a bottle of rubber cement."

He obviously doesn't know what you are talking about. However, rather than finding out what rubber cement is, he gives you a strange look, then turns his back and goes on to serve another customer. Needless to say, after that incident you will take all your hardware business elsewhere.

A final bit of advice about customer service; "If you aren't taking care of your customers, your competitors will." Print that advice out in large, bold letters and paste it above your cash register.

 ### Words and Expressions to Learn

loyalty / ˈlɔɪəltɪ / n. 忠诚

chit-chat / ˈtʃɪtˌtʃæt / n. 闲谈,聊天

concern / kənˈsɜːn / n. 关心,担心

admission / ədˈmɪʃən / n. 录取,大学许可

spying / ˈspaɪɪŋ / n. 窥探

cliché / ˈkliːʃeɪ / n. 陈词滥调

personalized / ˈpɜːsənəlaɪzd / a. 个性化的,
　　针对个人的

purchase / ˈpɜːtʃəs / n. 所购物品

coupon / ˈkuːpɒn / n. 优惠券,赠券

compensate / ˈkɒmpənseɪt / v. 补偿

address / əˈdres / v. 解决,处理

wholesaler / ˈhəʊlseɪlə / n. 批发商

reject / ˈriːdʒekt / n. 次品

enhance / ɪnˈhɑːns / v. 加强

bold / bəʊld / a. (印刷)黑体的,粗体的

***　　***　　***　　　***　　***　　***

bread and butter 必需品

shed light on 解释,使人了解

at a profit 以获利的结果

qualify for 有资格,合格

count on 指望,料想到,依靠

for life 终生

home delivery 送货上门

repeat business 回头生意

kiss ... goodbye 吻别,丧失,放弃

bottom line 账本底线,盈亏一览结算线

in the long run 从长远看

rubber cement 橡胶泥,橡胶黏合剂

needless to say 自不必说

cash register 收银机,现金出纳机

I. *Translate the following dialogue into English.*

—晚上好。能为你们做点什么？

—晚上好。我们刚从上海过来。你们这儿有房间让我们住一晚上吗？

—你们有几个人？

—八个人。

—需要什么样的房间呢？

—我们需要六个单人间，一个双人间。

—恐怕我们没有那么多单人间了。套房可以吗？

—套房多少钱一晚？

—880元人民币。

—噢，太贵了。有没有便宜一些的套间？

—这是我们这儿最便宜的套间了。如果你们订两套，可以给你们九折优惠。

—那好吧。我们要两套。

—请填一下登记表。

—好的。给你。

—这是你们的钥匙。套房和双人间都在12楼。单人间在9楼。房间号在钥匙卡上。

—谢谢。晚安。

—晚安。

II. *Answer the following questions according to the Reading Passages.*

1. Why is the way I answer the phone important to my business?

2. Why should I report your name and the name of my business when answering the phone?

3. How can I make sure the person at the other end of the line understands me easily?

4. How would the caller feel if I use a speaker phone when answering his call?

5. What can I do to make sure the phones in my business are answered in a professional manner?

6. Why do you think the hotel mentioned in Reading Passage 2 requires all its staff members to know as much about their customers as possible?

7. What does the underlined sentence in Reading Passage 2 mean?

8. Why does the author say "even more damaging to a small business is the 'silent complainer'"?

9. What benefits can honesty bring to a business?

10. How do you explain the statement "If you aren't taking care of your customers, your competitors will"?

III. *Fill in the blanks with proper expressions chosen from the list. Change the form where necessary.*

> put ... through to   deal with   shed light on   kiss ... goodbye   count on
>
> come off   concentrate on   qualify for   in the long run   needless to say

1. Sorry, Sir, I can not decide this. May I _____ the manager?
2. This new rule may not bring immediate benefits, but _____ it will have far better results.
3. That article in the newspaper _____ the situation in the Middle East.
4. He is a person you can _____ when you are in trouble, and I don't believe he has cheated you.
5. Johnny is only 16 years old and too young to _____ a driving license.
6. The boss said to the new employees that if they didn't work hard, they would _____ their bonus (奖金) _____.
7. You won't be able to solve the problem unless you _____ it.
8. His best friend died suddenly, which shocked him and _____ made him very sad.

IV. Topics for discussion.

1. Among the 12 phone answering tips listed in Reading Passage 1, which do you think is the most important one? Why?
2. Suppose you are the general manager of a large hotel, how can you practice the five secrets of good customer service?

UNIT 2 Lesson 6
Complaints and Emergencies

Part A Conversation

Dialogue 1 　 What a Mess!

(R: Hotel Receptionist　G: Guest　M: Manager)

R: Hello. Can I help you, Sir?

G: Yes. Where can I find the manager, please? I have a complaint to make.

R: His office is the first room on your left.

(Guest knocks on the door.)

M: Come in, please. Yes, Sir?

G: May I speak to the manager, please?

M: Yes. I am the manager here. What can I do for you?

G: Had anyone checked the room before we moved in?

M: Is there any problem?

G: Any problem? Many problems! The sheets and the carpets are dirty; the toilet doesn't work; the sink is clogged with hair; the ashtray is full, and the room still smells of cigarettes!

M: Wow, there are really many problems. Which room is this, Sir?

G: Room 1205. I can't imagine such kind of things happening at a famous hotel like yours.

M: I'm terribly sorry, Sir. I will take care of all of them immediately. Usually we check each room before new guests move in. But recently we have been awfully busy with an international conference.

G: Still I did not expect to live in such a messy room at a four-star hotel.

M: Sure. I do apologize. And I promise such things will never happen again.

G: Then what now?

M: We'll change your room at once and you can have two free meals at our restaurant. What do you think?

G: That is a fair solution and I accept. Thank you for your help.

M: Sorry for all the inconvenience. Enjoy your stay.

Dialogue 2　Help!

(R: Hotel Receptionist　G: Guest　D: Doctor)

R: Front desk. Can I help you?

G: Yes, please! I need to talk to a doctor, or maybe we need a taxi. No. An ambulance is better.

R: You sound nervous. Do calm down a bit and tell me what the problem is. Then I will figure out how to help you.

G: Yes, you are right. My wife doesn't feel well.

R: Don't worry. We have a clinic in our hotel. Let me put you through to the doctor.

G: Thank you.

D: Hello. Clinic.

G: Doctor, my wife is feeling very bad.

D: Can you describe it in detail?

G: She has chest pains, and she is short of breath. She looks very pale.

D: Does she have a history of heart trouble?

G: Yes. But that's long ago.

D: Please don't move her and I will call in a heart specialist immediately and see your wife in your room.

G: Oh, thank goodness.

D: What's your room number, please?

G: 1212. Please be quick.

D: Don't worry. Everything will be fine.

G: Thank you.

complaint / kəmˈpleɪnt / n. 投诉，抱怨

emergency / ɪˈmɜːdʒənsɪ / n. 紧急情况

clog / klɒg / v. 堵塞

ashtray / ˈæʃtreɪ / n. 烟灰缸

messy / ˈmesɪ / a. 乱糟糟的

ambulance / ˈæmbjuːləns / n. 救护车

clinic / ˈklɪnɪk / n. 诊所

specialist / ˈspeʃəlɪst / n. 专家

***　　***　　***　　　***　　***　　***

smell of 闻起来有……气味

figure out 弄清楚

in detail 详细地

be short of breath 呼吸困难

Part **B** Reading ·····························

Passage 1　Hotel Front Desk Clerk

Do you think you could deal with a tired, angry person who's unhappy about his pillow? Or a kid who demands that he gets Nintendo hooked up in his room? If you're a front desk clerk for a hotel, you'll be faced with these situations and more. But most of the time people are friendly and pleasant. Really.

Front desk clerks are always in the public eye and are the first line of customer service for a hotel. Their attitude and behavior greatly influence the public's impressions of the hotel. So they must always be polite and helpful. Most employers look for people who are friendly and customer-service oriented, well dressed, and display the maturity and self-confidence to show good judgment. Front desk clerks, especially in famous hotels should be quick thinking, show initiative, and be able to work as a member of a team.

Whether it's a fancy four-star hotel or a small one, front desk clerks are the "front line". They have similar responsibilities: they take reservations over the phone, greet customers in person, register arriving guests, and assign rooms. They keep records of room assignments and other registration-related information on computers. They also answer questions about services, checkout times, the local community, or other matters of public interest. They also report problems with guest rooms or public facilities to members of the housekeeping or maintenance staff for them to solve the problems. In larger hotels, front desk clerks may refer difficult questions to the manager.

In some smaller hotels and motels, where fewer staffs are employed, clerks may take on additional responsibilities, such as bringing clean sheets to rooms, which are usually done by employees in other departments of larger hotels. In the smaller places, front desk clerks often take care of all front-office operations, information, and services.

Hotels are open around the clock creating the need for night and weekend work. Most clerks work in areas that are clean, bright, and relatively quiet, although lobbies can become crowded and noisy when busy. Many hotels have strict dress code for desk clerks.

Desk clerks may experience very hectic times during check-in and check-out times or feel great pressures when dealing with convention guests or large groups of tourists. Moreover, dealing with angry guests can be stressful. Computer failures can further complicate an already busy time and add to stress levels. Hotel desk clerks may be on their feet most of the time and may sometimes be asked to lift heavy guest luggage.

 Words and Expressions to Learn

pillow / ˈpɪləʊ / *n.* 枕头
oriented / ˈɔːrɪentɪd / *a.* 以……为导向/目标的
maturity / məˈtjʊərɪtɪ / *n.* 成熟
initiative / ɪˈnɪʃətɪv / *n.* 主观能动性
assign / əˈsaɪn / *v.* 分配

maintenance / ˈmeɪntənəns / *n.* 维护,维修
motel / məʊˈtel / *n.* 汽车旅馆
hectic / ˈhektɪk / *a.* 忙乱的,闹哄哄的
convention / kənˈvenʃən / *n.* (大型)会议
stressful / ˈstresfəl / *a.* 充满压力的,紧张的
complicate / ˈkɒmplɪkeɪt / *v.* 使复杂化

***   ***   ***   ***   ***   ***

Nintendo 日本电子游戏机商标名
hook up 给……接通电源或中央系统
be faced with 正视,面对
in person 亲自

refer ... to ... 涉及,参考,指的是
take on 承担
around the clock 昼夜服务
dress code 着装规定

A comfortable room, good food, and a helpful staff can make being away from home an enjoyable experience for both families on vacation and business travelers. In full-service hotels, managers help their guests have a pleasant stay by providing many of the comforts of home, as well as services like hotel clinic. For business travelers, they often provide meeting rooms and electronic equipment.

Hotel managers are responsible for keeping their hotels running well and profitable. In a small hotel with a limited staff, the manager may oversee all operations. However, large hotels may have hundreds of workers, and the general manager usually is helped by a number of assistant managers of different departments.

General managers have overall responsibility for the operation of the hotel. Within rules made by the owners of the hotel, the general manager sets room rates, allocates funds to departments, and ensures expected standards for guest service, décor, housekeeping, food quality, and banquet operations.

Resident managers are responsible for the day-to-day operations of the hotel. In larger ones, more than one of these managers may assist the general manager, dividing responsibilities between the food and beverage operations and the room services. At least one manager, either the general manager or a resident manager, is on call 24 hours a day to resolve problems or emergencies.

Assistant managers help run the day-to-day operations of the hotel. In large hotels, they may be responsible for activities such as personnel, accounting, office administration, marketing and sales, security, maintenance, and recreational facilities. Assistant managers may adjust charges on a hotel guest's bill when a manager is away.

Executive housekeepers ensure that guest rooms, meeting and banquet rooms, and public areas are clean, orderly, and well maintained. They also train, schedule, and oversee the work of housekeepers, check on rooms, and order cleaning supplies.

Front office managers are in charge of reservations and room assignments, as well as train and direct the hotel front desk staff. They ensure that guests are treated politely, complaints and problems are resolved, and requests for special services are carried out. Front office managers may adjust charges on a customer's bill.

Convention services managers coordinate the activities of different departments in larger hotels to accommodate meetings, conventions, and special events. They meet members of groups or organizations to plan the number of rooms to reserve, the desired equipment of the meeting space, and banquet services. During the meeting or event, they resolve unexpected problems and oversee activities to ensure that hotel operations conform to the expectations of the group.

Food and beverage managers are in charge of all food service operations of the hotel. They discuss menus with the executive chef for the hotel restaurants, lounges, and room service operations. They oversee the ordering of food and supplies, direct service and maintenance within the kitchens and dining areas, and manage food service budgets.

Catering managers take care of food service in a hotel's meeting and convention rooms. They coordinate menus and costs for banquets, parties, and events with meeting and convention planners or individual customers. They coordinate staffing needs and arrange schedules with kitchen personnel to ensure good food service.

Sales or marketing directors and public relations directors oversee the advertising and promotion of hotel operations and functions, including lodging and dining specials and special events, such as holiday or seasonal specials. They direct the efforts of their staff to market their hotel to organizations or groups looking for a place for conferences, conventions, business meetings, trade shows, and special events. They also coordinate media relations and answer questions from the press.

Human resources directors manage the personnel functions of a hotel, ensuring that all accounting, payroll, and employee relation matters are handled according to hotel policy and laws. They also oversee hiring practices and standards and ensure that training and promotion programs reflect the employee development plans.

Finance directors monitor room sales and reservations. In addition to overseeing accounting and cash-flow matters at the hotel, they also calculate occupancy levels, decide which rooms to discount and when to offer it.

To be a hotel manager you should have a good head for business; be able to manage staff; have good written and spoken communication skills; enjoy working with people; have the ability to be tactful and diplomatic; keep calm under pressure and solve problems quickly; have energy and enthusiasm; be well organized.

 Words and Expressions to Learn ·················

profitable / ˈprɒfɪtəbl / *a.* 盈利的

oversee / ˌəʊvəˈsi: / *v.* 监察,监督

allocate / ˈæləkeɪt / *v.* 划拨

beverage / ˈbevərɪdʒ / *n.* 饮品,饮料

accounting / əˈkaʊntɪŋ / *n.* 账目,账单

adjust / əˈdʒʌst / *v.* 调整

schedule / ˈʃedju:l / *v.* 安排（日程）

accommodate / əˈkɒmədeɪt / *v.* 为……提供
     住宿

lounge / laʊndʒ / *n.* 休息室,休息厅

budget / ˈbʌdʒɪt / *n.* 预算

payroll / ˈpeɪrəʊl / *n.* 在职人员名单,发放工
     资总额

tactful / ˈtæktfl / *a.* 圆滑的,机敏的

diplomatic / ˌdɪpləˈmætɪk / *a.* 婉转的,说话办
     事得体的

enthusiasm / ɪnˈθju:zɪæzəm / *n.* 激情,热情

*** ··· *** ··· ***   *** ··· *** ··· ***

on vacation 度假

be responsible for 负责

general manager 总经理

assistant manager 副经理

resident manager 驻店经理

on call 随叫随到,随时待命

executive housekeeper 客房部经理

front office manager 前台经理

convention services manager 会务部经理

conform to 遵从

food and beverage manager 餐饮部经理

executive chef 厨师长

catering manager 承办酒席的经理

sales or marketing director 销售部总监

public relations director 公关部总监

the press 媒体

human resources director 人力资源部总监

finance director 财务总监

occupancy level 客房入住率

Part  Exercises

I. *Make up dialogues according to the given situation.*

You work at the front desk of a hotel. A guest comes to you to check out. You tell him to wait a minute while you prepare his bill. The guest checks the bill and finds a mistake in it. You apologize and correct it. The guest says his flight is 17:40 and asks if he can still rest in the room until then. You tell him no, because it is the rule of the hotel for guests to check out before

14:00 noon. But you suggest staying in the lobby drinking coffee or tea while waiting for his flight. He agrees and thanks you.

II. *Decide whose responsibilities the following statements describe and put the letter in front of each job title on the line in front of the statements.*

a. General managers   b. Assistant managers

c. Resident managers   d. Executive housekeepers

e. Front office managers   f. Convention services managers

g. Food and beverage managers   h. Catering managers

i. Sales and marketing directors and public relations directors

j. Human resources directors   k. Finance directors

1. _____ They monitor rooms sales, oversee the accounting and cash-flow at the hotel and decide which rooms to offer for discount.

2. _____ They talk about menus with the chef, oversee all food service and manage food service budget.

3. _____ They take care of food and beverage operations, room service and stay on call 24 hours a day to solve any unexpected problems.

4. _____ They are in charge of advertising and promoting hotel operations and services, contacting groups or individual customers for special events, and keeping good relations with and answer questions from the media.

5. _____ They make sure the right people are hired, train and promote them according to the employee development plans.

6. _____ They are responsible for the day-to-day operations of the hotel including activities such as personnel, accounting, office administration, security and so on.

7. _____ They coordinate activities of different departments to accommodate meetings, conventions or special events, and take care of the equipment needed in the meeting space and resolve unexpected problems.

8. _____ They ensure that guest rooms, meeting rooms and public areas are kept clean and in order.

9. _____ They ensure good food service in the meeting or convention rooms, calculate the costs for parties and other events.

10. _____ They are in charge of room reservations, assignment, resolve guests' complaints and satisfy their special needs.

11. _____ They set room rates, provide funds to different departments and ensure high standards for customer services.

III. Translate the following English passage into Chinese and the Chinese one into English.

1. Computers are used extensively by hotel managers and their assistants to keep track of guests' bills, reservations, room assignments, meetings, and special events. In addition, computers are used to order food, beverages, and supplies, as well as to prepare reports for hotel owners and top-level managers. Managers work with computer specialists to ensure that the hotel's computer system functions properly. Should the hotel computer system fail, managers must continue to meet the needs of hotel guests and staff.

2. 酒店前台服务员直接和公众打交道,因此职业化的外表和友善的性格很重要。口齿清楚,言语流畅也是很必要的,因为这些雇员直接与酒店客人和公众交谈,经常使用电话和广播系统。他们需要有良好的拼写水平和电脑知识,因为多数工作需要用电脑完成。此外,由于许多酒店里外国客人越来越多,流利地说一门外语也越来越有帮助。

IV. Topics for discussion.

1. Among the qualities listed in the last paragraph of Reading Passage 2, which do you think is the most important one in the making of a successful hotel manager?
2. Comment on the advantages and disadvantages of working as a hotel front desk clerk.

UNIT 3
Food Culture

UNIT **3** Lesson 7
Chinese Food
Culture Overview

Part **A** Conversation

(R: receptionist   S: Mr. Stevens   A: Angel, Mr. Steven's wife

G: Guide, Mr. Li   W: Waiter)

R: Good evening. Welcome to our restaurant. Do you have a reservation, please?

S: Yes. The name is Stevens.

R: (The receptionist checks the reservation list.) Mr. Stevens. Three of you?

S: Yes.

R: This way, please.

W: Here is the menu, Madam.

A: Thank you. What shall we have tonight?

S: I think Beijing duck is a must.

A: That's the main course. Chinese dishes have such wonderful names. Look at this "red-beaked green parrot with gold-trimmed jade cake". Do you know what it is, Mr. Li?

G: No, sorry. Sometimes it's hard to tell from the menu. (To the waiter.) Could you please tell us something about this dish?

W: That's mainly spinach and fried bean curd.

S: What are your specialties today?

W: The chef's specialties today are sweet and sour fish, and braised prawn in shell with tomato sauce.

S: All right, we'll take both.

A: Maybe you can order for us. (She gives the menu to Mr. Stevens.)

S: Help me, Mr. Li. Mm — let's try the chicken, the pork fillet, braised beef. What's this, Mr. Li, "Bean curd in earthen-pot?"

G: A small earthen-pot with bean curd and soup. It's a nice dish.

S: OK, we'll take that.

A: Shall we have some vegetables?

S: Let's have the mixed vegetables and the stuffed tomato. What is this sea slug?

G: It's a kind of seafood also called sea cucumber.

A: We don't really like sea cucumber.

G: It's one of the delicacies in Chinese cuisine.

S: Well, why don't we try the sea cucumber tonight?

A: OK. Maybe I'll come to love it. (To the waiter.) Do you think the food we've ordered is enough for us?

W: I think so. If you want more, you can order other dishes later on.

S: OK.

W: Here is the wine list. What drinks would you like?

G: (To Mr. Stevens.) Would you like to try Maotai — the best Chinese spirits?

S: Is it strong?

G: Yes. It's strong liquor made from sorghum grain.

A: Oh, that's not for me.

S: Fine, I'd like to try a small glass. A glass for you, Mr. Li?

G: Thank you.

S: And you, darling?

A: (To the waiter.) Do you have any special drinks?

W: May I suggest the Chinese red wine? It's sweet.

A: Fine, I'll try that.

 Words and Expressions to Learn

spinach / ˈspɪnɪtʃ / n. 菠菜

delicacy / ˈdelɪkəsɪ / n. 美味

liquor / ˈlɪkə / n. 酒，酒精饮料

main course 主菜

red-beaked green parrot with gold-
   trimmed jade cake 红嘴绿鹦金玉糕

fried bean curd 炸豆腐

braised prawn in shell with tomato sauce
   茄汁明虾

pork fillet 里脊肉

braised beef 炖牛肉

bean curd in earthen-pot 砂锅豆腐

mixed vegetables and the stuffed tomato
   八宝酿西红柿

sea slug 海参

sorghum grain 高粱

Part B Reading

Passage 1 Chinese Cooking History

China is a country where the preparation and appreciation of food has been developed to the highest level.

The art of Chinese cooking has been developed and perfected over many centuries. Emperor Fuxi taught people to fish, hunt, grow crops and cook twenty centuries before Christ. However, cooking was not considered an art until the Zhou Dynasty.

The two dominant philosophies of the Chinese culture are Confucianism and Taoism. Each influenced the course of Chinese history and the development of the culinary arts. Confucianism concerned itself with the art of cooking and placed great emphasis on the enjoyment of life. To the Chinese, food and friends are inseparable. A gathering without food is considered incomplete and improper.

Confucius loved and respected the art of cooking. He established culinary standards and proper table etiquette. Most of these are still considered to be the standards today. The tradition of cutting foods into bite size pieces during preparation is unique to the Chinese culture.

Confucius taught that good cooking depends on the blending of various ingredients and condiments rather than the taste of the individual elements. He believed that in order to become a good cook one must first be a good matchmaker. The flavors of the ingredients must be blended with harmony. Without harmony there is no taste. He also stressed the use of color and texture in preparing a dish. Most certainly Confucianism helped raise cooking from a menial task to the status of an art.

Taoism was responsible for the development of the hygienic aspects of food and cooking. The chief objective of this philosophy was people's wish for long life. In contrast to supporters of Confucianism who were interested in taste, texture and appearance, Taoists were concerned with the life-giving attributes of various foods.

Over the centuries Chinese people have explored the world of plants, roots, herbs, fungi and seeds to find life-giving elements. They discovered that the nutritional value of vegetables could be destroyed by improper cooking and that many items had medicinal value. For example, ginger, a favorite condiment, is also used to ease an upset stomach and as a cold remedy.

Unlike the majority of Eastern cuisines, most Chinese dishes are low-calorie and low-fat. Food is cooked using polyunsaturated oils; milk, cream, butter and cheese are not a part of the daily diet. Animal fats are kept to a minimum due to the small portions of meats used. However, some dishes served in Chinese restaurants may be considerably higher in calories and fats than those you prepare at home.

With this basic understanding of Chinese culinary history, you are ready to begin cooking in Chinese style.

 Words and Expressions to Learn

dominant / ˈdɒmɪnənt / a. 占优势的，支配的
culinary / ˈkʌlɪnərɪ / a. 厨房的，烹调用的
condiment / ˈkɒndɪmənt / n. 调味品
element / ˈelɪmənt / n. 元素，成分
menial / miːnɪəl / a. 低微的
status / ˈsteɪtəs / n. 地位，状况
hygienic / haɪˈdʒiːnɪk / a. 卫生的
philosophy / fɪˈlɒsəfɪ / n. 哲学，宗旨，观点

attribute / ˈætrɪbjʊt / n. 属性，品质，特征
fungi / ˈfʌngaɪ / n. 真菌；菌类（fungus 的复数）
medicinal / məˈdɪsɪnəl / a. 药用的
ginger / ˈdʒɪndʒə / n. 姜，生姜
polyunsaturated / ˌpɒlɪʌnˈsætʃəreɪtɪd / a. 多不饱和的
minimum / ˈmɪnɪməm / n. 最小值，最小化

＊＊＊　＊＊＊　＊＊＊　＊＊＊　＊＊＊　＊＊＊

before Christ 公元前（略作 B.C.）

in contrast to 与……形成对比

Yang and yin. Hot and cold. Male and female. The philosophy of yin and yang lies at the heart of Chinese culture. The first references to yin and yang come from the I Ching, one of the five classic works compiled and edited by Confucius. Taken literally, yin and yang mean the dark side and sunny side of a hill. People commonly think of yin and yang as opposing forces. However, it is really more appropriate to view them as complementary pairs. The Chinese believe problems arise not when the two forces are battling, but when there is an imbalance between them in the environment. Floods, divorce, or even a fire in the kitchen — all can be attributed to imbalance in the forces of yin and yang.

How does the concept of yin and yang relate to food? A basic adherence to this philosophy can be found in any Chinese dish, from stir-fried beef with broccoli to sweet and sour pork. There is always a balance in colors, flavors, and textures. However, belief in the importance of following the principles of yin and yang in the diet extends further. Certain foods are thought to have yin or cooling properties, while others have yang or warm features. The best is to consume a diet that contains a healthy balance between the two. When treating illnesses, a Chinese physician will frequently advise dietary changes in order to restore a healthy balance between yin and yang in the body. For example, let's say you're suffering from heartburn, caused by consuming too many spicy (yang) foods. Instead of antacids, you're likely to take home a prescription for herbal teas to restore the yin forces. Similarly, coughs or flu are more likely to be treated with dietary changes than antibiotics or cough medicines.

Almost no foodstuff is purely yin or yang — it's simply that one characteristic tends to dominate. This is why there is not complete agreement among experts as to which foods show yin or yang forces. Individual ingredient is not so important as the balance and contrast between ingredients in each dish. Interestingly, cooking methods also have more of a yin or yang property. Cooking methods with yin qualities are boiling, poaching, and steaming; and those with yang qualities are deep-frying, roasting, stir-frying. Accordingly, bean sprouts, cabbage, carrots, crab, cucumber, duck, doufu, watercress, etc. can be classified into yin foods while foods like bamboo, beef, chicken, eggs, ginger, glutinous rice, mushrooms, sesame oil belong to yang.

Words and Expressions to Learn

literally / ˈlɪtərəli / *ad.* 从字面上讲

complementary / ˌkɒmplɪˈmentəri / *a.* 互为补充的

arise / əˈraɪz / *v.* 出现，发生，起因于

imbalance / ɪmˈbæləns / *n.* 不均衡

property / ˈprɒpəti / *n.* 特征，特性

heartburn / ˈhɑːtbɜːn / *n.* 烧心，心痛

antacid / ænˈtæsɪd / *n.* 抗酸剂

antibiotic / ˌæntɪbaɪˈɒtɪk / *n.* 抗生素

dominate / ˈdɒmɪneɪt / *v.* 支配，占优势

poach / pəʊtʃ / *v.* 水煮

steam / stiːm / *v.* 蒸

deep-fry / ˈdiːpfraɪ / *v.* 油炸

watercress / ˈwɔːtəkres / *n.* 豆瓣菜，水田芥

***   ***   ***   ***   ***   ***

I Ching《易经》

be attributed to 归功于，认为是

adherence to 坚持，遵守

bean sprouts 豆芽

glutinous rice 糯米

Part **C** Exercises

I. *Complete the dialogue by translating the Chinese sentences into English.*

— 1. _____ (请问您有两个人的桌子吗？)

— 2. _____ (你们预订桌位了吗？)

— No, we don't.

— OK, let me have a look. We still have some vacancies.

— Great. 3. _____ (我们可以在非吸烟区坐在靠窗的桌位吗？我们想享受一下上海的夜景。)

— No problem. 4. _____ (请这边走。这是菜单。)

Moments later.

— 5. _____ (打扰一下，您现在可以点菜了吗？)

— Yes. 6. _____ (但是我们是初次来到这个城市，可以给我们点建议吗？)

— Sure. I'd like to recommend our beef. It enjoys a long history here.

— But beef is a rather traditional dish. 7. _____ (我们想尝一下你们酒店的特色菜。)

— 8. _____ (我们酒店烹制牛肉的方法与众不同，我保证您吃过之后定会十分满意的。)

— OK. I'll take that.

— 9. _____ (这道小牛肉要多大火候，嫩一些，适中，还是老一些呢？)

— Well done, please.

— OK. Anything to drink?

— I'd like a glass of wine.

— Anything else?

— No. Thank you.

After the meal.

— 10. _____（请拿账单来,好吗?）

— Here you are. How would you like to pay?

— In cash. Here is the money and keep the change.

— Thank you.

II. *Decide whether the following statements are true or false according to the passages.*

1. Cooking was considered an art in China even before Christ.

2. According to Confucianism, cooking is a menial task.

3. The Chinese people today still keep most cooking standards and table manners set by Confucius.

4. Confucianism and Taoism have played different roles in the development of the Chinese cooking art.

5. Taoism was much concerned about the life-giving value of different foods.

6. The principles of yin and yang are observed in cooking some Chinese dishes.

7. A sick person can regain a healthy balance between yin and yang in the body through dietary changes.

8. Yin and yang forces can be shown in each kind of food.

III. *Translate the following passage into Chinese.*

Chinese cuisine is healthier and more tasteful. Most Chinese dishes are cooked with meat and vegetables together, so the food contain lower calories and are less rich than Western food. Vegetables stay bright and crisp by cooking for a short time over high heat, either in their own juice or in a small amount of water. This method retains most of the vitamins and minerals.

IV. *Topic for discussion.*

What influences have the philosophies of Confucianism, Taoism, yin and yang exerted on the development of Chinese culinary arts respectively?

UNIT 3

Lesson 8
Table Manners and Cooking Techniques

Part **A** *Conversation*

Dialogue | **How to Prepare Food**

(D: Diner, chef's friend   C: Chef)

(They are talking in the kitchen.)

D: Mr. Hu, that chicken was delicious. Please tell me how to make it.

C: Oh, it's very easy. You need about six pieces of chicken for two people. First, roll each piece of chicken in a little flour.

D: Just ordinary flour?

C: Well, I usually use seasoned flour just to give it a little extra flavor.

D: All right. And then what would you do?

C: Then you heat a little oil in a frying pan. You'll need about half a cup.

D: I see.

C: And then you fry the chicken in the oil for a couple of minutes until it's nice and brown all over.

D: Just two or three minutes?

C: That's right. Now you take your vegetables — you'll need celery, carrots, onions, and some mushrooms — and you chop them up. And the next step is to add them to the chicken. And after you've done that, you add the spices. I like to put in some parsley, dill, tarragon, and a bit of salt and pepper. Just a pinch of each will do.

D: Let me go through that again. After you brown the chicken, you chop up the vegetables, put them in the frying pan, and then add the spices.

C: Right. Now you cook the vegetables and the chicken for another five minutes and then you're ready to add some wine. You'll need about half a bottle of dry white wine. Pour it over the chicken together with about a cup of water.

D: That's enough liquid?

C: Oh, yes, that's plenty. Then put the lid on the frying pan and cook the chicken for another 30 or 40 minutes on very low heat.

D: Oh, it sounds easy. I'm going to try it next weekend.

 Words and Expressions to Learn ·

season / ˈsiːzən / v. 给……调味   dill / dɪl / n. 小茴香
spice / spaɪs / n. 香料,调味品   tarragon / ˈtærəgən / n. 龙嵩,龙嵩叶
parsley / ˈpɑːslɪ / n. 荷兰芹,欧芹   pepper / ˈpepə / n. 胡椒,花椒

     ***   ***   ***   ***   ***   ***

frying pan 煎锅,长柄平锅   a pinch of 一撮,少量
chop up 切开,切细

Part B Reading

 **Passage 1**   Table Manners

Unlike in the West, where everyone has their own plate of food, in China the dishes are placed on the table and everybody shares. If you are treated by a Chinese host, be prepared for a ton of food. Chinese are very proud of their culture of cuisine and will do their best to show their hospitality.

There are some rules to follow to make your stay in China happier, though you may have no idea of what they are.

1. Never stick your chopsticks upright in the rice bowl, lay them on your dish instead. Otherwise, it is deemed extremely impolite to the host and old people present. The reason for this is that when somebody dies, the shrine to them contains a bowl of sand or rice with two sticks of incense stuck upright in it. So if you stick your chopsticks in the rice bowl, it looks like the shrine and is equal to wishing death upon a person at the table.

2. Make sure the spout of the teapot does not face anyone. It is impolite to set the

teapot down where the spout faces somebody. The spout should always be directed to where nobody is sitting, usually just outward from the table.

3. Don't tap on your bowl with your chopsticks, since that will be deemed an insult to the host or the chef. Beggars tap on their bowls, and also, when the food is coming too slow in a restaurant, people will tap their bowls. If you are in someone's home, it is like insulting the host or the cook.

4. Never try to turn a fish over and debone it yourself, since the separation of the fish skeleton from the fish will usually be done by the host or a waiter. People will deem that bad luck will follow and a fishing boat will turn upside down if you do so. This is especially true to southerners in China since, traditionally, southerners are the fishing population.

The meal usually begins with a set of at least four cold dishes, to be followed by the main course of hot meat and vegetable dishes. Soup then will come to be followed by staple food ranging from rice, noodles to dumplings. If you wish to have your rice to go with the dishes, you should say so in good time, for most of the Chinese choose to have the staple food at last or have none of them at all.

Perhaps one of the things that surprise a westerner most is that some of the Chinese hosts like to put food into the plates of their guests. In formal dinners, there are always "serving" chopsticks and spoons for this purpose, but some hosts may use their own chopsticks. This is a sign of true friendship and politeness. It is always polite to eat the food. If you do not eat it, just leave it in the plate.

People in China tend to over-order food, for they will find it embarrassing if all the food is eaten up. When you have had enough, just say so. Or you will always overeat!

 Words and Expressions to Learn

cuisine / kwɪˈziːn / *n.* 烹饪，饮食
hospitality / ˌhɒspɪˈtælɪtɪ / *n.* 热情
yummy / ˈjʌmɪ / *a.* 美味的，可口的
deem / diːm / *v.* 视为，认为
shrine / ʃraɪn / *n.* 神龛
spout / spaʊt / *n.* (茶壶) 嘴

insult / ˈɪnsʌlt / & / ɪnˈsʌlt / *n.* & *v.* 侮辱
debone / dɪˈbəʊn / *v.* 将 (鸡、鸭、肉等) 去骨
skeleton / ˈskelətən / *n.* (动物的) 骨架
embarrassing / ɪmˈbærəsɪŋ / *a.* 令人难堪的
overeat / əʊvəˈiːt / *v.* 吃得过多

a ton of 许多   turn over 翻身
have no idea of 不知道   staple food 主食
two sticks of incense 两炷香   range from ... to 在……范围内变动
be equal to 等于, 等同于   eat up 吃光

Passage 2 **Ways of Cooking**

In China, there are 40 to 50 different methods of heat control used in cooking. In practice, you need only be acquainted with a few of them.

Stir-frying is usually done in a wok. You can use a large thin-bottomed pan or frying pan instead. The essence of the technique is that the food is cooked quickly, over high heat, in very little oil. The food to be cooked is finely sliced or shredded into similar sized pieces, using a very sharp knife or Chinese cleaver.

Shallow-frying is a slower method of cooking than stir-frying. Again, a wok or frying pan is used. More oil is used and the cooking is done over moderate heat.

Deep-frying is used in the same way as in the West, to produce crisp-textured food. Sometimes the food is deep-fried, removed from the oil and drained. The oil is then reheated and the food deep-fried again, so that it is extremely crispy.

Small pieces of meat or fish are seasoned, then wrapped in cellophane paper to form little parcels, and deep-fried until tender. This is called paper-wrapped deep-frying. The food is served in its paper wrapping and opened by the diner with chopsticks. The paper is of course thrown away.

Steaming is an official way of cooking. The Chinese use bamboo steamers which stack on top of each other, so that four or five dishes can be steamed at the same time. Dishes requiring most cooking are placed on the bottom layer, near the boiling water, while those requiring less are placed on the top "floor".

Roasting is used less in China than in the West as most Chinese kitchens do not contain an oven: the best known dishes are restaurant ones, such as Roast Peking Duck. Chashao is a method of quick-roasting meat or poultry at a high temperature for a short time.

Red cooking is a unique Chinese method, used primarily for cooking large cuts of meat or poultry. Dark soy sauce is used, which imparts a rich flavor and dark reddish-brown color to the food.

Stews usually refer to meat cooked on its own with herbs and spices, rather than with vegetables. In China, stews are usually cooked in an earthenware pot over a slow charcoal fire. The stew is cooked for a very long time — up to four hours — producing meat almost jelly-like in tenderness.

 Words and Expressions to Learn

wok / wɒk / *n.* 锅,炒菜锅

slice / slaɪs / *v.* 切(片)

shred / ʃred / *v.* 撕碎,切碎

cleaver / 'kliːvə / *n.* 宽刃大刀

drain / dreɪn / *v.* 排干,控干

cellophane / 'seləfeɪn / *n.* 玻璃纸

stack / stæk / *v.* 堆放

impart / ɪm'pɑːt / *v.* 给予,传授

stew / stjuː / *n.* 炖,焖,炖肉(或菜)

earthenware / 'ɜːθənweə / *n.* 土器,陶器

charcoal / 'tʃɑːkəʊl / *n.* 木炭

heat control 火候

be acquainted with 熟悉,了解

red cooking 红烧

Part **C** *Exercises*

I. *Describe to your classmates your favorite dish and how to cook it.*

II. *Decide whether the following statements are true or false according to Reading Passage 1.*

1. Sticking one's chopsticks upright in the rice bowl at the dinner table is considered extremely impolite in China.
2. It's not proper to direct the spout of the teapot outward from the table.
3. It will be deemed an insult to the host or the chef if you tap on your bowl with your chopsticks.
4. There are good reasons behind most taboos (禁忌) with table manners in China.
5. Westerners tend to have their own plates of food to share with others.

III. *Indicate the basic cooking techniques according to Reading Passage 2.*

1. Cooking several dishes at the same time in a bamboo steamer _____

2. Quickly cooking meat at a high temperature for a short time _____

3. Cooking large cuts of meat with dark soy sauce _____

4. Cooking meat in an earthenware pot over low heat for a long time _____

5. Quickly cooking food over high heat in very little oil _____

6. Cooking foods over moderate heat in moderate amount of oil _____

7. Producing crisp-textured food in reheated oil _____

8. Cooking pieces of seasoned dish in cellophane paper _____

IV. *Put the following passage into Chinese.*

Chopsticks play an important role in Chinese food culture. Chopsticks were called "zhu" in ancient times. Chinese people have been using chopsticks as one of the main tableware for more than 3,000 years. Experts believe the history of wood or bamboo chopsticks can be dated to about 1,000 years earlier than ivory chopsticks. Bronze chopsticks were invented in the Western Zhou Dynasty. Lacquer (漆 器) chopsticks from the Western Han were discovered in Mawangdui. Gold and silver chopsticks became popular in the Tang Dynasty. It was believed that silver chopsticks could detect poisons in food. Chopsticks can be classified into five groups based on the materials used to make them, i.e., wood, metal, bone, stone and synthetic materials. Bamboo and wood chopsticks are the most popular ones used in Chinese homes. There are a few things to avoid when using chopsticks. Chinese people usually don't beat their bowls with the chopsticks while eating, since the behavior used to be practiced by beggars. Also don't insert chopsticks in a bowl upright because it is a custom exclusively used in sacrifice.

V. *Put the following sentences into English.*

1. 一些人说,如果不做下面三件事而离开中国,是一件非常遗憾的事。那就是:参观长城、吃北京烤鸭和喝茅台酒。

2. 对于经验丰富的厨师,他们是真正的艺术家,食谱仅仅是作为参考,他们常常一边做菜,一边依照他们宴请的人数,现有的佐料以及个人的口味来调整食谱。

3. 有些厨师们很少参照食谱,反而比较喜欢凭自己的直觉加一点这个,加一点那个来做出刚好的味道。

4. 烹饪是一种人人皆懂的语言。在中国,名厨对于几种烹饪"方言"都很"流利"。

5. 中国烹饪艺术十分讲究菜肴的色、香、味、形、声。

6. "南淡北咸,东甜西辣"精确地描述了中国烹饪的特色。

Topics for discussion.

1. Do you like to eat out or prepare dinner at home? Give your reasons according to the suggested points.

   Eating out: avoid the boring processes of preparation and cleaning up; better flavor; variety of dishes; good environment; avoid quarrel or argument over chores involved in cooking and cleaning up

   Eating at home: less expensive; enhance relationship; sometimes romantic; more personal; enjoy cooking

2. What differences do you know about the table manners in China and in the Western countries?

UNIT **3**

Lesson 9
Famous Dishes and Their Stories

Part **A**   *Conversation*

Dialogue   Having Hot Pot

(G: Guide   T: Tourist   W: Waiter)

T: It's terribly cold today! I'd really like something to warm up.

G: For that, hot pot is a good choice.

T: Hot pot? What's that? What's special about it?

G: It's very popular throughout China because it is fresh, fragrant, tingling, and hot, but more importantly, it creates a warm atmosphere.

T: How?

G: When having hot pot, people sit around the pot in a circle, which represents happiness and reunion, eating, chatting and laughing.

T: Can we get balanced nutrition from hot pot?

G: Don't worry about that. Hot pot only uses a single pot, yet has many ingredients, such as beef, lamb, and various vegetables, especially leafy ones.

T: That's quite amazing. I can't wait to have a try.

G: Let's go to "Little Lamb Hot Pot". It's very famous and not far from here.

(In the hot pot restaurant.)

W: What soup base would you like?

G: Do you like spicy food?

T: No, I can't take it.

G: Then we'll get the yuanyang soup base.

T: Isn't yuanyang a bird?

G: Here, yuanyang soup base means two bases in one pot, but divided in the middle.

The food tastes different depending on which soup base you cook it in.

W: The lamb here is really good. Would you like to try some?

G: We'll get two plates of lamb and some vegetables.

T: (To the waiter.) Chinese cabbage, bean curd and vermicelli.

W: What sauce would you like?

G: What do you have?

W: Sesame oil, sesame paste, smashed garlic and seafood sauce.

G: A bowl of sesame oil, and you?

T: The same for me.

(The hot pot is brought to the table.)

W: The pot is served, Sir.

T: Wow, it's half white and half red. It looks great.

G: The pot is boiling. Let's start putting stuff in.

T: Oh, look, the meat's changed color.

G: That means it's cooked. Lamb slices cut as thin as paper can be eaten immediately after they are dipped into the boiling water. Quick, the meat tastes good while it's hot!

T: What shall I do now?

W: Take out the lamb slices with chopsticks and dip them in the mixture of condiments and relishes.

T: Let me try. Hmm, yummy yummy! The lamb cooked this way is very tender and delicious. I think it takes great skill to slice the meat into such thin slices.

G: Of course. The thinner, the better.

 Words and Expressions to Learn · · · · · · · · · · · · · ·

tingle / ˈtɪŋɡl / *v.* 麻
reunion / riːˈjuːnɪən / *n.* 团圆

vermicelli / vɜːmɪˈtʃelɪ / *n.* 粉条
relish / ˈrelɪʃ / *n.* 作料，调味品

***　　***　　***　　***　　***　　***

soup base 锅底汤
sesame paste 芝麻酱

seafood sauce 海鲜酱
lamb slices 涮羊肉片

Part **B** *Reading*

Passage 1 **Roast Duck**

Roast Beijing Duck is thought to be one of the most delicious dishes all over the world. Some find it a bit too greasy, but others get hooked after one taste. In any case, a Beijing Duck dinner is usually a fixed item on any Beijing tour itinerary. Most visitors coming to Beijing will never forget to have a try.

The places that serve the best Roast Beijing Duck are Bianyifang Roast Duck Restaurant and Quanjude Roast Duck Restaurant, both of which have a history of over one hundred years. They represent two different schools of roasting duck. Bianyifang, founded in 1855, makes use of a closed oven and straw as the fuel. Quanjude, a better known one, founded in 1864, uses an oven without a door.

To cook ducks by direct heat dates back at least 1,500 years to the period of the Northern and Southern Dynasties, when "broiled duck" was mentioned in writing. About eight hundred years later, an imperial dietician to an emperor of the Yuan Dynasty, listed in his book the "grilled duck" as a banquet delicacy. It was made by cooking the duck — stuffed with a slice of sheep's tripe, parsley, scallion, and salt on a charcoal fire.

Before being put in the oven, the inside of the duck is half filled with hot water, which is not released until the duck has been cooked. For oven fuel, jujube-tree, peach or pear wood is used because these types of firewood emit little smoke and give steady and controllable fires with a faint and pleasant aroma. In the oven, each duck takes about forty minutes to cook, and the skin becomes crisp while the meat is tender. When roasted and dried, the duck will look brilliantly dark red, shining with oil and with crisp skin and tender meat. Few people could resist the temptation of it.

Now it's time to serve it! First, the chef will show you the whole duck. Then, he will slice it into about one hundred and twenty pieces with both skin and meat for each. Usually the duck is served together with special pancakes, hollowed sesame bun, green onions and sweet bean sauce. People can wrap duck slices, onion, and sauce in a pancake or a sesame bun with their bare hands. Sometimes people would like to put in mashed garlic and cucumber or carrot strips as well. Other parts of the duck will be served as either cold dishes with its livers, wings, stomach, webs and eggs, or hot dishes with its heart, tongue and kidneys. The bones can even be decocted together with Chinese watermelon and Chinese cabbage.

 Words and Expressions to Learn ·····················

greasy / ˈɡriːzɪ / *a.* 油腻的

hook / hʊk / *v.* 沉迷，上瘾

broil / brɔɪl / *v.* 烤（肉）

imperial / ɪmˈpɪərɪəl / *a.* 帝王的，皇帝的

dietitian / daɪəˈtɪʃən / *n.* 营养学家

grill / ɡrɪl / *v.* 烤

tripe / traɪp / *n.* 肚子，内脏片

jujube / ˈdʒuːdʒuːb / *n.* 枣

web / web / *n.* 蹼足

kidney / ˈkɪdnɪ / *n.* 肾

decoct / dɪˈkɒkt / *v.* 熬，煎（药等）

***   ***   ***   ***   ***   ***

in any case 无论如何

a slice of 一片，一部分

hollowed sesame bun 芝麻饼圈

mashed garlic 大蒜泥

Chinese watermelon 冬瓜

Chinese cabbage 白菜

Passage 2 | Some Traditional Foods

Beggar's Chicken

It is said in the Qing Dynasty, at the foot of Yushan Mountain in Changshu, a beggar caught a chicken. He just killed the chicken and got out its viscera. Because there was no boiler or cooking stove, he wrapped the chicken with several lotus leaves, and sealed the chicken with mud, then baked it on a simple furnace. He removed the mud after the chicken was cooked, and the good smell came out immediately. A lot of people stopped walking, just to breathe the fragrant and delicious smell. Later on, this cooking method has spread away wildly. People call this dish beggar's chicken.

Stinky Tofu

Chowdoufu, also called "stinky tofu", is a favorite in China. It leaves an unforgettable impression upon foreigners, who either love it or wish they have never smelt it. Stinky tofu is a form of fermented tofu, which, as the name suggests, has a strong odor. However, it is a popular snack in East China. They are usually found at night markets, roadside stands, and temple fairs and often as a side dish in lunch bars. Wide regional and individual variations exist in its manufacture and preparation. Most typically, it consists of tofu which has been marinated in a brine made from fermented vegetables for as long as several months. It can be eaten cold, steamed, stewed, or most commonly, fried. It is often accompanied by chili sauce.

It is recorded that chowdoufu originated from Wang Zhihe, a scholar who went to Beijing for imperial examinations. Unfortunately, he failed many times. In order to earn his bread, he could do nothing but make tofu. One day, his tofu sold badly and many remained. So he chopped them into small blocks and bloated them with seasonings. Until autumn, when he opened the jar, the tofu changed its color into cyan, emitting a strong odor, but with a unique flavor. He let his neighbors have a taste; however, to his surprise, they all loved it. Soon, chowdoufu found great favor in the royal court. Dowager Empress Cixi liked it very much, giving it a name of "Qingfang". Since then, chowdoufu has become an imperial dish.

Jaozi

Jiaozi or dumpling is a traditional and popular food with a long history in China. There is a popular saying in China, "There is nothing more delicious than jiaozi." So you could imagine how much Chinese love it. In the later years of Eastern Han period, an official called Zhang Zhongjing created a kind of food to help poor people keep warm in cold winter. It was made with all kinds of fillings such as mutton, hot pepper and some medicinal materials. Afterwards people began to make dumplings as well. Jiaozi is the food that will no doubt appear on tables during the Spring Festival. Generally, people prepare it before midnight on the last day of the passing lunar year and eat it after the New Year's bell is sounded.

Jiaozi looks like gold and silver ingots so when people eat it during festivals they really hope it could bring fortune and good luck to them. Sometimes people will add some sweets, Chinese dates and chestnuts in the fillings of some dumplings to express their wishes. They hope those who get sweets could have a sweeter life. Those who get dates and chestnuts could have babies early, because dates (zao), are homonymic with "early" in Chinese, and chestnuts (lizi) with "smoothly". Zi is homonymic with children. Today jiaozi has already become an important part of Chinese cuisine.

Words and Expressions to Learn

viscera / ˈvɪsərə / n. 内脏

furnace / ˈfɜːnɪs / n. 火炉

stinky / ˈstɪŋkɪ / a. 发臭的

ferment / ˈfɜːment / v. (使) 发酵

odor / ˈəʊdə / n. 气味，臭气

snack / snæk / n. 小吃

variation / ˌveərɪˈeɪʃən / n. 变化形式，变体

marinate / ˈmærɪneɪt / v. 浸泡

brine / braɪn / n. 盐水

chili / ˈtʃɪlɪ / n. 辣椒

bloat / bləʊt / v. 使膨胀，腌制

cyan / ˈsaɪən / n. 蓝绿色，青色

ingot / ˈɪŋgət / n. 元宝

homonymic / ˌhɒməˈnɪmɪk / a. 同音异义字的

***　　***　　***　　　***　　***　　***

originate from 起源于

no doubt 无疑地

lunar year 农历年

Part C Exercises

I. *Make up a brief dialogue according to the given situation.*

　　Suppose you are a chef, familiar with different styles of hot pot in China. You are to introduce to foreign guests hot pots of Sichuan, Cantonese, and Beijing style. You can refer to the following.

Sichuan hot pot: noted for its spiciness, pepper oil added to the stock, an insulator on the surface of the soup, special ingredients: beef tripe, beef marrow, and pig brain.

Cantonese hot pot: most popular in Southeast Asia, its sauce: dried shrimp, peanuts, garlic, hot pepper, tea leaves, and salt, soy sauce and fresh raw egg added to it to make a dip (调味汁).

Beijing style: including both chrysanthemum (菊花) and mutton hot pots. Chrysanthemum hot pot: when chrysanthemums bloom, it's time to start eating hot pot. Main ingredients: shrimp, thin slices of pork kidney and liver, and fish fillet (鱼片，鱼柳). Chrysanthemum leaves are actually scattered (撒，撒播) into the pot to add a touch of the flavor of the plant. Mutton hot pot: choose only young lambs from Inner Mongolia, tender meat.

II. *Complete the dialogue by translating the Chinese sentences into English.*

(T: Tourist　W: Waiter)

(At a Roast Duck Restaurant.)

W: Here is your Roast Beijing Duck, Sir.

T: 1. _____ (看起来很像我们在美国感恩节吃的烤火鸡).

W: Maybe. But it is absolutely unique in China.

T: Really? 2. _____ (请你给我示范一下怎样吃这道菜,好吗)?

W: Sure. 3. _____ (首先,左手拿薄饼,用大葱段蘸少量面酱涂到上面,然后将葱段放在薄饼中间,再用筷子夹几片鸭肉在上面。最后将薄饼卷起来便可食用).

T: Let me have a try. Is this right?

W: Yes. You are great.

T: 4. _____ (真是皮脆肉嫩！我从来没有尝过如此好吃的烤鸭). It's very difficult to make it, isn't it?

W: The preparation is a bit complicated.

T: How long does it take to roast the ducks?

W: About 40 minutes. 5. _____ (等鸭皮发脆呈暗红色,鸭子就烤好了).

T: Quite interesting. I hope someday I will come again to taste the dish.

W: You are always welcome.

III. *Decide whether the following statements are true or false according to the Reading Passages.*

1. The most famous restaurants for serving Roast Beijing Duck are Bianyifang and Quanjude.
2. It was during the Northern and Southern Dynasties that the grilled duck was served as a banquet delicacy.
3. In the roasting process some fruit tree wood is used to give the meat its unique flavor.
4. Tourists can't help trying the roast duck mainly due to its color, aroma and taste.
5. The chef needs to be very much skilled in slicing the roast duck.
6. The way the beggar roasted a chicken is to put the lotus leaves in between the chicken and clay and baked it on a simple furnace.
7. Stinky tofu can't be found in bars but at markets, roadside stands and temple fairs.
8. People in East China often eat stinky tofu with different kinds of sauce.
9. Stinky tofu used to be one of the favorite dishes in the royal court of the Qing Dynasty.
10. Chinese people have given symbolic meanings to dumplings.

IV. *Put the following sentences into English.*

1. 约一万年前,我们祖先发明了三条腿和四条腿的陶器鼎,放在火上煮东西吃。
2. 那时人们将所有可以食用的食物放在鼎里加热直到煮熟为止。人们称这种食物为"羹"。
3. 一般认为用火锅速煮羊肉可以追溯到元朝开国皇帝忽必烈。
4. 涮羊肉火锅起源于中国北方,已有上千年的历史了。

5. 火锅下面有火能使火锅里的汤水保持沸腾。

6. 将煮熟的羊肉片放进备有各种调味品的佐料中沾一沾，就可以吃了。

7. 叫花鸡是我们餐厅的特色菜。

8. 饺子看似金银元宝，所以在节日里人们吃饺子，真诚希望自己财运亨通。

V. *Topic for discussion.*

List some famous dishes in Chinese Cuisine and tell the interesting stories behind them.

UNIT 3 Lesson 10
Chinese Tea Culture

Part A *Conversation*

Dialogue 1   At a Teahouse

(G: Guide   T: Tourist   W: Waiter)

G: We'd like some tea. What kinds are you serving today?

W: We have green tea, black tea, and herbal tea. They're listed on our menu.

G: Do you have any flower-scented tea?

W: Yes, we do. We have an excellent selection of them.

G: Great. We'd like a pot of jasmine tea for two.

T: Well, do you have any iced tea or cold drinks?

W: Of course. We have iced milk tea and iced pearl tea. They are both very popular here.

T: OK. I'll get a large glass of iced pearl tea. Not too sweet, please. I'm on a diet.

W: No problem. We also have a great choice of herbal teas. It's on the first page of the menu.

T: I see.

G: Do you have any afternoon tea specials?

W: Yes. We serve all-you-can-eat cakes with our Chinese tea collection.

G: Sounds good. How much is it?

W: It's 30 *yuan* each. It's really a good deal for a cake lover.

T: We'll take two. My treat.

G: Thank you.

Dialogue 2　At a Tea Store

(T: Tourist　S: Shop Assistant)

S: Hello. What can I do for you?

T: I want to buy some local specialties for my parents. They are very fond of Chinese tea.

S: Really? We have a good selection of black tea and green tea.

T: What do you recommend?

S: You may try some green tea. Green tea contains more Vitamin C. This category includes Longjing tea of Zhejiang Province, Maofeng of Huangshan Mountain in Anhui Province and Biluochun produced in Jiangsu. Longjing tea is believed to be the best brand. Or, you can try some Oolong tea. It's mainly produced in Fujian, Guangdong and Taiwan.

T: Well, I'd like both Longjing and Oolong tea. What are the prices?

S: 480 *yuan* per kilo for each.

T: One kilo of Longjing and one kilo of Oolong, please.

S: That'll be 960 *yuan*.

T: Here is 1,000 *yuan*.

S: Thank you. Here's your change, Sir. Have a nice day.

 Words and Expressions to Learn · · · · · · · · · · · · · · · · · · ·

category / ˈkætəgrɪ / *n.* 类别, 范畴

***　　***　　***　　***　　***　　***

black tea 红茶	all-you-can-eat 自助的
flower-scented tea 花茶	My treat. 我请客。
a selection of 许多, 精选的	Longjing tea 龙井茶
jasmine tea 茉莉花茶	Maofeng 毛峰
iced pearl tea 冰镇珍珠奶茶	Biluochun 碧螺春
on a diet 节食	Oolong tea 乌龙茶
afternoon tea specials 午后茶点	

Part B Reading

Passage 1 China, the Homeland of Tea

China is the homeland of tea. Of the three major beverages of the world — tea, coffee and cocoa — tea is consumed by the largest number of people in the world.

At present more than forty countries in the world grow tea with Asian countries producing 90% of the world's total output. All tea trees in other countries have their origin directly or indirectly in China. The word for tea leaves or tea as a drink in many countries are derivatives from the Chinese character "cha." The Russians call it "cha'i", which sounds like "chaye" (tea leaves) as it is pronounced in North China, and the English word "tea" sounds similar to the pronunciation of its counterpart in Xiamen. The Japanese character for tea is written exactly the same as it is in Chinese, though pronounced with a slight difference.

The habit of tea drinking spread to Japan in the 6th century, but it was not introduced to Europe and America till the 17th and 18th centuries. Now the number of tea drinkers in the world is legion and is still on the increase.

In the past dynasties, people not only formed a special way of tea-drinking, but also developed an art form called tea-drinking. This art form includes many aspects. The most noticeable ones are the making of tea, the way of brewing, and the drinking utensils such as teapot. The art of making tea is called "chadao", translated as "the way of tea" by Westerners, which was soon accepted as something that Japan and Korea learned from China. There are four basic principles in "chadao" — harmony, respect, purity and tranquility. Tea is by no means a meditation medicine. However, it is very important for people who want to taste the sweetness behind the bitterness in tea to have a peaceful mind. Every tea has different flavor and sweetness.

In China, a host will pour tea into teacup only seven tenths full, and it is said the other three tenths will be filled with friendship and affection.

Tea plays an important role in Chinese emotional life.Tea is always offered immediately to a guest in Chinese home. Serving a cup of tea is more than a matter of mere politeness; it is a symbol of togetherness, a sharing of something enjoyable and a way of showing respect to visitors. Not to take at least a sip might be considered rude in some areas.

Though never drunk with milk and only very rarely with sugar, the method of serving tea also varies from place to place: sometimes it comes in huge mugs with a lid, elsewhere in exquisite cups served from a miniature pot. When drinking in company, it's polite to top up others' cups before your own whenever they become empty; if someone does this for you, lightly tap your first two fingers on the table to show your thanks. If you've had enough, leave your cup full. In a restaurant, take the lid off or turn it over if you want the pot refilled during the meal.

It's also a good idea to try some Muslim tea during your stay in China. This involves dried fruit, nuts, seeds, crystallized sugar and tea heaped into a cup with the remaining space filled with hot water, poured with panache from an immensely long-spouted copper kettle. Also known as Eight Treasures Tea, it's becoming widely available in restaurants everywhere, and is sometimes sold in packets from street stalls.

Today, just as coffee in the West, tea has become a part of daily life in China. You can see teahouses scattered on streets like cafes in the West. Despite Western culture's impacts on China, the tea ceremony is still very popular and the Chinese people would like to hold on to their traditional tea culture.

 Words and Expressions to Learn ·

derivative / dɪˈrɪvətɪv / *n.* 派生物, 派生词
counterpart / ˈkaʊntəpɑːt / *n.* 对方相应的人 或物, 配对物
legion / ˈliːdʒən / *a.* 众多的, 大批的
brew / bruː/ *v.* 泡制
utensil / juːˈtensl / *n.* 器皿, 用具

tranquility / trænˈkwɪlɪtɪ / *n.* 宁静
meditation / medɪˈteɪʃən / *n.* 静坐, 默祷
sip / sɪp / *n.* 呷, 喝 (一小口)
miniature / ˈmɪnɪətʃə / *a.* 微型的, 缩小的
Muslim / ˈmʊzlɪm / *n. & a.* 穆斯林 (的)
panache / pəˈnæʃ / *n.* 神韵, 神气十足

∗∗∗　　∗∗∗　　∗∗∗　　∗∗∗　　∗∗∗　　∗∗∗

take over 接管, 获得对……的控制
on the increase 正在增长
by no means 决不

top up 加满
crystallized sugar 冰糖
Eight Treasures Tea 八宝茶

Passage 2　Category of Chinese Teas

Tea cultivation was first recorded in China in 350 AD. But according to legends, tea had been known in China since 2700 BC. Today, tea is widely consumed in the world, either hot or cold, by half of the world's population.

Tea is traditionally classified according to the degree or period of fermentation or oxidation that the leaves have gone through.

White tea is resulted when young leaves or new buds have undergone no oxidation. The buds may be shielded from sunlight to prevent formation of chlorophyll. White tea is produced in less quantities than most of the other kinds, and can be more expensive than tea from the same plant processed by other methods. It is also less well-known in countries outside China, though this is changing with the introduction of white tea in bagged form.

Green tea is produced when the oxidation process is stopped after a minimal amount of oxidation by heating, either with steam, a traditional Japanese method; or by dry cooking in hot pans, the traditional Chinese method. Tea leaves may be left to dry as separate leaves or rolled into small pellets. The latter process takes more time and is typically done only with pekoes of higher quality. The tea is processed within one to two days of harvesting.

Oolong tea is when oxidation is stopped somewhere between the standards for green tea and black tea. The oxidation process will take two to three days.

With black tea, the tea leaves are allowed to completely oxidize. The literal translation of the Chinese name is red tea. Chinese people call it red tea because the tea liquid is red. Westerners call it black tea because the tealeaves used to brew it are usually black. The oxidation process will take around two weeks and up to one month.

Pu-erh tea includes two types: raw and cooked. Raw or green pu-erh may be consumed young or aged. During the aging process, the tea undergoes a second, microbial fermentation. "Cooked" pu-erh is made from green pu-erh leaf that has been artificially oxidized to approximate the flavor of the natural aging process. This is done through a controlled process similar to composting, where both the moisture and temperature of the tea are carefully controlled. Both types of pu-erh tea are usually compressed into various shapes including bricks, discs, bowls, or mushrooms. This is used to start the second fermentation process, as only compressed forms of pu-erh will age. While most teas are consumed within a year of production, pu-erh can be left there to age for many years to improve its flavor with up to 30 to 50 years for raw pu-erh and 10 to 15 years for cooked pu-erh. Teas that undergo a second oxidation are collectively referred to as "black tea" in Chinese. This is not to be confused with the English term black tea, which is known in Chinese as red tea.

The category of yellow tea usually implies a special tea processed similarly to green tea, but with a slower drying process. The tea generally has a very yellow-green appearance and a smell different from both white tea and green tea, but similarities in taste and smell can still be drawn between yellow, green and white teas.

Flower tea is processed or brewed with flowers. Typically, each flower goes with a specific category of tea, such as green or red tea. The most famous flower tea is jasmine tea, a green or oolong tea scented or brewed with jasmine flowers. Rose, lotus, lychee, and chrysanthemum are also popular flowers.

As far as tea preparation is concerned, typically, the best temperature for brewing tea can be determined by its type. Teas that have gone through little or no oxidation period, such as green or white tea, are best brewed at lower temperatures around 80℃, while teas with longer oxidation periods should be brewed at higher temperatures around 100℃.

 Words and Expressions to Learn ·

cultivation / ˌkʌltɪ'veɪʃən / n. 培养,耕作

fermentation / ˌfɜːmen'teɪʃən / n. 发酵

oxidation / ˌɒksɪ'deɪʃən / n. 氧化

chlorophyll / 'klɒrəfɪl / n. 叶绿素

minimal / 'mɪnɪməl / a. 最小的,最小限度的

pellet / 'pelət / n. 小球

pekoe / 'piːkəʊ / n. 香红茶(用茶树嫩叶制的高级红茶)

microbial / maɪ'krəʊbɪəl / a. 微生物的,由细菌引起的

artificially / ˌɑːtɪ'fɪʃəlɪ / ad. 人工地

approximate / ə'prɒksɪmeɪt / v. 近似,接近

compost / 'kɒmpɒst / v. 混合,合成

moisture / 'mɒɪstʃə / n. 湿度

compress / kəm'pres / v. 压缩

lychee / 'liːtʃiː / n. 荔枝,荔枝树

*** *** *** *** *** ***

be shielded from 保护, 防护   be referred to as 被称作

pu-erh tea 普洱茶

Part C Exercises

I. *Make up a brief dialogue between a tourist and a guide according to the following passage.*

How to Pick a Good Teapot

In China, people think different teas prefer different tea wares. Green tea prefers glass tea ware; scented tea porcelain ware while Oolong tea performs best in purple clay tea ware.

In fact, tea wares not only improve tea quality but also by-produce a tea art. Skilled artisans bestow them artistic beauty. A good teapot is not only a piece of good tea ware but also a piece of great artwork that its value can never be understated. The way to pick a good teapot can be summarized as follows:

1. A great teapot is one that you don't want to drink tea without it. You pick a good teapot like you pick a wife. You want to look at your teapot for the next 50 years and it will still be beautiful.

2. The teapot can be clay or porcelain. A good clay teapot needs to be bright and hard. Put the teapot on your palm and tap it with your finger. Listen to the sound. With a few practices, you will be able to tell how hard the clay is.

3. Smell! A brand new clay teapot will come with the smell of clay. If you pick a new teapot that smells charcoal, oil or other smell, chances are that it is not a good one.

4. The lid of the pot should be tight. The clay teapot has a vent on the lid. Fill the pot with water and press your index finger on the vent as you tilt the teapot. If you see water coming out from the spout, it is not a good teapot.

5. Release your finger from the vent as indicated in step 4. A better teapot will have water flow out of the spout smoothly with an open vent.

6. The gravity center of the teapot is also very important. Fill the teapot (75% filled) with water. Lift the teapot and try to pour the water out of the teapot. If you feel your hand a bit out of balance when you try to pour water out, it is not a good teapot.

7. What kind of tea are you going to use in the pot? The character of tea is an important factor for the type of teapot you are going to choose. The tea that emphasizes "smell" such as flower flavored tea needs to retain heat in the pot in order to bring out the smell. In this case, a high frequency teapot is better (referred to #2 for tapping sound). The tea that emphasizes taste such as Oolong tea needs a teapot with sound of lower frequency.

Complete the dialogue by translating the Chinese sentences into English.

> (T: Tourist   S: Shop Assistant)
>
> T: Excuse me, can you recommend some good tea?
>
> S: Yes, of course. 1. _____ (砖茶在这儿很受青睐).
>
> T: I see. How do you pack the tea?
>
> S: 2. _____ (大多是袋装茶).
>
> T: All right.
>
> S: Any particular type of tea you are looking for?
>
> T: Yes. 3. _____ (我要茉莉花茶。我听说中国人喜欢花茶). So I want to have a taste of it.
>
> S: OK. 4. _____ (花茶在中国北方尤其受欢迎).
>
> T: Please show me some herbal tea, too.
>
> S: OK. Anything else?
>
> T: I also want some green tea to take home. 5. _____ (哪一种牌子的绿茶好呢)?
>
> S: 6. _____ (本店供应大量中国绿茶精品。所有精品茶叶都在货架上，任您挑选).
>
> T: OK. I want to buy four tins, each one with a different brand.

III. *Decide whether the following statements are true or false according to the Reading Passages.*

> 1. Tea did not become the most popular beverage among the Chinese until the 7th century.
>
> 2. Now tea has become the most popular beverage in the world and the number of tea drinkers is still on the rise.
>
> 3. Tea ceremony is rooted as one of the most important aspects of Asian cultures like those of Japan and Korea.
>
> 4. The method of serving tea in China varies little as most people never drink tea with milk and rarely with sugar.
>
> 5. Tea also plays an important part in Chinese emotional life.
>
> 6. Today, just like coffee in the West, tea has become a part of people's daily life in China.
>
> 7. With less production, white tea is generally more expensive and better known than any other tea.
>
> 8. The oxidation process of Oolong tea will take more time than that of black tea.
>
> 9. Tea that undergoes a second oxidation is referred to as black tea in Chinese.

10. It can be inferred that tea bricks will taste much better if it is brewed at the temperature about 100℃ .

IV. *Fill in the blanks with a suitable preposition or the proper form of the word given in brackets.*

People in different regions might use different tea sets 1. _____ tea serving. While large teapots are favored in North China, those 2. _____ (common) used in South China are pretty small, sometimes even as tiny as a fist.

No matter what kind of teapot they use, however, most Chinese people might regard the teapot produced in Yixing 3. _____ the best. It is said that if you have used a Yixing teapot for decades, you can brew 4. _____ (taste) tea by simply pouring 5. _____ (boil) water into it. This is because the special porous (能渗透的) clay called "zisha" (purple clay) from which the teapots are made can absorb the flavor of tea, and become more and more seasoned after years of use. So, people are often suggested to prepare just one kind of tea with a pot, in case that the 6. _____ (mix) of different teas will affect the flavor.

This porous nature gives another outstanding attribute (特性) 7. _____ Yixing teapot: the ability to retain heat. 8. _____ this advantage, a master of tea ceremony can fully bring 9. _____ the special flavors of certain types of tea. There are also many other features 10. _____ its credit. Free of any toxic (有毒的) element that is often found in other clay wares, it also has a solid texture, an appropriate 11. _____ (absorb) rate, as well as a low thermal (热量的) 12. _____ (conduct). The history of Yixing teapot can be dated back to the Song Dynasty. While it was gradually growing popular 13. _____ Chinese, many noble people and scholars began to collect those 14. _____ (beauty) made. From then on, potters have added much more 15. _____ (art) creations into the daily article, and meanwhile, established the tradition of hand making.

V. *Translate the following passage into Chinese.*

In one popular Chinese legend, Shennong, the legendary emperor of China, inventor of agriculture and Chinese medicine, was on a journey about five thousand years ago. The Emperor, known for his wisdom, believed that the safest way to drink water was by boiling it. One day he noticed some leaves had fallen into his boiling water. The ever inquisitive and curious monarch took a sip of the brew and was pleasantly surprised by its flavor and its restorative (有恢复健康和体力作用的) properties. Variant of the legend tells that the Emperor tried medical properties of various herbs on himself, some of them poisonous, and tea worked as an antidote. Shennong is also mentioned in Lu Yu's *Cha Jing*, the earliest work on the subject of tea.

VI. *Topic for discussion*

Discuss the advantages and disadvantages of tea drinking with your classmates.

UNIT 4
Tourist Attractions

UNIT 4 Lesson 11
Heilongjiang, Jilin and Liaoning

Part A *Conversation*

Dialogue   **Enjoying the Night View of Harbin**

(G: Guide   T: Tourist)

T: Wow, the whole city is like a crystal town. It's so beautiful.

G: Exactly. In other places, such a cold winter night usually calls for an early bedtime, but here in Harbin, when the night falls, the more wonderful side of life begins. You see there are so many people!

T: Yeah! Look, those children are eating ice cream! And it's 30 degrees centigrade below zero!

G: The local people often say there is no wrong weather here. Blame yourself for wrong clothes.

T: That's interesting!

G: Here is the Sophia Square.

T: Wait, I know how it got the name. Because of the church over there, right?

G: Yes. The Sophia Cathedral is the biggest Orthodox church in the Far East.

T: When was it built?

G: It used to be a small church built in 1907. With an increase in believers of the Orthodox, the St. Sophia Cathedral was rebuilt in 1923. It took 9 years to finish it.

T: I can see the Russian style has greatly influenced the buildings in Harbin.

G: Yeah. If you want to see the old Harbin, there's another place you should never miss, the central boulevard.

T: Old Harbin?

G: Well, Harbin has adopted the Paris model in city planning, building modern buildings as the new town outside and leaving the old buildings as the old town.

T: That adds modern features to the long history of the city.

G: You said it. Look down at the stones of the street!

T: Oh, yes! They are so different.

G: The streets were paved a hundred years ago. You know, before it was paved, the whole street got very muddy on rainy days and a Russian engineer got the idea of paving it with these stones.

T: I love these stones!

G: The local people call these stones "bread stones".

T: Oh, they look exactly like bread. How amazing! What is that? An ice carving?

G: Yes. This is the Ice and Snow Wonderland on the frozen Songhua River.

T: There are snow carvings too! It is a Disneyland on ice!

G: You know people here often say "What is Harbin without ice, snow and joy?"

T: Sure, now I understand ice and snow are the soul of Harbin in winter.

G: You know, Harbin International Ice and Snow Festival is held annually from January 5 to February 5.

T: That's a wonderful idea to have a festival. Who first came up with such a good idea?

G: Your guess is as good as mine.

 Words and Expressions to Learn ·

crystal / ˈkrɪstəl / *a.* (水晶般)透明的
Orthodox / ˈɔːθədɒks / *n.* 东正教

adopt / əˈdɒpt / *v.* 采用
annually / ˈænjʊəlɪ / *ad.* 每年一次地

***　　***　　***　　***　　***　　***

Sophia Square 圣索菲亚广场
the central boulevard 中央大街
ice carving 冰雕
snow carving 雪雕
Disneyland on ice 冰上迪斯尼乐园

Harbin International Ice and Snow Festival
　哈尔滨国际冰雪节
Your guess is as good as mine. 我和你一样
　不知道。

Passage 1　Changbai Mountain

Changbai Mountain is situated in northeast China, bordering the Democratic People's Republic of Korea in the south. As a dormant volcano, Changbai Mountain boasts rare animals, marvelous lakes, amazing hot springs, and forests that stretch to the horizon. There is splendid scenery during the four seasons, but it is especially beautiful in winter.

The most beautiful part of Changbai Mountain is undoubtedly Tianchi, or the Heavenly Lake. The lake was formed in the crater of Changbai Mountain, and it is the source of the Songhua, Tumen and Yalu Rivers. Changbai Mountain is also the cradle of Manchu, Korean and Han nationalities. The altitude of the Heavenly Lake is 2,189 meters, and so the average temperature is 7.3 ℃ (45.14 ℉). With clouds everywhere, the Heavenly Lake is like a piece of jade in the sky. You can find a very interesting phenomenon while walking around the Heavenly Lake. On many occasions sunshine and rain occur at the same time. It may rain very hard one minute, but you may soon find the sun shining warmly the next minute. Sometimes, you can even watch it rain in the west and shine in the east. Besides the wonderful scenery and extraordinary climate, many visitors have claimed that there are monsters in the lake! Some of them even took photos as proof, but there is still no conclusion.

To the north of the Heavenly Lake is the Chengcha River. Running gently for about 1,200 meters, the river suddenly becomes a churning rapids and drops from a 68-meter-high cliff. This is the famous Changbai Waterfall, the highest volcanic waterfall in the world. Watching it from far away, the waterfall appears like a white ribbon hanging in midair. As you go nearer, you can hear the loud roar and feel the cold of the waterfall. Another good place to watch the waterfall is Heifengkou on the main peak of Changbai Mountain. Strong winds blow endlessly here, making it hard for visitors to walk and climb. But it remains the best place to enjoy the beauty of the waterfall. Apart from Changbai Waterfall, more than ten smaller waterfalls are also available in Changbai Mountain. Visitors have to climb the north slope to see the

Changbai Waterfalls.

Less than 2 kilometers away from Changbai Waterfall lie the Changbai Hot Springs. All kinds of minerals in the water have dyed the rocks around the hot springs many bright colors. Most of the hot springs have temperatures over 60 ℃ (140 ℉); the highest is 82℃ (179.6 ℉). Hot Spring Eggs have become a special local snack. Visitors can bathe in the hot springs, which are very effective for some diseases, such as arthritis, dermatitis and exhaustion.

Underground Forest in Changbai Mountain is famous for its view of virgin forests. Ancient tall trees, huge rocks, rare animals and cliffy canyons have attracted many scientists, explorers and photographers in recent years. Twin Lakes and Natural Museum on the north slope are also worth visiting. Additionally, the Great Valley, Jinjiang Waterfall, King's Lake, Tiger's Back and so on on the west slope also attract many visitors. If visitors want to closely observe the borders of the PRC and the DPRK and enjoy the beautiful alpine flowers, they can climb Changbai Mountain from the south slope.

During the peak seasons, namely June through September, hundreds of flowers blossom on the south and west slopes. It is very cool in Changbai Mountain, so it's an ideal place for escaping from the summer heat. But it is also very rainy in July and August, and visitors cannot watch the Heavenly Lake clearly at that time. The best time to visit Changbai Mountain is September. Generally, it snows from October. The best time to view snow and to ski is from November to March. Ice and snow begin to melt from April, but visitors can still find snow even in May.

Visitors can stay with Korean families to experience the local life, or they can camp in the forest to breathe the fresh air. Changbai Mountain is also an area rich in wild fungi and medicinal herbs. Visitors can find them in most local shops.

 Words and Expressions to Learn

boast / bəʊst / v. 自豪地拥有

crater / ˈkreɪtə / n. 火山口

cradle / ˈkreɪdl / n. 摇篮

churning / ˈtʃɜːnɪŋ / a. 翻滚的，汹涌的

rapids / ˈræpɪdz / n. 急流，湍流

ribbon / ˈrɪbən / n. 缎带，丝带

roar / rɔː / n. & v. 吼叫，咆哮

arthritis / ɑːˈθraɪtɪs / n. 关节炎

dermatitis / dɜːməˈtaɪtɪs / *n.* 皮炎

exhaustion / ɪgˈzɔːstʃən / *n.* 疲劳

canyon / ˈkænjən / *n.* 大峡谷

namely / ˈneɪmlɪ / *ad.* 就是，既是

ideal / aɪˈdɪəl / *a.* 理想的，完美的

***　　***　　***　　***　　***　　***

the Democratic People's Republic of Korea
朝鲜人民民主共和国

a dormant volcano 休眠火山

Heifengkou 黑风口

apart from 除了

Twin Lakes 双湖

Passage 2　Harbin Snow and Ice Festival

The temperature in Harbin reaches forty below zero, and stays below freezing nearly half the year. This Chinese city is actually further north than Vladivostok, Russia, which is just 300 miles away and known for being cold. So what do people do here in winter? Rather than suffer the cold, the people of Harbin celebrate it, with annual festival of snow and ice sculptures and competitions. The festival officially runs from January 5 through to February 5, but often opens a week earlier and runs into March, since it's usually still cold enough.

Snow and ice sculpture show in Harbin was first organized in 1963, and the festival itself only started in 1985. Since then, the festival has grown into a massive event, bringing in over a million tourists from all over the world every winter. The sculptures have become more elaborate and artistic over time.

The snow festival is actually separated from the ice festival; both take place on the wide open spaces of Sun Island Park north of the Songhua River.

Most of the sculptures appearing at the snow festival are competitive entries. Each team starts with a cube of packed snow that measures about three meters on each side, and then starts carving away. Teams come in from all over the world — Russia, Japan, Canada, France, even South Africa. Part of the fun is guessing the nationality of the team, based on their sculpture's artistic style, before reading the signs.

The ice festival, a few miles away from the snow festival, is anything but dull and colorless. Crowds flocking to the entrance are greeted by loud dance music in the distance, as if at an outdoor pop concert. And colorful lights shine everywhere, buried within huge blocks of ice structures as high as thirty meters. You can make out people standing on its blue and red stairway.

Looking at the ice festival site from the top of a huge sculpture, you will feel it's like a Disney theme park, with all kinds of attractions and food hawkers and kids running around and people lining up for bathrooms. The only differences are that the temperature is about a hundred degrees lower than that of the typical Disney Park, and all the structures are made out of ice rather than plastic — and slipping and falling here doesn't result in lawsuits.

One of the popular activities at the festival is climbing a wall of solid ice. All the ice comes from the Songhua River, which provides a limitless supply; huge chainsaws are required to cut through the ice, which can be meters thick.

The snow festival is mostly a display of art; the ice festival is mostly a display of architecture. Long ago, Disney made a circle-vision 360 film called "Wonders of China" — still showing at the China Pavilion in the world showcase at EPCOT — which includes a brief section about Harbin's ice festival. In the movie, the sculptures are quite low-key, with only some light bulbs inside small globes and ice carvings. Things have changed a lot since those days.

 Words and Expressions to Learn ·

massive / ˈmæsɪv / *a.* 规模庞大的
elaborate / ɪˈlæbərət / *a.* 精致的，复杂的
entry / ˈentrɪ / *n.* 参赛作品
cube / kjuːb / *n.* 立方体状的东西
flock / flɒk / *v.* 蜂拥，簇拥

hawker / ˈhɔːkə / *n.* 叫卖的小贩
lawsuit / ˈlɔːsuːt / *n.* 诉讼，官司
chainsaw / ˈtʃeɪnsɔː / *n.* 链锯
showcase / ˈʃəʊkeɪs / *n.* 玻璃陈列柜
low-key / ˈləʊˈkiː / *a.* 低调的，不招摇的

***   ***   ***   ***   ***   ***

Vladivostok 符拉迪沃斯托克（即海参崴）
anything but 决不，一点儿不
a Disney theme park 迪斯尼主题公园
a circle-vision 360 film 全景电影
EPCOT=Experimental Prototype Community

of Tomorrow 迪斯尼世界的埃布克特中心（即由迪斯尼乐园创始人迪斯尼设想出的未来社区实验原型）
light bulb 灯泡

Part C Exercises

I. Make up a brief dialogue according to the given situation.

Suppose you are Li Ming. You and your friend Mr. Smith are visiting the Harbin Snow and Ice Festival. Prepare a dialogue.

II. Answer the following questions about the Reading Passages.

1. What kind of mountain is Changbai Mountain?
2. What is unusual about Tianchi, the Heavenly Lake?
3. Why is the Changbai Waterfall so famous?
4. Which month is the best time to visit Changbai Mountain? Why?
5. Besides enjoying the artistic snow and ice sculptures, what fun can visitors also get from visiting the Ice and Snow Festival?
6. According to the author, what are the differences between a Disney Park and the Ice Festival in Harbin?
7. Where does the ice used at the Ice Festival come from?
8. What is the difference between the Ice Festival and the Snow Festival?

III. Translate the following two passages into Chinese.

1. In recent years, elderly people in Harbin's suburbs have been organizing themselves into many yang ko (秧歌) teams, and their purpose is to enjoy themselves while keeping fit. In the countryside, big yang ko teams are organized for wedding celebrations, birthday parties and so on. During the busy farming season the dancers work in the fields, but when the lunar New Year comes around they put on their costumes (服装, 演出服) and go to private homes to perform the yang ko dance, celebrating the new year and carrying on an age-old tradition.

2. Hunting is still the principal means of livelihood for the majority of Elunchun (鄂伦春) people. Some of the Ewenki (鄂温克族) people rely on the raising of reindeer, supplemented by some hunting, while the rest of them conduct seasonal hunting. A minority of the Dawo'er (达斡尔) people still hunt for a living. The combined hunting way of life of these peoples, which has been passed down from generation to generation, forms the hunting culture circle of the north.

IV. *Topics for discussion.*

1. Talk about the benefits the Harbin Snow and Ice Festival might bring to the Northeast.
2. Zhao Benshan is a well-known skit actor. Comment on his performance in skits or TV series.

UNIT 4 Lesson 12
Beijing

Part **A** *Conversation*

Dialogue 1   Ascending the Great Wall

(G: Guide   T: Tourist)

G: Have you heard of the story of Meng Jiangnü?

T: It has something to do with the Great Wall, isn't it?

G: Quite right. And now we are arriving at the Great Wall!

T: Would you please tell us the story? We'd like to hear it.

G: Sure. In the construction of the Great Wall many laborers lost their lives. Meng Jiangnü came to the Great Wall to bring winter clothes to her husband Fan Xiliang only to find that he had died. She was heartbroken and wept so bitterly that part of the Wall fell down. When Meng Jiangnü found her husband's body lying under the wall, she killed herself by jumping into the sea.

T: What a tragedy! Can you take us to the place where Meng Jiangnü cried her eyes out?

G: That's only a legend. Don't take it seriously. Meng Jiangnü lived in the reign of Emperor Qin Shi Huang, the first emperor of Qin Dynasty, but Badaling, the part of the Great Wall we see today was mainly built in Ming Dynasty.

T: Oh, I see.

G: The construction of the Great Wall started in Zhou Dynasty in the 7th century B.C. and continued until Ming Dynasty in the 15th century, taking altogether more than 2,000 years. So we Chinese often proudly say the Great Wall stands for the industry and wisdom of the Chinese people and is also a symbol of ancient Chinese culture.

T: You said it! How long is the Great Wall? It is said you can even see it from the moon.

G: The total length of the Great Wall is about 6,000 kilometers. Look! The Great Wall is built on the mountain and goes higher and higher. Isn't it beautiful, rising and falling, like a dragon?

T: It is beautiful, even better than the Great Wall I've seen in photographs. What are the towers for on the wall?

G: Oh, they are called beacon-fire towers. You know, the Great Wall was built to guard against invasion by nomadic tribes from the north. When people found the enemy approaching, they would send smoke signals from the tower as a warning. When the guards in the neighboring tower saw the signals, they would do the same. In this way, the signals would be sent all the way to the capital.

T: How clever the ancient people were!

G: Come on! Let's keep climbing up; the view's even more breathtaking up there.

T: Oh, the top of the Great Wall is really wide.

G: Yes. Five horses and ten soldiers could stand side by side. Come and have a look at the huge bricks of the Great Wall. How do you think they moved these bricks up here? There weren't even roads up here on the mountain, not to mention trucks and machines.

T: The ancient Chinese were really clever! I'm already tired. Hey, do you think anyone's ever walked to the end of the Great Wall?

G: Sure, some people have walked from Shanhaiguan all the way to Jiayuguan.

T: Really? Look, there are even people up there. Let's climb up and have a look. Race you!

G: I'll win for sure!

Dialogue 2   Visiting the Summer Palace

(G: Guide   T: Tourist)

G: Here we are. The Summer Palace.

T: But there are so many entrances. Which one should we go in?

G: This is called the East Palace Gate. It's the formal entrance for the Summer Palace.

The middle of the entrance was reserved for the emperor and empress. There was no way other people could go in through here.

T: Then how did people go in?

G: Through the small gates at both sides.

T: Who would have thought there would be so many rules even for gates?

(After entering the gate.)

T: This place is big! Which way should we go?

G: The Summer Palace has over three thousand rooms, and is made up of three parts — the Palace area, Longevity Hill and Kunming Lake. Which part would you like to see?

T: We want to see them all. Let's start from the Palace area. Is it where the emperor used to live?

G: That's where the Dowager Empress Cixi and the emperor attended to political affairs. You can see the Dowager Empress's Qingong.

T: Qingong? What's that?

G: Oh, "qin" means sleep. Qingong is the place where the emperor and the Dowager Empress used to rest.

T: The Dowager Empress and the emperor lived at the Summer Palace as well? Didn't they live in the Forbidden City?

G: Yes. But the Dowager Empress liked here a lot. Sometimes she'd stay for as long as half a year or more.

T: (Coming out of the Qingong.) This must be the famous Long Corridor? I've seen it many times on postcards.

G: You got it!

T: All these paintings are wonderful! I think this long corridor is a good idea. It separates the mountain and lake, and it's a shelter against the wind and sun while you enjoy the sights.

G: Exactly.

T: Oh, this lake is so pretty!

G: This is Kunming Lake. It's shaped like a peach, whereas the Longevity Hill behind it is shaped like a bat.

T: Why a bat? How ugly!

G: Bat in Chinese is pronounced "bianfu", and the "fu" sound in "bianfu" is the same as the "fu" in "xingfu" or happiness in Chinese.

T: So the design is for good luck.

G: You are right again!

 Words and Expressions to Learn

construction / kən'strʌkʃən / *n.* 建筑	breathtaking / 'breθteɪkɪŋ / *a.* 惊险的，激动人心的
tragedy / 'trædʒədɪ / *n.* 悲剧	shelter / 'ʃeltə / *n.* 遮蔽物
industry / 'ɪndʌstrɪ / *n.* 勤劳	
invasion / ɪn'veɪʒən / *n.* 侵略	

***   ***   ***   ***   ***   ***

cry one's eyes out 哭得死去活来	not to mention ... 更不用说……
in the reign of 在……统治时期	the Summer Palace 颐和园
beacon-fire tower 烽火台	Longevity Hill 万寿山
guard against 防御	Dowager Empress Cixi 慈禧太后
nomadic tribe 游牧部落	Long Corridor 长廊

Part B Reading

 **The Forbidden City**

Also known as the Palace Museum, the Forbidden City was the place where the emperors of Ming and Qing Dynasties worked and lived. It lies at the center of Beijing. Rectangular in shape, the Forbidden City is the world's largest palace complex. It is 960 meters long and 750 meters wide, having 9,999 rooms. Opposite the Tian'anmen Gate in the south, to the north is the Gate of Devine Prowess, which faces Jingshan Park.

The Forbidden City is surrounded by a 52-meter-wide, 6-meter-deep moat and a 10-meter-high, 3,400-meter-long city wall which has one gate on each side. There are four corner towers overlooking the city inside and outside on the four corners.

The Forbidden City is divided into two parts: the southern half, or the Outer Court where emperors executed their power over the nation and the northern half, or the Inner Court where they lived with their family. Until 1924 when the last emperor in China was driven out of the Inner Court, 14 emperors of Ming Dynasty and 10 emperors of Qing Dynasty had ruled here. About 500 years being the imperial palace, it houses numerous rare treasures. It is now listed by the UN among the World Cultural Heritage in 1987.

Meridian Gate is the main gate and south gate. Standing on the bridges stretching over the gorgeous Golden Water River, you can see Gate of Supreme Harmony (Taihemen), which is the most marvelous gate in the city.

Hall of Supreme Harmony (Taihedian), Hall of Central Harmony (Zhonghedian) and Hall of Preserved Harmony (Baohedian), three main halls of the outer court, sit in line inside the gate. The first and grandest hall is Taihedian, where emperors executed their rule over the whole country. It was the place where emperors ascended the throne and gave formal interviews to officials and where important events were celebrated. The hall is flanked by Hall of Literary Glory (Wenhuadian) and Hall of Martial Velour (Wuyingdian). The former, on the right side, used to be the study of the royal princes. Dinner parties and some rites were held here, too. The latter, on the left side, was the imperial press where many books were compiled and published and where Li Zicheng, the famous peasants uprising leader, ascended his throne after having pulled down Ming Dynasty. To the north of Wenhuadian lies Pavilion of Literary Source (Wenyuange), the imperial library where the world largest encyclopedia Complete Library of the *Four Treasures of Knowledge* (Sikuquanshu) was housed. South Fragrance Hall near Wuyingdian was where portraits of emperors are kept.

Zhonghedian is behind Taihedian, a square building much smaller than Taihedian. It was the place where the emperor rested on his way to Taihedian and interviewed his ministers or officials from the Ministry of Rites and preparations for ceremonies were also held here.

Baohedian, the second largest architecture in the palace, is the rear hall of the Outer Court. Imperial parties were often given here. Emperors presided over the final stage of national examinations to select officials from all over the country in this hall.

Words and Expressions to Learn ·······························

rectangular / rek'tæŋɡjʊlə / *a.* 长方形的	rite / raɪt / *n.* （宗教等的）仪式
moat / məʊt / *n.* 护城河	compile / kəm'paɪl / *v.* 编纂
execute / 'eksɪkjuːt / *v.* 执行	encyclopedia / ɪn,saɪklə'piːdɪə / *n.* 百科全书
marvelous / 'mɑːvələs / *a.* 不可思议的	portrait / 'pɔːtrət / *n.* 画像
throne / θrəʊn / *n.* 宝座	ceremony / 'serɪmənɪ / *n.* 仪式，典礼
flank / flæŋk / *v.* 位于……的侧面	preside / prɪ'zaɪd / *v.* 主持（典礼、会议等）

***   ***   ***   ***   ***   ***

Gate of Devine Prowess 神武门	Meridian Gate 子午门
imperial palace 皇宫	crown prince 王储
World Culture Heritage 世界文化遗产	Ministry of Rites 礼部

Passage 2   **The Temple of Heaven**

The Temple of Heaven was where the emperor came every winter solstice to worship heaven and to pray for a good harvest. In ancient China, only the emperor was allowed to directly worship heaven. The subjects were permitted only to worship their ancestors and river and mountain gods. Therefore, the ceremony at the Temple of Heaven was an act of national importance. Since the emperor ruled the country on behalf of heaven, a bad harvest could be understood as his fall from heaven's favor and a threat to his reign. So, it was a measure of self-interest that the emperor prayed to heaven for a good crop every year. During Ming Dynasty, the holy ceremony was combined with the emperor's worship of his ancestors.

The design of the Temple of Heaven complex, true to its purpose, follows the mystical cosmological laws believed to be central to the workings of the universe. Hence, complex numerological rules operate within its design. For example, because the number nine was considered to be the most powerful number, you will see the Altar of Heaven, built entirely of white marble, has a flight of nine steps leading down in every direction. Similarly within the Hall of Prayer for Good Harvest, the interior twenty-eight columns represent the 28 constellations, the four central pillars represent the four seasons, twelve inner columns represent the months and twelve outer columns represent the twelve shichen that make up a day. There are many examples showing the emphasis on these lucky numbers.

Whereas in old times common people were not allowed to enter the huge park, now for a low fee Chinese citizens can enjoy it all day long. If you visit it at dawn you'll be surprised by the number of people there doing their morning exercises. Next to an older person practicing the slow and flowing movements of taiji, there might be a younger one doing vigorous karate-like punches and kicks. One group might be learning the ancient martial art of sword-fighting, while another might be practicing a traditional dance. It is well worth waking up early one morning and visiting this park to watch such events if you have the energy and the interest.

 Words and Expressions to Learn ·

subject / ˈsʌbdʒekt / *n.* 臣民
cosmological / kɒzməˈlɒdʒɪkəl / *a.* 宇宙学的
numerological / njuːməˈrɒdʒɪkəl / *a.* 数字占星术的

marble / ˈmɑːbl / *n.* 大理石
flight / flaɪt / *n.* 楼梯的一段
column / ˈkɒləm / *n.* 支柱, 纪念柱
karate / kəˈrɑːtɪ / *n.* 空手道

***　　***　　***　　***　　***　　***

the Temple of Heaven 天坛
winter solstice 冬至
Altar of Heaven 圜丘祭坛

Hall of Prayer for Good Harvest 祈年殿
shichen 时辰
martial art 武术

Part C Exercises · · · · · · · · · · · · · · · · · ·

I. *Make up a brief dialogue according to Reading Passage 2 and the given situation.*

Xiao Wang, a tour guide, shows Mr. Smith around the Temple of Heaven. Mr. Smith asks Xiao Wang some questions about the imperial temple and Xiao Wang answers these questions.

II. *Answer the following questions according to the dialogues and passages.*

1. The Great Wall has always been regarded as one of the most remarkable accomplishments of the Chinese people. Why?
2. What is the grandest hall in the Forbidden City? What did the emperors do there?
3. For what purpose was the Temple of Heaven built?
4. If you visit the Temple of Heaven in the early morning, what events will you most likely see?

III. *Translate the following dialogue between a guide and a tourist into English.*

—瞧,这就是我跟你说过的地方。

—这里的胡同可真多,我们从哪儿开始啊?

—俗话说,在北京,有名的胡同三千六,无名的胡同赛牛毛。

—比牛毛还多呀?

—那当然!往这儿走。看,这些都是四合院。

—咱们走近点儿看看。这是门墩儿吗?

—对,而且不同的门墩儿也有不同的意思,你从门墩儿就可以知道这家人是做什么工作的。

—哦,原来是这样的。一个四合院里可以住四家人吗?

—不一定。以前,有钱的人是一家人住一个或者好几个四合院,没钱的就很多家人合住一个四合院。

—这儿的四合院还和以前一样吗?

—不,已经有很大的不同,大部分四合院的格局都已经改变了。

—你看,空调机,看来四合院的生活也现代化了。

—在我看来,无论怎么变,四合院都是北京生活最重要的代表。

IV. *Topics for discussion.*

1. In order to build Beijing into a modern international city, many courtyards and hutongs in Beijing have been removed or destroyed. Comment on this.
2. Beijing is facing serious sand storms, especially in spring and autumn. Do you think it advisable to move our capital to another city?

UNIT 4

Lesson 13
Shanxi and Inner Mongolia

Part **A** *Conversation*

Dialogue   Visiting the Tomb of Zhaojun

(G: Guide   T: Tourist)

G: This is the Tomb of Zhaojun, one of the four beauties of ancient China.

T: If only there were cameras back then! I really want to see with my own eyes.

G: Well, you can get some idea from the statues of her and her husband on horseback over there.

T: Hmm, really charming. The real person must be a lot more beautiful.

G: You bet. You know the four beauties of ancient China were said to be able to make swimming fish sink, to cause flying geese to fall, to send the full moon hiding behind the cloud, and to render the flowers ashamed. And Wang Zhaojun was the one to cause the flying geese to fall down.

T: Wow, what beauty!

G: Actually Wang Zhaojun has earned so much respect not only because of her beauty, but also because of what she did.

T: What did she do, then?

G: She married the Xiongnu Chanyu, the chief of the Xiongnu People.

T: What is Xiongnu?

G: It was an ancient nomadic tribe in China. It started in the third century BC and declined in the first century AD. Some people said Xiongnu People were the ancestors of the Huns in Europe.

T: Oh, I see. Then why was her marriage so unusal?

G: Good question! West Han Dynasty used to be at war with Xiongnu and the people suffered a lot from the wars. When Emperor Yuan came into power, Xiongnu was on the decline but still very aggressive.

T: What does this have to do with a common girl?

G: Wang Zhaojun was not a common girl. She was actually a palace lady-in-waiting.

T: What is that?

G: Oh, this is another long story. In ancient times the emperor usually rounded up all the beauties in the country into his court so as to choose concubines from among them. Those who were not chosen remained palace ladies-in-waiting. It means they were waiting to be summoned by the emperor.

T: But you said Wang Zhaojun was famous for her beauty. How could the emperor be blind to her?

G: The emperor could not possibly meet all those beauties in person, so he ordered some painter to paint the beauties for him to look at and choose. In order to get a chance to be chosen by the emperor, the beauties usually bribed the painter so that he would paint them prettier. But Wang Zhaojun was an upright and honest girl and she refused to bribe the painter. So the painter painted her badly. She waited several long years, but failed to get the emperor's attention.

T: Didn't the emperor find out the truth?

G: Not until when Wang Zhaojun was presented to the Xiongnu Chanyu. The emperor was reluctant to give her away at the sight of her beauty, but it was too late. So the emperor punished the painter seriously later.

T: So after the marriage, did the wars stop?

G: You said it. Sixty years of peace between Xiongnu and Han after the marriage.

T: Wow, amazing! So she made great contributions to the relationship between Han and Xiongnu.

G: Absolutely. Besides peace for sixty years, she also spread Han culture and knowledge to the Xiongnu People.

T: Maybe that is why she deserved such a huge tomb?

G: Probably. The tomb is 33 meters high with an area of 13,000 square meters. And to tell you the truth, Wang Zhaojun was not buried here. It is only her clothes and other belongings in there.

T: Really?

G: In old times, nobles, especially royal families, tended to bury their members in secret places so as to avoid theft and other trouble. It is the same case with Wang Zhaojun.

T: That makes sense. But I heard some people called the tomb "Qingzhong". Why?

G: Well, in Chinese "qing" means "green". "Zhong" means "tomb". It is said that each year when it turns cold and grasses and leaves on other trees become yellow, the plants on this tomb remain green and so it got the name.

T: That's amazing!

 Words and Expressions to Learn

render / ˈrendə / v. 使成为，致使
aggressive / əˈgresɪv / a. 有攻击性的
concubine / ˈkɒŋkjʊbaɪn / n. 嫔妃

bribe / braɪb / v. 贿赂，收买
upright / ˈʌpraɪt / a. 正直的

***   ***   ***   ***   ***   ***

if only 要是……多好
make swimming fish sink 沉鱼
cause flying geese to fall 落雁
send the full moon hiding behind the cloud 闭月
render the flowers ashamed 羞花
Chanyu 单于
the Huns 匈奴人

be at war with 与……交战，冲突
on the decline 在衰落，在下降
a palace lady-in-waiting 宫女，待诏
round up 收罗
be blind to 对……视而不见
be the same case with ……也是如此
make sense 有道理

Part B Reading

 Passage 1   Xilamuren Grassland

Xilamuren, meaning "yellow river" in Mongolian, is located 100 kilometers north of Hohhot. Xilamuren Grassland is covered with green grass and fresh flowers every summer and autumn. It has become a popular scenic spot in Inner Mongolia.

The main reason for most visitors to come to Inner Mongolia is for a grassland experience, and Hohhot is well set up to satisfy this need with its plentiful tourist facilities. If you have not experienced the grasslands before, you can have fun simply by having a walk on your own into the rolling grass.

Although it is possible to visit one of the grassland areas in one day, it is far nicer to spend a night or two out here in a Mongolian traditional yurt. These yurts are made of sheep wool, have thick rug floors and are usually furnished with many blankets, low beds, quilts, pillows. The yurts were designed to be easily folded up and carried by camel, however nowadays most of them are more solidly built on concrete yards. In yurt camps there are numerous yurts with usually a dining area, a washroom with occasional hot water and even electric light.

There are various entertainments in these areas. You may try activities such as Mongolian wrestling, horse and camel riding, archery, visiting traditional families, and trips to the aobaos (rock mounds that are normally decorated with flags, meant for worship). The best time to do all this is during Nadam Festival, in the second half of August, when the crowds are out in full and a fair-like atmosphere is created and there is a better chance to both take part in and feel the lively atmosphere of the grassland life. In the evenings the camps provide interesting activities, including a baijiu (white wine) dinner and traditional dancing, singing and music from traditional Mongolian instruments, including the horsehead fiddle. The white yurts, bright sky, fresh air, rolling grass and the flocks and herds moving like white clouds on the remote grassland, all contribute to making the scenery a very relaxing one for every visitor.

 Words and Expressions to Learn

quilt / kwɪlt / *n.* 被子

concrete / ˈkɒnkriːt / *a.* & *n.* 水泥，混凝土（的）

wrestle / ˈresl / *n.* 摔跤

archery / ˈɑːtʃərɪ / *n.* 射箭

***　　***　　***　　***　　***　　***

Xilamuren Grassland 希拉穆仁大草原

Hohhot 呼和浩特

Mongolian traditional yurt 蒙古包

aobao 敖包

Nadam Festival 那达慕节

horsehead fiddle 马头琴

In the middle of Shanxi Province, covering an area of 2.25 square kilometers, 90 kilometers southward from Taiyuan, the capital city of Shanxi Province, Pingyao Ancient Town is one of the four best-preserved ancient cities in China. Being well developed both in Ming and Qing Dynasties as a financial and business center, Pingyao was the assembly place of wealthy merchants who built the eye-catching courtyards one after another. With a history of more than 1,700 years, the Ancient Town is the birthplace of the earliest banks in China named Piaohao, meaning the firm for exchanging and transferring money.

The town's history goes back to Western Zhou Dynasty. The present wall is one of the best examples from Ming Dynasty when China saw a construction campaign. The city wall is a rammed-earth-and-brick structure that goes 6.2 kilometers around. It rises 10 meters high with a width of 8 to 12 meters at the bottom and 2.5 to 6 meters on the top. Interestingly, the city is shaped like a tortoise, a traditional Chinese symbol of longevity. Around the wall there are altogether six gates with one in the north and one in the south while the east and west walls each opened two. The south and north gates are regarded as the head and the tail while the east and west gates as four feet. Two wells stand just outside the south gate like the eyes of the tortoise and the crisscrossing streets inside the town are taken as the streaks on the shell. Thus Pingyao got the name "the tortoise city", which shows a good and naive wish for the town to last forever.

As an outstanding example of Chinese Han Nationality cities in Ming and Qing Dynasties, Pingyao's ancient buildings fully reflect the historical flavor of those periods. The ancient town has 4 main streets, 8 smaller streets and 72 lanes which form a cross shape. Shops, firms and houses were built symmetrically along a 750-meter-long street which runs from north to south as the axis, with the Market Tower located in the center.

Along the central street there used to be over 220 banks, hotels, pawn shops, Chinese herb shops, silk shops, tea stores, antique stores and restaurants. The most famous one was Rishengchang, the first private bank in China. The buildings in Pingyao display a combination of artistry and practicability.

There are many temples inside and around Pingyao. Shuanglin Temple, 6 kilometers southwest from Pingyao is famous for its colorful sculptures. Zhenguo Temple, 12 kilometers to the northeast has unique wooden buildings. In November 1986, the town was listed by UNESCO in the world heritage catalogue.

 Words and Expressions to Learn ·······················

transfer / træns'fɜː / v. 转移，调动
crisscrossing / 'krɪskrɒsɪŋ / a. 纵横交错的
naive / naɪ'iːv / a. 幼稚的，天真的

lane / leɪn / n. 巷子
artistry / 'ɑːtɪstrɪ / n. 艺术性

***　　***　　***　　　***　　***　　***

Pingyao Ancient Town 平遥古城
assembly place 集中的地方
rammed-earth-and-brick structure 夯土和
　　砖结构
streaks on the shell 龟壳上的条纹
Han Nationality 汉族
pawn shop 当铺

Chinese herb shop 中药店
antique store 古玩店
combination of artistry and practicability
　　艺术性和实用性的结合
Shuanglin Temple 双林寺
Zhenguo Temple 镇国寺

Part  *Exercises*

I. *Collect information about Mt. Hengshan in Shanxi Province and make up a dialogue about it.*

II. *Answer the following questions according to the dialogue and the two passages.*

1. Why was Zhaojun married to the chief of Xiongnu?

2. What was the result of Wang Zhaojun's marriage to the Xiongnu Chanyu?

3. Why is the tomb of Wang Zhaojun also called "Qingzhong"?

4. What is the main reason for visitors to come to Inner Mongolia?

5. What are the traditional activities visitors can enjoy on the grasslands?

6. Where was the first bank in China established?

7. Why was Pingyao Ancient Town laid out like a tortoise?

III. *Fill in each of the blanks in the following sentences with the proper form of a suitable expression you have learned in the dialogue.*

1. We can no longer remain _____ the problem of noise pollution any longer, or our health will suffer great damage.

2. She doesn't like jazz very much, but if there is no other choice, she will listen to it. It is _____ me.

3. The dog helped the shepherd (牧羊人) _____ the sheep and lead them back to the pen (羊圈).

4. Those two countries _____ each other for a long time, which had brought about losses to both sides.

5. Thanks to the education of the people and the new rules, birth rate in the countryside areas is _____ .

6. It doesn't _____ for him to give up the golden chance to go abroad for further studies.

7. _____ he had taken my advice, he would not have got lost in the forest.

IV. *Translate the following Chinese dialogue into English and the English passage into Chinese.*

1. — 我听说山西人很爱吃醋(vinegar)。
   — 是的。山西产醋的历史很长。据说三千年前,山西有个村子的人就开始用一种神秘的配方(recipe)制醋。宋代,家家都有醋缸(jar),人人都会做醋。
   — 醋的制作过程很复杂吗?
   — 是的,要很多步骤呢。也要用很多不同的配料(ingredient)。
   — 好像山西人离了醋没法生活。
   — 说得没错。这是因为山西人不光喜欢醋的味道,还认为长期吃醋能延年益寿。
   — 真的吗?
   — 我不知道。不过吃醋能降血压,从这点说,应该是对人的健康有好处的。对了,有个醋文化博物馆。你想去参观吗?
   — 在哪里?
   — 在清徐县。离太原市区(downtown)很近。
   — 那我们去那里参观一下吧。
   — 好啊。这下我们就能知道过去人们用什么工具和原料造醋了。

2. When it comes to the beauty of Inner Mongolia, those who have never been there can hardly imagine it. The endless grasslands alone are enough to send you wowing, lingering on without the slightest wish to go home, not to mention the magnificent Daqingshan Mountain, the towering Helan Mountain, the roaring Yellow River or the luxuriant forests, the vast surging lakes and the borderless deserts. If you come in summer, spreading in front of you will be thousands of miles of green. The land is green, the stream water is green and the gently contoured mounds are also green. The green flows wherever your

eyes roam till the horizon. The vast green land is dotted with colorful wild flowers, making the land even more charming. The snow-white yurts sparsely scattered on the grassland with their chimney smoking, the cloud-like herds of horses, sheep and cattle flowing here and there, coupled with the song of the shepherds add even more vitality to the picturesque scenery. Looking to the horizon, you will find the sky so blue and so high, and the land so green, so vast. When stepping into such a place, how can anyone stay sober without being intoxicated?

V. *Topics for discussion.*

1. Many archeologists are still looking for the real tomb of Genghis Khan (成吉思汗), and many imperial tombs such as Qin Shi Huang's tomb have been found and excavated. Do you think it better to keep the tombs untouched or open them up for studies and tourism? Why?

2. It takes a lot of man power and money to preserve the cultural relics. Do you think it worthwhile to protect them? Why? Do you have suggestions to make the preservation more effective?

UNIT 4 Lesson 14
Gansu and Qinghai

Part **A** *Conversation*

Dialogue | Visiting Mogao Grottoes

(G: Guide T: Tourist)

T: My goodness, the Mogao Grottoes have five stories.

G: And they are more than 1,600 meters long from north to south.

T: Look! Some stand alone, and others are together. All are arranged in perfect order.

G: In the Yungang Grottoes and the Longmen Grottoes, statues are carved out of rock, but here they are sculpted out of clay.

T: How did they make it?

G: A local plant from the desert here was used to wrap the wooden skeleton, and then clay was used for sculpture.

T: Those ancient craftsmen were really smart.

G: There is a big collection of murals in the Mogao Grottoes, too. People believe there may be as many as 45,000 square meters of them. If they were put end to end, they would form a two-meter-high, 25-kilometer-long art gallery.

T: Wow, that's really amazing.

G: This is a mural of Tang Dynasty.

T: Look, are these people musicians? Are they performing for these singing and dancing fairies?

G: Yes. From the instruments the musicians were playing and the manner of the fairies, you can imagine the popularity of singing and dancing at that time and the instruments people used in Tang Dynasty. The murals show us various aspects of social life back then.

T: Wow, unbelievable! You Chinese people really should be proud of them.

G: Sure we are. Over there is the "Classics Cave" where a lot of historical documents are kept. Let's go and take a look.

T: OK.

(Coming out of the cave.)

T: I saw some murals have been seriously damaged.

G: Yes. Mold, fading and cracks have always been the most dangerous enemies to the murals. And don't forget the dry weather and the sandstorms from the nearby deserts and Gobi.

T: So what can be done now? Move them to another place?

G: Of course not. Experts have been working hard to repair the damaged murals using modern techniques.

T: I remember I read some reports about the repair work by Chinese and American experts.

G: Yes. The work started in 1999 and ended in 2005. Did you notice those plants at the foot of Mingsha Hill yesterday?

T: Anything unusual about them?

G: Those desert plants were planted about forty years ago to keep the sand in place. Remember before getting into the caves I told you that taking photos in the caves is forbidden?

T: Yeah, flashlight can damage the murals, right?

G: Yes. And the caves take turns to open to the public and there is a limit to the number of visitors in a cave.

T: You people have done so much to protect the place.

 Words and Expressions to Learn ·······················

statue / ˈstætjuː / *n.* 雕像

sculpt / skʌlpt / *v.* 雕刻

mural / ˈmjʊərəl / *n.* 壁画

gallery / ˈɡælərɪ / *n.* 画廊

mold / məʊld / *n.* 霉菌

fading / ˈfeɪdɪŋ / *n.* 褪色

crack / kræk / *n.* 裂缝

Gobi / ˈɡəʊbɪ / *n.* 戈壁

Mogao Grottoes 莫高窟　　　　　　　second to none 首屈一指
wooden skeleton 木胎　　　　　　　　Mingsha Hill 鸣沙山
painted sculpture 彩塑

Part B Reading

Passage 1　Gansu Travel Overview

Gansu Province is located in the upper reaches of the Yellow River, the middle part of the Silk Road in Northwest China. It covers an area of 454,000 square kilometers with a population of 24 million. Lanzhou is the capital city of the province.

Gansu is one of the cradles of ancient Chinese civilization. It is the birthplace of Fuxi, the ancestor of the Chinese people, the inventor of Diagram of the Eight Trigrams, the Chinese characters and calendar. Farming also started here in early Zhou period, 3,000 years ago. Cultural relics in Gansu fall mainly into the Neolithic culture, the Yellow River culture, and the Great Wall culture representing the history of the civilization of the Chinese people for 8,000 years. Meanwhile, the Silk Road culture in Gansu has drawn attention from other parts of the world.

Gansu has always been a must along the Silk Road, and an important thoroughfare of cultural exchange and trade between China and the West. Over the past 2,000 years, from the loess plateau in the east to the Gobi Desert in the west, there had been groups of famous figures like envoy Zhang Qian, monk Xuanzang and Marco Polo advancing through mountains and over rivers.

Gansu is richly endowed with cultural relics and natural beauty. Known as the Golden Section along the Road, Gansu is regarded as "the Hometown of Grotto Arts". The most popular ones are Mogao Grottoes, Maijishan Grottoes and Binglingsi Grottoes. Take for example the world-famous Mogao Grottoes. It is the largest and most well-preserved Buddhist art palace in the world and also a post along the ancient Silk Road. In addition, there are many attractive historical sites along the Silk Road including temples, monasteries, the Great Wall, towers, pagodas, tablets and ancient castles. The grand Jiayuguan is the west end of the Great Wall; the Labrang Monastery is one of the largest Tibetan Buddhist resorts in China. The majestic and charming natural scenery in Gansu includes the endless plateau prairie, vast expanse of Gobi-desert, magnificent loess plateau and grotesque Danxia landform as well as snow-capped mountains.

Gansu has a multi-ethnic population which includes ethnic groups of Kazak, Mongolian, Tibetan, Hui, Dong, Tu and Manchu. They influence each other in the fields of economics, politics and culture and hold close ties with the Han people. They have thus developed a unique cultural community.

Gansu Province sits between 1,000 and 3,000 meters above sea level. With more than 30 percent of its area covered by grassland, Gansu is a rural, agricultural province as well as the country's second-largest producer of traditional Chinese medicines, with over 9,500 types in production. It is also one of China's five bases of animal husbandry.

The traditional handicrafts in Gansu are archaized carpets (using patterns from ancient carpets), luminous cups and the duplicates of sculptures and murals of the Mogao Grottoes in Dunhuang.

 Words and Expressions to Learn

thoroughfare / 'θʌrəfeə / n. 大道, 通衢
envoy / 'envɒɪ / n. 使节, 使者
monk / mʌŋk / n. 和尚
endow / ɪn'daʊ / v. 恩赐, 赏赐
monastery / 'mɒnəstrɪ / n. 修道院, 寺院
plateau / 'plætəʊ / n. 高原
prairie / 'preərɪ / n. 大草原

component / kəm'pəʊnent / n. 成分, 部分
multi-ethnic / mʌltɪ'eθɪk / a. 多民族的
husbandry / 'hʌzbəndrɪ / n. 畜牧业
archaized / 'ɑːkeɪɑɪzd / a. 仿古的
luminous / 'luːmɪnəs / a. 发光的, 夜光的, 夜明的

***   ***   ***   ***   ***   ***

the upper reaches 上游
the Silk Road 丝绸之路
Fuxi 伏羲 (中国传说中的人类始祖)
Diagram of the Eight Trigrams 先天八卦图
the Neolithic culture 新石器时代文化
loess plateau 黄土高原
Zhang Qian 张骞 (西汉使节, 出使过西域各国)

Xuanzang 玄奘 (唐朝和尚, 西去天竺取佛经)
Marco Polo 马可·波罗 (意大利旅行家)
Maijishan Grottos 麦积山石窟
Binglingsi Grottos 炳灵寺石窟
the Labrang Monastery 拉卜楞寺
Danxia landform 丹霞地貌 (最主要的特点是赤壁丹崖)

Qinghai Province is located in the northeast of the Qinghai-Tibet Plateau with a vast territory, abundant resources, a long history and lovable landforms. The Kunlun Mountains run across the middle, the Tanggula Mountains stand in the south, and the Qilian Mountains tower in the north. Grasslands rise and fall endless; the Chaidamu Basin expands boundless. The Kekexili Natural Protection Zone is the paradise of wild animals. The sources of the Yangtze River and the Yellow River are here in Qinghai. The Qinghai Lake is the largest inland salt-water lake in China with the world famous Bird Island in the north of the lake. Famous for its Danxia landforms, the Kanbula Forest Park and the Mengda Natural Protection Zone are wonderlands enjoying world popularity. Qinghai Province is one of the five largest pastures in China. Galloping horses, numerous yaks, snow-white sheep, and herdsmen's tents form a peaceful landscape on the boundless pastureland.

Qinghai is home to several ethnic groups: Tibetan, Hui, Tu, Mongolian and so on. The folk customs in Qinghai vary a lot. Among the ancient culture remains, the painted potteries of Majiayao Culture of the Middle Stone Age, and the stone inscriptions, rock paintings and murals scattered in the province demonstrate the history and lifestyle of the ancient plateau nations. And then, there are more than 240 religious temples in Qinghai, most of which are Tibetan lamaseries. They have become important tourism resources in the province.

The protected area of river sources (the Yangtze River, the Yellow River and the Lancang River) is situated in the south of Qinghai. In this area, great glaciers grow over snow line of grand mountains. The Yangtze River, the Yellow River and the Lancang River rise from here. Twenty-five percent of the water of the Yangtze River, 49 percent of the Yellow River and 15 percent of the Lancang River come from this area, and that is why Qinghai is called Water Tower of China.

There are nearly 1,000 kinds of plants, 147 kinds of birds, 76 kinds of wild beasts, 48 kinds of amphibians and fishes, and nearly 10,000 kinds of insects and bacteria. The cold plateau is an ideal base for biological research. In August 2000, the state established a Natural Protection Area around the river sources with an area of 363,000 square kilometers. This is the largest natural protection area in our country. In 2000, the Three Rivers Natural Protection Area Monument was set up on the bank of the Tongtian River, with a base of 363 meters, symbolizing the protection area of 363,000 square kilometers. The height of the base is 4.2 meters, symbolizing the elevation of the area (4,200 meters above the sea).

 Words and Expressions to Learn

tower / taʊə / vi. 高耸，屹立
expand / ɪk'spænd / v. 扩张，延伸
pasture / 'pɑːstʃə / n. 牧场
yak / jæk / n. 牦牛
remains / rɪ'meɪnz / n. 遗迹

pottery / 'pɒtərɪ / n. 陶器
inscription / ɪn'skrɪpʃən / n. 碑文，献词
lamasery / 'lɑːməsərɪ / n. 喇嘛庙
glacier / 'glæsɪə / n. 冰川
amphibian / æm'fɪbɪən / n. 两栖动物

***   ***   ***   ***   ***   ***

the Qinghai-Tibet Plateau 青藏高原
the Chaidamu Basin 柴达木盆地
The Kekexili Natural Protection Zone 可可
  西里自然保护区
the Kanbula Forest Park 坎布拉国家森林
  公园

the Mengda Natural Protection Zone 孟达
  自然保护区
be home to 是……的家园
Majiayao Culture 马家窑文化
the Middle Stone Age 中石器时代
the Tongtian River 通天河

Part C Exercises

I. *Search and collect information about the Qinghai-Tibet Railway and make up a dialogue between a tourist and a guide about it.*

II. *Decide whether the following statements are true or false according to the passages.*

1. There are numerous cultural relics in Gansu partly because of its position on the Silk Road.
2. Gansu Province boasts various landforms including snow mountains, grasslands, deserts, plateaus and basins.
3. Mogao Grottoes are the largest and most well-preserved Buddhist art palace in the world and

have attracted worldwide attention.

4. Traditional Chinese medicine production is the economic mainstay in Gansu Province.

5. Qinghai Province is the largest pasture in China.

6. Qinghai is called the Water Tower of China because it is the place where three largest rivers originate.

7. The cold plateau in Qinghai is an ideal place for biological studies and researches because of its perfect weather.

III. Fill in the blanks with the proper forms of the given words.

Fuxi is the 1. _____ (legend) god in the mythology of ancient China. He is also called Taihao or Taihao Fuxi. Legend says, by 2. _____ (imitation) the spider, he created a net to catch fish and animals. He invented the 3. _____ (music) instrument, Se, a plucked instrument with 50 strings, and 4. _____ (creation) the Eight Diagrams used in divination. He 5. _____ (marriage) his younger sister, Nüwa, and started the 6. _____ (product) of offspring one generation after another. Thus they became the ancestors of the 7. _____ (China). In Han Dynasty, they were 8. _____ (carving) on stone as figures with human heads and bodies of the snake. They are human-shaped from the waist up, but are snake-like below. The lower bodies are entangled together with each other.

IV. Translate the following passage about Bird Island in the Qinghai Lake into Chinese.

Lying 180 kilometers from Xining and 3,200 meters above sea level, the Qinghai Lake is the largest salt-water lake in China. In the Qinghai Lake, Bird Island is the most charming and attractive place. Situated on the western shore of the Qinghai Lake, the island has largely been turned into a peninsula (半岛). Though it covers an area of less than 1,000 square meters, it attracts many migrating birds (候鸟) in every spring and summer. To these hundreds of thousands of migrant birds, the island has become a very important home. Thousands of birds of different kinds nest on the island and the birds' songs are carried far away. For these birds as well as bird watchers, the island is a real paradise.

V. Topics for discussion.

1. Find more information about the Silk Road and comment on its significance in ancient China.

2. The loess plateau is said to be the source of the sand storms affecting Beijing and many other cities in North China. Talk about the causes and make some suggestions about how to stop them.

UNIT 4 Lesson 15
Shaanxi

Part A *Conversation*

Dialogue Visiting the Big Goose Pagoda and the Daci'en Temple

(G: Guide   T: Tourist)

T: Where are we going next? Are there any other places with a long history like the terracotta warriors in Xi'an?

G: Xi'an is the oldest among the six ancient capitals in China. Whatever it's lacking in, it's certainly not lacking in historical sites: the Huanqing Pool, the Stone Tablet with No Writing, the Forest of Steles and so on. How about visiting the Daci'en Temple and the Big Goose Pagoda?

T: Good. I heard Daci'en Temple is one of the most important Buddhist temples in China.

G: Yes. Do you happen to know anything about Monkey King?

T: Oh, sure. When I was at university, I once took a course in Chinese classical literature. I read several chapters in the book *Journey to the West*. I like it very much. Later I watched the TV series based on the novel. Why are you asking this? Does it have anything to do with the Big Goose Pagoda?

G: You got it. The Pagoda was actually built in honor of the Monk in the novel. Look, in front of the temple stands the statue of the Monk.

T: So the Monk in the novel is a real historical figure? What was his name and what did he do to deserve the honor of being written in a novel and having a pagoda built to honor him?

G: His name is Xuanzang. He was born into a poor family, and became a monk at the age of eleven. By the time he was twenty-six, he'd grown so disappointed with poor translations of Buddhist works that he made up his mind to travel to India to find uncorrupted Sanskrit texts.

T: To India? That is a long journey!

G: You bet. And international travel was forbidden by the emperor.

T: Then how did he manage to go?

G: Xuanzang disguised himself and joined a group of Central Asian businessmen going west along the Silk Road.

T: How long did it take him to make the journey?

G: Seventeen years to and from India. In 645 AD, he returned to Chang'an, that is present Xi'an. His journey covered sixteen kingdoms.

T: It's amazing. I can't imagine how he managed to finish the journey without the help of modern transportation!

G: The novel will help you, if you read the whole of it.

T: Hmm, that's a good idea.

G: After he returned, he wrote *The Record of the Western Regions* to describe his travel and gave the government up-to-date information about Central Asian countries. The emperor ordered a translation of the new Sanskrit texts and built the Big Goose Pagoda, according to an Indian design to store them.

T: Oh, I see. Look, the pagoda is simple-styled but very attractive at the same time.

G: That is very true. The pagoda is 64 meters tall and has seven stories, each with large windows. Visitors nowadays often throw money through the windows for luck.

T: Let's go up and take a look.

G: OK. (Coming out of the Pagoda.) And this temple holding the Pagoda has a longer history.

T: It's called Daci'en Temple, right?

G: Yes. It was built in 648 AD to commemorate the dead queen, and named "Ci'en" (Mercy and Kindness). When it was first built, it was seven times its present size with more than 2,000 rooms, but it now still keeps its grandeur.

T: I can see that.

G: Monk Xuanzang was once its chief resident, and did his translation work here. When you have toured the inside of the temple and seen all the works of famous calligraphers and painters, you will have a deeper understanding of the historical importance of the Temple and the Pagoda.

T: I sure will.

 Words and Expressions to Learn ·

chapter / ˈtʃæptə / *n.* 章

up-to-date / ˌʌptəˈdeɪt / *a.* 包含最新信息的

disguise / dɪsˈɡaɪz / *v.* 伪装

***　　***　　***　　***　　***　　***

the Big Goose Pagoda 大雁塔

the Daci'en Temple 大慈恩寺

terracotta warriors 兵马俑

be lacking in 缺乏

the Stone Tablet with No Writing 无字碑

the Forest of Steles 碑林

Monkey King 美猴王孙悟空

Journey to the West《西游记》

have ... to do with 与……有关系

a historical figure 历史人物

uncorrupted Sanskrit texts 没有讹误的梵文经文

The Record of the Western Regions《大唐西域记》

Part B Reading

Passage 1　The Terracotta Warriors

The Terracotta Warriors and Horses are the most significant archeological excavations of the 20th century. Work is still going on at this site, which is about 1.5 kilometers east of Emperor Qin Shi Huang's Tomb, Lintong County, Shaanxi Province. It is a sight not to be missed by any visitor to China.

After becoming ruler of the Qin State at the age of 13 (in 246 BC), Qin Shi Huang, later the first emperor of all China, had begun the work on his tomb. It took 11 years to finish. It is believed that many treasures and sacrificial objects had been buried in his tomb. A group of peasants uncovered some pottery while digging a well near the royal tomb in 1974. It caught the attention of archeologists immediately. They came to Xi'an to study and to extend the digs. They had proved that these objects were from the Qin Dynasty.

The State Council decided to build a museum on the site in 1975. When completed, people from far and near came to visit. Xi'an and the Museum of Qin Terracotta Warriors and Horses have become a must for travelers.

Life size terracotta figures of warriors and horses are arranged in battle formations. They are replicas of what the emperor's guards should look like in those days.

The museum covers an area of 16,300 square meters, divided into three sections: No.1 Pit, No.2 Pit, and No.3 Pit. They were named in the order of their discoveries. No.1 Pit is the largest, first opened to the public on China's National Day, 1979. There are columns of soldiers at the front, followed by war chariots at the back. No.2 Pit, found in 1976, is 20 meters northeast of No.1 Pit. It contains over a thousand warriors and 90 chariots of wood. It was opened to the public in 1994. Archeologists came upon No.3 Pit also in 1976, 25 meters northwest of No.1 Pit. It looks like to be the command center of the armed forces. It went on display in 1989, with 68 warriors, a war chariot and four horses. Altogether over 7,000 pottery soldiers, horses, chariots, and over 10,000 bronze weapons have been dug out so far from these pits. Two bronze chariots were discovered in December, 1980, about 20 meters east of Emperor Qin's tomb. They were named Chariot No.1 and No.2. Both required much restoration. No.2 was displayed first in 1983, and then No.1 was displayed in 1988.

The Terracotta Warriors and Horses is a sensational archeological find of all times. It has put Xi'an on the map for tourists. It was listed by UNESCO in 1987 among the World Cultural Heritage.

 Words and Expressions to Learn

column / ˈkɒləm / *n.* 纵队，纵列

sensational / senˈseɪʃənəl / *a.* 轰动的

* * *

archeological excavation 考古发掘
sacrificial object 祭品，陪葬品
the State Council 国务院

No. 1 Pit 一号坑
war chariot 战车

Situated at the northern foot of Mt. Lishan in Lintong County, 30 kilometers from Xi'an City, Huaqing Hot Spring is famed for both its charming spring scenery and the romantic love story of Emperor Xuanzong (685–762) and Yang Guifei in Tang Dynasty. Its long history and location among the wonderful landscapes of Xi'an should entice any visitor to visit and bathe in this hot spring.

It is said that King You built a palace here during West Zhou Dynasty. Additions were made later in the Qin and West Han Dynasties. In Tang Dynasty, Emperor Xuanzong spent huge sums of money to build a luxurious palace, changing its name to Huaqing Hot Spring or Huaqing Palace. The palace thus has a history of 3,000 years and the hot spring a history of 6,000 years!

Entering the gate which bears the inscription "Huaqingchi" by Guo Moruo, a famous literary man in China, visitors are greeted by two giant cedars. Continuing inward, you will see the Nine-Dragon Lake. Despite the fact that the lake is man-made with an area of 5,300 square meters, it is one of the main sceneries in the Huaqing Palace. You will see water lilies floating on the lake, giving out a sweet smell, and a white marble statue of Yang Guifei — regarded as one of the four most beautiful women in ancient China — stands tall by the lake like a shy and charming fairy. Mirrored in the lake you will see surrounding buildings here and there among willows and rocks. The magnificent Feishuang Hall used to be the bedroom of Emperor Xuanzong and Yang Guifei, with red supporting pillars and beautiful carvings.

Walking southwards through Marble Dragon Boat and several pavilions, you will find the Imperial Pools, which is the only one of its kind to be discovered in China. The five remaining pools are the Lotus Pool, Haitang Pool, Shangshi Pool, Star Pool and Prince Pool. The Lotus Pool was made for the emperors, the Haitang Pool for concubines, and the Shangshi Pool for officials.

In the Huan Garden lie the Lotus Pavilion, the Viewing Lake Tower (Wanghulou), the Flying Rainbow Bridge (Feihongqiao), the Flying Glow Hall (Feixiage), and the Five-Room Hall (Wujianting). The Flying Glow Hall was said to be the place where Yang Guifei cooled down her long hair after bathing in the hot spring. The Five-Room Hall was built in the late Qing Dynasty. It was the shelter of Dowager Empress Cixi after the Eight-Power Allied Forces seized Peking in 1900. The Huan Garden also has a large-scale mural about the feast in which Emperor Xuanzong summoned Yang Guifei. Made up of 90 white marbles, the mural is 9.15 meters long and 3.6 meters high. The mural and poems written about Huaqing Hot Spring are all witnesses of the past glory of Tang Dynasty.

By visiting the Huaqing Hot Spring, you will not only enjoy the scenery, but also taste the joy of imagining yourself back in the days of Tang Dynasty.

The first pleasure is to have a bath in the imitational Guifei Pool. With a temperature of 43 degrees, the ever-flowing water of the hot spring contains minerals and organic materials that have therapeutic effects on the skin.

In the Exhibition Hall of Tang Art built in 1995, you can enjoy dance performances of the Tang style and a Chinese tea ceremony in the teahouse.

In the palace of Huaqing Hot Spring, visitors will be delighted to discover the inscriptions collected there. All of them represent the best work in the field of calligraphy art.

 Words and Expressions to Learn

entice / ɪn'taɪs / v. 诱惑, 吸引
imitational / ɪmɪ'teɪʃənəl / a. 仿造的, 模拟的

therapeutic / ˌθerə'pjuːtɪk / a. 有疗效的, 能治病的
calligraphy / kə'lɪgrəfɪ / n. 书法

***   ***   ***   ***   ***   ***

Huaqing Hot Spring 华清池温泉
Mt. Lishan 骊山
King You 周幽王
water lily 莲花

the Feishuang Hall 飞霜殿
the Huan Garden 环园
the Eight-Power Allied Forces 八国联军
organic materials 有机物质

Part  Exercises

I. *Make up a brief dialogue according to the given information in Reading Passage* 2.

II. Complete the dialogue by translating the Chinese sentences into English.

(L: Li Yang   S: Mr. Smith, Li's American friend)

S: Oh, there is a souvenir shop. 1 _____ (店里出售兵马俑复制品). I'd like to buy some.

L: Wait until you have seen the real terracotta warriors. 2. _____ (真的兵马俑和真人一样高, 非常壮观).

S: Look! They are even taller than me. 3. _____ (他们简直就像是一支军队嘛). Look, soldiers, chariots and horses.

L: 4. _____ (他们确实是和秦始皇葬在一起的一支军队啊). What you see now is only Pit One, only a part of the complete army.

S: Oh, gosh. This is only a part? How many are there all together?

L: 5. _____ (据说总共有七八千个吧, 我也不肯定). The first emperor had many things buried with him. 6. _____ (除了兵马俑, 还有铜车马之类的东西).

S: Really?

L: Yeah. 7. _____ (整个秦始皇陵已经发掘了三个坑). We're only seeing one of them today. Moreover, many objects are still buried underground.

S: Hey, do you know who discovered this place?

L: 8. _____ (是一位农民在挖井的时候发现的).

S: That's interesting. Cultural relics can be discovered like this. It seems we should be alert when we take a walk in Xi'an. 9. _____ (说不定我们也能发现点什么呢).

L: (Laughs.) I wish you good luck!

III. Decide whether the following statements are true or false according to the dialogue and the passages.

1. Xuanzang and Monkey King in the novel *Journey to the West* were real historical figures.

2. Unlike in the novel, Xuanzang's trip to India began as a secret.

3. It took Xuanzang 17 years to get to India and 17 years to come back to Xi'an.

4. The Daci'en Temple was built for Xuanzang to translate the Sanskrit texts in.

5. Qin Shi Huang began to have his own tomb built when he was only 13 years old.

6. A group of farmers happened to discover Qin Shi Huang's tomb in 1974.

7. The Terracotta Museum was divided into three sections according to the order they were opened to the public.

8. Huaqing Palace has a longer history than Huaqing Hot Spring.

9. Huaqing Hot Spring has therapeutic effects because of various minerals and organic materials.

10. Tourists can also enjoy Tang-style dance performance and Chinese tea ceremony in Huaqing Hot Spring.

IV. *Translate the following passage into Chinese.*

Mt. Huashan is famous for its breath-taking cliffs. Along the 12-kilometer-long winding path up to the top are awe-inspiring (令人敬畏) precipices (悬崖峭壁), looking down which will take your breath away. Among the five peaks, East Peak (Facing Sun Peak), West Peak (Lotus Peak) and South Peak (Dropping Goose Peak) are comparatively high. Standing at the top of East Peak, one can enjoy the rising sun early in the morning. West Peak, which is shaped like a lotus flower, is the most graceful peak in Mt. Huashan. In addition, there are Middle Peak (Jade Maiden Peak) and North Peak (Clouds Stand Peak). The middle peak got its name because of a story telling that once a young lady rode a white horse among the mountains. North Peak, like a flat platform in the clouds, is the place where the story Capturing Mt. Huashan Wisely took place.

V. *Topics for discussion.*

1. Some people say that the government should not spend so much money restoring the Ancient City Wall of Xi'an. Do you agree with them? Why or why not?

2. Some people think it a good idea to sell some terracotta warriors to foreign countries since we have so many of them. Comment on this statement.

UNIT 4 Lesson 16
Xinjiang

Part A Conversation

Dialogue | **At the Kanas Lake**

(G: Guide   T: Tourist)

G: Here we are. The Kanas Nature Reserve. I'm sure you will find the scenery more beautiful than in pictures. The surrounding glaciers, the tranquil lake, and the vast grassland ...

T: This place is really like a wonderland.

G: Exactly. The Kanas Lake is beautiful. If you look at the map, China looks like a rooster, and the Kanas Lake should be the most beautiful tail plume of the rooster.

T: That's a nice analogy.

G: Now let's see how beautiful this plume is. The Wolongwan, Yueliangwan, Yaze Lake and Guanyu Pavilion around the lake are all worth seeing. If you are interested, we can also boat on the lake.

(Arriving at the Yaze Lake.)

T: Wow, no wonder people say water is the soul of Kanas. It's absolutely true.

G: Of course. The water of the Kanas Lake is especially beautiful under the sunshine. And the trees over there also sparkle with light. Come here.

T: I'll take some pictures to show my friends back home.

G: The Yaze Lake is also called the Wild Duck Lake.

T: Look, there are really wild ducks over there! One, two, three ... more than ten!

G: In this wetland, there are not only wild ducks. If you are lucky, you'll see many other kinds of birds.

T: Look! What fun those wild ducks are having!

(Arriving at the Guanyu Pavilion.)

G: What are you looking for?

T: I'm looking for fish. You said this is the famous Fish Observing Pavilion. But it's so high, how can you see any fish from here?

G: The fish we want to see are not ordinary fish.

T: What kind of fish is it, then?

G: It's the lake monster in Kanas.

T: What? A lake monster here?

G: Don't be afraid. Let me finish. Some people say the lake monster is a kind of huge red fish, called Hucho taimen. The biggest is about four meters long, weighing 500 kilograms.

T: No way. How can there be such huge fish in the lake?

G: Well, I have no idea. It may be a rumor. But this is Kanas. You know, the word Kanas, in Mongolian, means beautiful, rich and mysterious. Do you know the most unusual thing about the Kanas Lake?

T: No. What is it? Not the lake monster?

G: Seeing is believing. Just stare at the surface of the lake.

T: I am, but I don't see anything unusual.

G: Look carefully and you will find every time you look at the lake, the color of the water is different.

T: (Looking at the water again.) Yeah, you are right. The color of the water can change. That's amazing! How come?

G: Some people say it is because of the minerals in the water. Others say it is the light.

T: So what's the answer?

G: I don't know. It's still an unsolved puzzle. But if you think about it another way, it just adds to the beauty of this mysterious lake.

 Words and Expressions to Learn

wonderland / ˈwʌndələnd / *n.* 仙境   analogy / əˈnælədʒɪ / *n.* 类比

***   ***   ***   ***   ***   ***

the Kanas Nature Reserve 喀纳斯自然保护区（位于新疆）

tail plume 尾羽

Wolongwan, Yueliangwan, Yaze Lake and Guanyu Pavilion 卧龙湾、月亮湾、鸭泽湖和观鱼亭

lake monster 湖怪

Hucho taimen 哲罗鲑

Seeing is believing. 眼见为实。

an unsolved puzzle 一个未解之谜

Part B Reading

Farming has always played the most important role in Turpan, the famous "home of fruits" in China. As early as 70 BC, large-scale farming was carried out. During Wei and Jin and Southern and Northern Dynasties, grape vines were widely cultivated in Turpan. The Turpan area made a name in the world with its seedless white grapes, Hami melons and long-staple cotton.

More than 100 kinds of grape grow in the vineyards stretching for 15 kilometers in the suburbs of Turpan. On the mountain slopes there are many drying houses with openwork walls in which hang strings of grapes drying slowly in a natural process. The raisins, when they are ready, are freshly green and extremely sweet. The grape harvest season is also a season to harvest happiness and love. Grapes are presented among friends and relatives. People sing of grapes and paint grapes and hold parties in vineyards where Chinese and foreign tourists gather to taste the Xinjiang specialty. The happy life is the result of the Turpan people's hard work in building oases. Over the centuries, they have dug under the land to store up water for irrigation.

Looking at the Flaming Mountains in the distance from the city of Turpan, one can see nothing but barren red sand. But the Grape Valley of the Flaming Mountains, 15 kilometers from the city center, is a world of unique beauty, giving a great contrast to the hot and dry outside.

The Grape Valley is a world of green. Scattered everywhere in the valley are trees. Different fruit trees have turned the valley into a "garden of flowers" in spring and an "orchard of all kinds of fruits" in summer. Grapes growing in the valley are of several kinds, including the seedless white, rose-pink, mare-teat, black. There is a fruit winery producing several kinds of wines and canned grapes.

The Flaming Mountains, lying in the middle of the Turpan Depression and running from east to west, are part of the Tianshan Mountains and appeared fifty million years ago. The Flaming Mountains are so hot and so dry that "flying birds even 500 kilometers away dare not come". Yet, the mountains at the same time are a giant natural dam of the underground water.

Under the blazing sun, the red rock glows and hot air goes up like smoke as though it were on fire, so it got its name. The mountains are 98 kilometers long and 9 kilometers wide. The highest peak is 40 kilometers east of the city of Turpan and 831.7 meters above sea level.

Situated on the north route of the ancient Silk Road, Turpan has many cultural relics and many beautiful ancient tales. The Gaochang Ancient Town and the Bizaklik Thousand-Buddha Caves have attracted a lot of tourists.

 Words and Expressions to Learn

cultivate / ˈkʌltɪveɪt / *v.* 种植，培育

vineyard / ˈvɪnjɜːd / *n.* 葡萄园

raisin / ˈreɪzən / *n.* 葡萄干

oases / əʊˈeɪsiːz / *n.* 绿洲 (oasis 的复数)

irrigation / ɪrɪˈɡeɪʃən / *n.* 灌溉

barren / ˈbærən / *a.* (土地) 贫瘠的

orchard / ˈɔːtʃəd / *n.* 果园

mare-teat / ˈmeətiːt / *n.* 马奶子 (一种葡萄)

dam / dæm / *n.* 坝

route / ruːt / *n.* 路线，航线

*** *** ***   *** *** ***

Turpan 吐鲁番

seedless white grapes 无籽白葡萄

Hami melon 哈密瓜

long-staple cotton 长绒棉

the Flaming Mountains 火焰山

the Grape Valley 葡萄沟

Turpan Depression 吐鲁番盆地

the Gaochang Ancient Town 高昌古城

Bizaklik Thousand-Buddha Caves 柏孜克里

克千佛洞

Passage 2   **The Ancient City of Loulan**

On the west bank of the Lop Nur Lake, which is now a lake of sand instead of water, the Ancient City of Loulan was founded in the 2nd century BC in an oasis with advanced water network. It suddenly disappeared after about 800 years of flourish. The city, once the capital of State Loulan which was one of the 36 Western Region States, occupied very important position on the Silk Road. However it declined in the middle of the 6th century AD. At the beginning of last century, a Swedish explorer Sven Hedin discovered by accident the city buried in desert in his exploration. Discovery surprised the world from then to present.

The city has already totally collapsed into dust. The only recognizable structures are a pagoda, which is the largest structure in the ruins, and a seems-to-be office which still has painted wooden structures.

Archeologists believe there was once a water tunnel running through the city and dividing it into two parts. Large amounts of wood pieces, coins, jewelries and wood slip documents are listed in the archaeological finds, which provide us with many clues of the ancient city.

Archaeologists have also found a graveyard which was lost after its previous discovery. Hundreds of boat-shaped coffins scatter around, while most of them are broken, with mummies lying around. Among them, one coffin contains a well-preserved female mummy. Archaeologists also found colorfully painted coffins. A real size wood statue with clear female characteristics proves that early Loulan people could produce very artistic works. The graveyard is, archaeologists believe, a holy place where early Loulan people prayed for strong reproductive ability.

The discovery may explain why the active and flourishing oasis suddenly disappeared. It is discovered that early Loulan people preferred Sun Tomb which consists of 7 circles of logs thicker and thicker from the center to the outer circle like the sun. The unique burying form led to Loulan's destruction. A large number of trees were cut down before Loulan people realized the importance of controlling wood use and of protecting woods and trees. Aa a result, the city was soon buried under the desert.

 Words and Expressions to Learn ·

flourish / ˈflʌrɪʃ / n. 繁荣   preserve / prɪˈzəːv / v. 保存
graveyard / ˈɡreɪvjɑːd / n. 墓地

✱✱✱   ✱✱✱   ✱✱✱   ✱✱✱   ✱✱✱   ✱✱✱

the Ancient City of Loulan 楼兰古城（遗址）
　（位于新疆）

the Lop Nur Lake 罗布泊

by accident 偶然，碰巧

collapse into dust 坍塌为灰烬

a seems-to-be office 看上去像办公室一样

的东西

water tunnel 水渠

a real size wood statue 一个和真人一样大
　小的木制雕像

reproductive ability 生育能力

Part **C** Exercises

I.　Read the following brief introduction of Xinjiang and then make up a dialogue between a guide and a tourist about visiting Xinjiang.

Xinjiang boasts rich and diverse tourist resources. Landscapes here are both unique and beautiful. If you come here, you will be attracted by wild landscapes and peculiar combination of natural sights. Here, you can see snow-capped mountains stand in very hot land, and deserts neighbor on oases. Over 1,000 kinds of wild animals and plants live in Xinjiang, including many unique grasses, trees, and animals. Here 23 nature reserves have been established, of which 4 are at the national level. Some famous scenic spots may have already been known to you, such as the Tianchi Lake, the Kanas Lake, the Bosteng Lake and the Bayanbulak Grassland. In Xinjiang there are many historical sites. Of them, well known both at home and abroad are Jiaohe Ancient City, Gaochang Ancient City, Loulan Ancient City, Kizil Thousand-Buddha Cave and Apak Hoja Tomb (commonly known as Xiangfei Tomb). Xinjiang is well known as the home of songs and dance, where folk customs are unique.

Superlatives are often used when describing Xinjiang: It is the most arid province; also contains the hottest and the coldest places; the longest inland river, the Tarim; the lowest marsh, the Aydingkol Lake (Moonlight Lake) (艾丁湖) in the Turpan Basin; the largest inland lake and the largest desert. In Xinjiang, tourists can visit the world-famous Yardang Spectacle (雅丹地貌) in Korla (库尔勒), stone forests, and enjoy the mystery of the desert with its spectacular sand mountains. The ancient Silk Road had brought Xinjiang a mix of Eastern and Western cultures which left behind stunning relics. Today, those ancient cities, caves, temples and tombs attract countless tourists from home and abroad.

II.　Answer the following questions according to the passages.

1. How did the Flaming Mountains get its name?

2. Besides the Flaming Mountains and the Grape Valley, are there any other tourist attractions

in Turpan?

3. What are the most famous fruits in Turpan?

4. When and how was the ancient Loulan discovered?

5. What can we learn from the disappearance of ancient Loulan?

III. Fill in the blanks with the proper form of the words given in brackets.

1. _____ (Know) as Yaochi (Jade Lake) in ancient times, Tianchi is one of the main tourist 2. _____ (attract) in China. 3. _____ (Surround) by a group of mountains west of Mount Bogda, Tianchi is 4. _____ (geology) a moraine lake (冰碛湖) 3,400 meters long, 1,500 meters wide, 105 meters at the deepest point and lies 1,980 meters above sea level. This giant bowl of sapphire water is surrounded by mountains with 5. _____ (majesty) snow-crowned peaks 6. _____ (reflect) on the lake, 7. _____ (make) the beauty of the lake and mountains an integral whole. Mountainsides are covered with green and luxuriant pines and cypresses 8. _____ (extend) as far as the eye can see. The open spaces between trees are decorated with rainbows of flowers, dotted with white yurts, and roamed by flocks of sheep that look like clouds 9. _____ (float) past. This picturesque scene on a day after a rain is especially enchanting. In summer, the lake sees an 10. _____ (end) stream of visitors from around China and abroad.

IV. Translate the following passage into Chinese.

Tianshan literally means "the Heavenly Mountains." At about the center of the Xinjiang region, Tianshan spans 2,500 kilometers from east to west, of which 1,700 kilometers is located in the Xinjiang Uygur Autonomous Region. The width from north to south is about 250 to 300 kilometers. At the northern foot a dense (茂密的) primeval forest (原始森林) shades the earth from the sun and the sky. Tianshan also holds a rich reserve of glacial water and fertile basins which support both abundant agriculture and thriving cattle stocks. Visitors to the region may find that the most attractive areas of the beautiful and richly endowed Tianshan range are the vast grasslands and graceful grazing lands. Bayinbuluke Grassland, the largest grazing land near the middle of the Tianshan range, is situated in a basin at more than 2,500 meters above sea level. Vast plains of grass, enormous lakes, rivers, roving cattle and round yurts (蒙古包) collectively form a breathtaking scene.

V. Topic for discussion

Xinjiang is rich in natural resources, and now our government is trying to promote economic development in the west regions including Xinjiang. Comment on the advantages and disadvantages of Xinjiang in terms of economy and give your suggestions in promoting Xinjiang's development.

UNIT 4

Lesson 17
Shandong and Jiangsu

Part A Conversation

Dialogue 1   Climbing Mount Tai

(G: Guide   T: Tourist)

G: Mount Tai is one of the greatest mountains in China. It is famous not only for its scenery but for its cultural contents as well. Many famous people in Chinese history have climbed it.

T: I hope we can find some trails they've left. How far do you think we are from the top?

G: We're at Zhongtianmen, which means we're almost halfway up.

T: Really? I'm too tired. Can we have a rest here?

G: Sure. Let's slow down a bit. Look, over there are the Wudafu Pines. Dafu was an official title in ancient times. These pines have the same status as officials.

T: Ha, that's interesting. But who would appoint pine trees as officials?

G: Emperor Qin Shi Huang!

T: Really? He'd come to Mount Tai as well?

G: Yes. Once he came here to offer sacrifice to heaven. There was a sudden downpour. He took shelter under the five pines and didn't get wet. So he gave them the title of Dafu in gratitude.

T: Looks like Mount Tai is full of stories.

G: Sure, and they are all interesting.

T: Yes. Very interesting!

Dialogue 2   In Suzhou

(G: Guide   T: Tourist)

G: Suzhou gardens are very famous. The Humble Administrator's Garden, the Lingering Garden, the Master-of-Nets Garden and the Lion Forest Garden are the four most famous.

T: I'd like to visit all of them.

G: No problem. Suzhou gardens are nothing compared to Beijing's royal gardens in terms of size. But they have their own flavor. Today I will first take you to the Canglang Pavilion, one of the oldest gardens in Suzhou.

T: It's been around longer than the Humble Administrator's Garden?

G: That's right. The Canglang Pavilion is more than a thousand years old.

T: I can't wait. Let's go in and have a look. Wow, it's beautiful with a hill and a lake.

G: Actually, the beauty of the Canglang Pavilion is the corridor between the mountain and the water.

T: It divides the garden into two parts.

G: Why not have a look out from these windows in the corridor wall?

T: Wonderful! It's like looking at a magical scene through a crystal ball.

G: Yes. Not only does the man-made corridor not spoil the view, it enhances it.

T: You said this is a garden from Song Dynasty. What about other gardens?

G: The Lion Forest Garden is from Yuan Dynasty.

T: The Lion Forest Garden? Sounds like a zoo.

G: Well, it is not a zoo, but it's animal-related. Some say it's a kingdom of rockeries.

T: The rockeries look like lions?

G: Bingo! You are very good at guessing.

T: I've seen the model of a hall in a museum back in the US. It was supposed to be a replica of some garden in Suzhou.

G: That must be the Lingering Garden. It's best known for its halls.

T: I haven't seen any halls like them since I've come to China.

G: Then we'll save the Lingering Garden for tomorrow.

T: OK.

Words and Expressions to Learn

trail / treɪl / n. 遗迹，足迹

appoint / əˈpɔɪnt / v. 任命

downpour / ˈdaʊnpɔː / n. 倾盆大雨

rockery / ˈrɒkərɪ / n. 假山园

replica / ˈreplɪkə / n. 复制品

***　　***　　***　　***　　***　　***

Mount Tai 泰山

Wudafu Pines 五大夫松

official title 官衔

offer sacrifice to heaven 祭天

take shelter 躲避

in gratitude 感激地

the Humble Administrator's Garden 拙政园

the Lingering Garden 留园

the Master-of-Nets Garden 网师园

the Lion Forest Garden 狮子林

Venice of the East 东方威尼斯

the Canglang Pavilion 沧浪亭

spoil the view 破坏风景

Bingo. 说得对。/ 当然。

Part B Reading

Passage 1   The Confucius Temple and the Cemetery of Confucius in Qufu

Confucianism has had the most lasting and profound effect on Chinese culture. As time went on, Confucius became respected as a sage, and the temples of Confucius were built all over China. Among them, the Temple in Qufu, the hometown of Confucius, is the most famous and the largest. Located inside the south gate of Qufu, Shandong Province, the Temple of Confucius is a group of grand buildings built in traditional Chinese style.

The Temple started as three houses in the year of 478 BC, the second year after the death of Confucius. Each year as Confucianism became the backbone of Chinese culture, the Temple was expanded. Sacrifices were often made to the sage, either by emperors, or by high officials. In Qing Dynasty, Emperor Qianlong offered sacrifices here eight times. Sacrifices to Confucius were as grand as those given to the heavens. This gives us an idea of the importance of the Temple of Confucius in history.

The existing Temple of Confucius was rebuilt and repaired during Ming and Qing Dynasties. Patterned after a royal palace, it is divided into nine courtyards. The main buildings run along a north to south axis, with the other buildings symmetrically in line. The whole group includes three halls, one pavilion, one altar, and three ancestral temples. Altogether there are 466 rooms and 54 gateways covering an area of 218,000 square meters. The yellow tiles and red walls are all covered with beautiful decorations.

After Great Sage Gate (Dashengmen), the buildings are divided into three parts. The central part is for offering sacrifices to Confucius and other scholars and sages while the eastern part is for sacrifices to the ancestors of Confucius. The west is for his parents.

However, the Temple wins its fame not only for its grandness, but also for the rich cultural relics found there. The 2,100 pieces of steles from various dynasties make a fine exhibition of calligraphy and stone sculpture.

At a location 1 kilometer north of Qufu, people can visit the Cemetery of Confucius where the family and descendants were buried. This cemetery has the longest line of descendants in the world. Record has it that this cemetery has already lasted 2,340 years. At the time Confucius was buried there, the cemetery was about 66,700 square meters. It was continually expanded to over 2,000,000 square meters in the following dynasties. The walls around the cemetery are 7 kilometers long surrounding more than 10,000 tombs.

The path that leads up to the cemetery is 1,266 meters long and is lined with pines and cedars. At the end of the path stands a wooden archway — called the Most Sacred Cemetery (Zhishenglin), and is the gate to the Cemetery of Confucius.

The changes and development of the Cemetery reflect the role of Confucianism through history. During his eventful life, Confucius traveled from one place to another, trying to persuade the rulers to adopt his philosophy, but with little success. It was during later dynasties that Confucianism gained popularity among the rulers.

Beside the tombs stand steles with handwritings of notable people of the times, and stone sculptures. The Cemetery is known for its more than 1,000 ancient trees. It is said that after Confucius's death, disciples planted rare trees from all over China. Some of the trees are so rare that their proper names are yet unknown. When one walks into the cemetery and fully enjoys the treasures here, one will certainly be impressed by the role of Confucius in Chinese culture.

sage / seɪdʒ / *n.* 圣人   disciple / dɪ'saɪpl / *n.* 门徒，学生

axis / 'æksɪs / *n.* 轴

***   ***   ***   ***   ***   ***

patterned after a royal palace 按照皇宫的   ancestral temple 宗祠
样式

Passage 2 | Nanjing Travel Overview

Nanjing is located on the lower bends of the Yangtze River, making its location extremely important throughout Chinese history. Nanjing was the capital of China for 6 dynasties. It is now the capital of Jiangsu province, the home to several high ranking universities, a major economic center and a very popular place with tourists.

The Purple Mountain, a green hill on the eastern side of Nanjing, is home to many important historical sights. Some say the Purple Mountain is all about Tombs. The area is home to the tombs of many famous historical figures, among which the three best-known are the Tomb of Sun Quan, a late Han Dynasty general and leader of the State of Wu during the Three Kingdoms period; Ming Xiaoling, mausoleum of Zhu Yuanzhang, the first emperor of Ming Dynasty, which was listed as an UNESCO World Heritage Site; and the Mausoleum of Sun Yat-sen, the leader of the 1911 revolution and first president of China. A visit to these tombs will give you a chance to appreciate the wonderful stone animal figures, tablets and monuments as well as architectures of traditional Chinese and Western styles.

The Linggu Temple has seen many ups and downs in Chinese history. The Three Superb Tablet stands in the temple which features a painting of Monk Baozhi by Wu Daozi, a memorial poem written by Li Bai and calligraphy by Yan Zhenqing. The original tablet was destroyed in a battle and the current one is a replica created in Qing Dynasty.

The City Wall of Nanjing was designed by Emperor Zhu Yuanzhang after he founded Ming Dynasty and made Nanjing the capital. Building the wall took 21 years, and involved 200,000 laborers. Zhonghuamen is the southern gate of the city wall, one of the best preserved parts of the ancient city wall, and one of the best remaining examples of early Ming defensive architecture anywhere.

The Confucius Temple, now a museum, was once an imperial examination center for the entire Jiangsu region. The museum now comprises only a tiny fraction of the once-massive original buildings. The rest of the site is a massive, buzzing market, a top tourist draw in Nanjing where you can have a taste of the countless local snacks and delicacies.

Ming Dynasty Imperial Palace was completely destroyed in Qing Dynasty and its ruins today barely hints at its size. The site was a prototype of Beijing's Forbidden City as the layout was copied by the Emperor's grandson when he moved the capital to Beijing in 1421.

The Nanjing Massacre Memorial is a chilling reminder of the brutality of *the Nanjing Massacre*, one of the most horrific war crimes in human history. Its chill can still be felt in the city to this day. Two partially excavated mass-burial sites reveal victim remains in site, accompanied by insightful information boards around the walkway. The elongated sites, restrained architecture, well-maintained gardens, interspersed sculptures and other artworks inspire solemn meditations. Close to the entrance is a *museum* showing *multitudes of* photos, videos and objects to tell the full story, and can easily occupy you for hours.

The 6 km-long Nanjing Yangtze River Bridge is worth a visit since it's the first major project built entirely by Chinese people without foreign help.

Nanjing is an old city, and a modern one at the same time. It boasts the tenth tallest building in the world — Zifeng Tower (450-metre, 89-story), which hosts a fancy restaurant and a bar on the 78th floor and a public observatory on the 72nd floor.

There are many other places you can go, such as the Nanjing Museum, the Qinhuai River, the Presidential Palace, Jiangsu Kunqu Theatre and so on to learn about the colorful local culture and long history of Nanjing.

 Words and Expressions to Learn

mausoleum / ˌmɔːsəˈlɪəm / *n.* 陵墓
memorial / mɪˈmɔːrɪəl / *a.* 纪念的，追悼的

current / ˈkʌrənt / *a.* 现存的
defensive / dɪˈfensɪv / *a.* 防御性的

comprise / kəmˈpraɪz / v. 包括，由……组成

fraction / ˈfrækʃən / n. 小部分

buzzing / ˈbʌzɪŋ / a. 忙乱的，嘈杂的

hint / hɪnt / v. 暗示

prototype / ˈprəʊtətaɪp / n. 原型

layout / ˈleɪaʊt / n. 布局，格局

brutality / bruːˈtælɪtɪ / n. 残忍，暴行

accompany / əˈkʌmpənɪ / v. 伴随

elongate / ˈiːlɒŋɡeɪt / v. 伸长

restrained / rɪˈstreɪnd / a. 谨严的

intersperse / ɪntəˈspɜːs / v. 散布，点缀

meditation / ˌmedɪˈteɪʃən / n. 沉思

observatory / əbˈzɜːvətərɪ / n. 天文台，瞭望台

***   ***   ***   ***   ***   ***

the Purple Mountain 紫金山

The Linggu Temple 灵谷寺

the Three Superb Tablet 三绝碑

the Confucius Temple 南京夫子庙

imperial examination 科举考试

The Ming Dynasty Imperial Palace 明故宫

the Nanjing Massacre Memorial 侵华日军
    南京大屠杀遇难同胞纪念馆

multitudes of 众多，大量

Zifeng Tower 紫峰大厦

Part **C** Exercises

I. *Make up a dialogue about traveling in Nanjing according to the information in Reading Passage 2.*

II. *Answer the following questions according to the dialogues and the passages.*

1. What kind of cultural contents does Mount Tai have?

2. How did Wudafu pines get their title?

3. What can visitors see at the Confucius Temple?

4. What is Confucius's status in Chinese history?

5. How many years has the Cemetery of Confucius lasted? What about its expansion in the later dynasties?

6. Is Nanjing still an important city in modern China? Why do you say so?

7. Why do people say the Purple Mountain is all about tombs? Share with your classmates stories of any one of the famous people buried there.

8. Why was the tablet in the Linggu Temple called Three Superb Tablet?

9. What is the Confucius Temple in Nanjing famous for now?

10. Though the Ming Dynasty Imperial Palace was completely ruined in history, we can still learn about its layout and scale. How and why?

III. Fill in the blanks with suitable prepositions.

Qin Huai River, a tributary (支流) of the great Yangtze River, is 110 km 1. _____ length and covers a drainage area of 2,631 km². The river used to be called Huai River, and it is said that the river was channeled 2. _____ the city of Nanjing 3. _____ the reign of Emperor Qin Shi Huang, so it was named Qin Huai River 4. _____ then on. Qin Huai River is the largest river in the Nanjing City area, other 5. _____ the Yangtze River, and is the "life blood" of the city. There are many sites of interest 6. _____ its banks, such 7. _____ Zhanyuan Garden, Zhonghua Gate. Taking a painted boat to cruise 8. _____ the Qinhuai River, visitors can not only enjoy the sights along the river but can also experience the traditional culture of Nanjing.

IV. Translate the following dialogue between a guide and a tourist into English.

— 对, 我在明信片上看到的就是这样的亭阁。

— 这是苏州园林中最大的亭阁。这些家具都是楠木 (cedar) 的, 所以这里也叫楠木厅。

— 这两个房间完全不一样, 我的眼睛都不够用了。

— 这里叫鸳鸯厅。

— 鸳鸯不是鸟的名字吗? 鸟跟这个亭阁有什么关系?

— 鸳鸯是一种鸟, 不过这里的鸳鸯亭呢, 是一对的意思。你看, 这边是男亭, 是专门为招待男客人用的, 那边是女亭, 当然是为了招待女客人用的了。

— 我明白了。

V. Translate the following passage into Chinese.

Baotu Spring, the symbol of Jinan, is known not only as the first of the 72 springs in Jinan but as the "No.1 Spring under Heaven". With its earliest account in "Spring and Autumn Annals", it has a history of more than 2,600 years. Because of its pure quality and mellow taste, the natural spring water could be directly used for drinking. When water bursts out through the three outlets (出口, 泉眼), the spring gives thunderous (雷鸣般的) sounds, and water columns (水柱) surge upward, looking like spinning wheels. The spring keeps its temperature at about 18 degrees centigrade all year round. In cold winter, mist rises from and hangs over the spring pond, and the clear spring water reflects the ancient-styled buildings with colorful carvings and upturned eaves, presenting the visitors with a picturesque view of a paradise on earth. Together with its environs (周边区域), it has been turned into a park of the same name that is now one of the three major places of interest in Jinan.

VI. *Topics for discussion.*

1. Confucianism has extensive and deep-rooted influence on Chinese culture. Please cite some examples to illustrate it.
2. Collect information from all possible sources and talk about the differences between the Royal gardens in Beijing and the scholastic gardens in Suzhou.
3. On Feb.27, 2014, our government decided to set December 13th the National Memorial Day for the Nanjing Massacre Victims. Comment on the decision.

UNIT 4

Lesson 18
Anhui, Shanghai and Zhejiang

Part A Conversation

Dialogue   **Climbing Mt. Huang**

(G: Guide   T: Tourist)

T: If I remember correctly, Huang in Chinese means yellow. But why do you call this mountain Mt. Huang? To me, it is very green, not yellow at all.

G: In ancient times Huangdi, the ancestor of the Chinese nation, made pills of immortality here, so the mountain got the name.

T: I see. It's named after Huangdi.

G: Yes. Mt. Huang is known for its different charm in different seasons. The snow scenery is extremely stunning but there's been very little snow in winter in the past years, so now the best season to visit Mt. Huang is late spring and early summer.

T: Look! Isn't that the famous "Guest-greeting Pine"? I once saw a huge painting of it.

G: You said it. Pine trees are one of the Four Wonders of Mt. Huang. There are a lot of pine trees in different shapes. They all grow out of rocks and they are evergreen all the year round.

T: You said Four Wonders? What are the other three?

G: The second one is grotesque rocks in different shapes. Some of them look like people, some look like different animals such as rabbits, squirrels, monkeys, and so on. The Lotus Flower Peak looks like a newly opened lotus bloom.

T: Amazing!

G: The third wonder is the sea of clouds. When you stand high looking down at the drifting clouds, you'll feel like there are thousands of horses galloping under your feet!

T: Can we see the sea of clouds today?

G: Climb a bit higher, and we'll find out. You know, the sea of clouds appears only when the weather conditions are just right.

T: Wow! What a view!

G: Yes, indeed! We're really lucky.

T: And the sea is changing! Wait, I'll take some photos. (After a while.) Come on, tell me the fourth wonder.

G: The hot spring. There used to be a big hot spring swimming pool at the foot of the mountain, but there is not much water getting out now.

T: What a pity!

G: On your right is Tiandu Peak, one of the three main peaks of Mt. Huang and also the steepest It is 1,810 meters high. Look up there. Can you see a cliff? It's called Jiyubei, or the Carp's Backbone.

T: Oh, I can see why it got its name. Is it the highest peak?

G: No. The highest peak is on your left, called Lotus Flower Peak, with the height of 1,860 meters. The summit is a rock only about six meters wide. Famous pine trees such as the "Flying Dragon" and the "Twin Dragons" are found there.

T: It sounds very exciting. Shall we climb the highest peak first?

G: Why not? Let's go.

 Words and Expressions to Learn ·

ancestor / ˈænsestə / *n.* 祖先   steep / stiːp / *a.* 陡峭的
stunning / ˈstʌnɪŋ / *a.* 令人吃惊的   cliff / klɪf / *n.* 悬崖
gallop / ˈgæləp / *v.* (马) 奔跑

***   ***   ***   ***   ***   ***

pills of immortality 长生不老丹   grotesque rocks 奇石
the Guest-greeting Pine 迎客松   the Lotus Flower Peak 莲花峰
the People's Great Hall 人民大会堂   the Carp's Backbone 鲫鱼背

Part B Reading

Passage 1   Hangzhou Attractions

Hangzhou, a city famous for its scenic splendor, attracts more than 20 million tourists from home and abroad every year.

The West Lake is the name tag of Hangzhou. Held in the embrace of hilly peaks on three sides, this water wonderland, with its ten famous attractions has all the elements of a traditional Chinese garden but on a very grand scale. The strangely shaped peaks, serene forests and springs, dense foliage and a myriad of blossoms in springtime are enhanced by a treasury of sculptures and architectures.

The Solitary Hill is an ideal spot to admire the vista. For those who have a love of sculpture and art and those who have a particular interest in Buddhism, the Peak Flown From Afar and the Temple of the Soul's Retreat are the must-see attractions. The nearby Mausoleum of General Yue Fei is a monument to the patriot murdered by his archrival Qin Hui in Song Dynasty. These buildings together with others add to the calm and beauty of the lake.

The Botanical Garden is both a beautiful park and a botanical research base. The Running Tiger Spring is famed for its crystal clear water.

No visitor to the West Lake and Hangzhou can fail to learn something about the city's most famous products, namely silk and Longjing Tea. Chinese National Silk Museum is the country's first national museum dedicated to silk culture and is the largest of its kind in the world. Located at the West Lake Dragon Well Tea Plantation, the National Tea Museum provides insights into the history and production of tea. Museum of Traditional Chinese Medicine is the only state-level professional Chinese medicine museum in the country. Southern Song Dynasty Official Kiln Museum will show you how the best and most valuable ancient chinaware was made.

Another natural spectacle to be found in the city is the Qiantang River Tide. Annually, millions of people from home and abroad flock there to watch the spectacular tide around the eighteenth day of the eighth lunar month.

Around the city area, there are also other places of interest like the famous ancient water towns Wuzhen and Xitang, beautiful moutains like Mogan Mountain and Tiantai Mountain.

Hangzhou, with its hills, waters, architectures and local culture has been ranked as one of the ten best tourist cities in the country.

 Words and Expressions to Learn

embrace / ɪmˈbreɪs / *n.* 怀抱,拥抱
serene / sɪˈriːn / *a.* 晴朗的,宁静的
foliage / ˈfəʊliːdʒ / *n.* 叶子
vista / ˈvɪstə / *n.* 排成长列的景色

patriot / ˈpeɪtrɪət / *n.* 爱国者
archrival / ˈɑːtʃˈraɪvəl / *n.* 劲敌,主要对手
spectacle / ˈspektəkl / *n.* 景象,奇观

***   ***   ***   ***   ***   ***   ***

name tag 名片,标签
on a very grand scale 规模巨大
a myriad of 无数的,极大数量的
the Solitary Hill 孤山

the Peak Flown From Afar 飞来峰
the Temple of the Soul's Retreat 灵隐寺
the Mausoleum of General Yue Fei 岳飞祠
the Running Tiger Spring 虎跑泉

Passage 2   The Bund of Shanghai

Shanghai is a city with a long history. In its development, it has formed its own unique city skyline and culture. A lot of cultural relics beginning in the Tang and Song Dynasties are well preserved till this day.

The most famous street of Shanghai is the Bund. The Bund lies to the west of the Huangpu River. It is a famous waterfront and is regarded as a symbol as well as the birthplace of Shanghai. It starts from Waibaidu Bridge, which is at the connecting point of the Huangpu River and the Suzhou Creek, to the East Jinling Road and winds a 1,500-meter length.

Shanghai used to be a small town on the shore of the Huangpu River. The Bund area covered with reeds used to be a piece of wasteland of old Shanghai. Today, the Bund is dotted with buildings of Western styles dating back to the early 20th century. Due to these buildings, the Bund is also reputed as "an international exhibition of architecture". This is a legacy to the world and makes it the most famous sight in Shanghai.

The Bund was the centre of Shanghai's politics, economy and culture hundreds of years ago. Consulates of other countries and many foreign banks, businesses, newspaper offices were settled there. Known as "the Wall Street of the East" then, it was a miniature of Shanghai in the colonial period. Some major firms of the Far East once had their offices in the buildings facing the river.

Among these buildings, former Shanghai and Hong Kong Bank and the Customs Building were designed by a famous British designer. People in Shanghai called them "Sister Buildings". At present, they remain an important mark of Shanghai. It is now the home of Shanghai Pudong Development Bank.

Walking along the Bund, the Oriental Pearl TV Tower can be seen on the opposite side and also the Jinmao Tower. The newly-built Flood Control Bank plays the role of preventing floods.

Standing on the Bund is Mr. Chen Yi's statue in commemoration of Mr. Chen's great contribution to the development of new Shanghai. He was the first mayor of Shanghai after liberation. The Monument to People's Heroes serves as a monument to the history of the people's brave struggle in Shanghai.

Now, a 646.7-meter-long sightseeing tunnel, connecting the Bund to the Oriental Pearl TV Tower, is open to the public, through which visitors can experience a wonderful trip under water.

Being one of the Top Ten Attractions in Shanghai, the Bund is a really beautiful and special place worth visiting.

 Words and Expressions to Learn

skyline / ˈskaɪlaɪn / n. (建筑物等在天空映衬
下的)空中轮廓线
waterfront / ˈwɔːtəfrʌnt / n. 滨水区

reed / riːd / n. 芦苇
legacy / ˈlegəsɪ / n. 遗产,财富
miniature / ˈmɪnɪətʃə / n. 微型画,缩影

***   ***   ***   ***   ***   ***

Waibaidu Bridge 外白渡桥
the Suzhou Creek 苏州河
be dotted with 点缀着……
date back to 追溯到

due to 由于,因为
be reputed as 有……的盛誉
in commemoration of 纪念

I. Make up a dialogue between a guide and a tourist about visiting Hangzhou according to the information given in Reading Passage 1.

II. Answer the following questions according to the dialogue and passages.

1. What is the legend about the name of Mt. Huang?

2. What are the four wonders of Mt. Huang?

3. Can visitors enjoy the sea of clouds every day? Why?

4. Why do we say Shanghai is a city with a long history?

5. Why is the Bund called "an international exhibition of architecture"?

6. Can people cross the Huangpu River on foot from the Bund? How?

7. How many attractions in and around Hangzhou are mentioned in Passage 1?

8. List at least five attractions of Hangzhou.

III. Fill in the blanks with the proper form of the words given in the brackets.

Qiantang River is the longest in Zhejiang Province, 1. _____ (run) from the west to the Hangzhou Bay in the east. It serves an important role in the water transportation between the east and the west. It is 2. _____ (circle) by a group of 3. _____ (economy) booming cities including Shanghai and Ningbo, one of China's 4. _____ (lead) port cities. The extraordinary 5. _____ (surge) tide of the Qiantang River is a world-renowned natural wonder 6. _____ (cause) by the gravitational pull of the stars and planets. The centrifugal force (向心力) produced by the 7. _____ (rotate) of the earth and the peculiar bottleneck shape of the Hangzhou Bay make it easy for the tide to come in, but difficult for it to ebb.

The tide of the Qiantang River is such a 8. _____ (marvel) spectacle that only the Amazon River's surging tide rivals it! 9. _____ (annual), millions of people from both home and abroad flock there to watch the magnificent tide on the eighteenth day of the eighth lunar month. When the surging tide comes, the water can rise up to a 10. _____ (high) of 30 feet and the noise it 11. _____ (generation) sounds like thunder, or thousands of horses galloping. 12. _____ (vary) activities will also be held to celebrate the annual Tide-Watching Festival, according to local custom. The custom of watching the bore tide has existed for more than 2,000 years. It first appeared during the first century. Then, it became popular in Tang Dynasty.

IV. *Translate the English passage into Chinese, and the Chinese one into English.*

1. The Taiping (Peace) Lake is located at the southern foot of Mt. Huangshan and to the southeast of Mt. Jiuhua, with an area of some 88 square kilometers, and water of 40 meters deep. It is the largest man-made lake in Anhui Province. There are more than 10 islets (小岛) of various shapes in the lake. Tea trees and simple-styled buildings with painted walls are reflected in the mirror-like lake, which is dotted with sails of fishing boats and bamboo rafts. The lake is home to many wild animals, such as deer and rabbits. Recently, tourist attractions including a Deer Island, a Monkey Island, an Egret (白鹭) Oasis, and ponds for snakes and crocodiles have been established in the lake. The lake is 40 kilometers from the northern entrance to Mt. Huangshan and 90 kilometers from Mt. Jiuhua. In December 1996, the Taiping Lake Bridge opened to traffic, thus offering more convenience for traveling.

2. 普陀山，中国最低的"圣山"，位于一个面积仅有12平方公里的小岛上，地处浙江省舟山岛以东五公里。普陀山最高峰海拔291米，1 060级石头台阶通往山顶。该岛在佛教到来之前就是一个神圣的地方，到处都是神秘的山洞，宁静的山谷，悬崖峭壁和金色的沙滩。除了许多庙宇外，该岛由于气候温暖湿润而植被葱郁，森林密布。身处这种环境中，环岛漫步和在沙滩上静静地待上一天同样惬意。更妙的是普陀山向游客提供中国最好的海鲜。品尝海鲜已成为任何普陀山游程必不可少的一部分了。

V. *Topic for discussion.*

Do some reading about Huizhou Village in Anhui Province and comment on the advantages and disadvantages of living in places like Huizhou in Anhui and places like Shanghai.

UNIT 4 Lesson 19
Fujian and Jiangxi

Part A *Conversation*

Dialogue | Climbing Mt. Lushan

(G: Guide   T: Tourist)

G: Have you heard of Li Bai, a poet of Tang Dynasty?

T: Of course. My Chinese teacher once introduced some of his poems to us.

G: Well, the beauty of Lushan greatly inspired him and it is said that he wrote over 900 poems about Lushan.

T: 900? I can't believe it! Look! What a beautiful garden.

G: This is the Flower Path.

T: Flower Path? But it looks like a garden. And there are not many flowers.

G: Don't forget this is late October. If you come in April or May, you will say it really deserves its name.

T: Flower Path. Sounds beautiful. I love the name.

G: In April, 817 AD, another famous poet of Tang Dynasty, Bai Juyi, came to Lushan. To his surprise, the peach flowers here were still in full bloom. He wrote in his poem, "The fragrance in the human world has withered in April, while flowers in the mountain (Mt. Lushan) are in full bloom".

T: So it was Bai Juyi who named it "Flower Path"?

G: You are very good at guessing. Here is the Three Tier Spring. It is the most famous attraction in the Lushan area. A famous saying says, "If there is no Three-Tier Spring, Mt. Lushan is not worth visiting."

T: Wow, look at the waterfall. So splendid!

G: Yeah! The water falls 155 meters from the Peak of Five Old Men to the multi-tiered rocks at the cliffs.

T: The Peak of Five Old Men? We will see it a little bit later, right?

G: Yes. Look! This is the Peak of Five Old Men. Can you see why it is called so?

T: Let me see. Oh, the five peaks stand side by side, like five old men talking with each other.

G: Right. The top of the mountain is a good place to enjoy sunrise. If it is foggy, people even can hear "the sound of the fog".

T: "The sound of the fog"? Really?

G: Let's come here again on a foggy day and see whether it is just a rumor.

T: I heard that the cloud sea at Mt. Lushan is really impressive.

G: Yes. Su Dongpo, a well-known poet of Song Dynasty described how he felt about the cloud sea of Mt. Lushan in one of his poems, "The failure to get the real looks of the mountain only results from the fact that you are right in the midst of it."

T: You Chinese have poems about almost anything! Look! What's that? A temple?

G: No. It is the Academy of White Deer Cave, an institution for higher learning.

T: Does it mean they taught in a cave called "White Deer"?

G: Well, it got its name because the founder raised a white deer as a pet.

T: I see. When was it established?

G: In Tang Dynasty during the 9th century.

T: A long time ago! I wonder what they taught back then.

G: Of course not English.

T: That's for sure!

 Words and Expressions to Learn · · · · · · · · · · · · · · · · · ·

wither / ˈwɪðə / v. 枯萎,凋谢
multi-tiered / ˈmʌltɪtɪəd / a. 多层的

rumor / ˈruːmə / n. 谣传

✦✦✦   ✦✦✦   ✦✦✦   ✦✦✦   ✦✦✦   ✦✦✦

the Flower Path 花径
in full bloom (花)盛开
the Three-Tier Spring 三叠泉
the Peak of Five Old Men 五老峰

stone engraving 石刻
the Academy of White Deer Cave 白鹿洞书院

Gulangyu Island, known as a garden on the sea, is located to the southwest of Xiamen City. Visitors can reach it by steamship from Xiamen City in about 5 minutes. Gulangyu Island is famous for its natural beauty, its ancient relics, and its various buildings as well.

During Ming Dynasty, the island was called "Yuanshazhou Island". It got its present name from the huge reef surrounding it. When the tide comes in, the waves hit the reef and it sounds like the beating of a drum. The island came to be named Gulang. Gu in Chinese means drum, and lang waves.

Gulangyu Island has a population of about 20,000. Only electricity-powered vehicles are allowed on the island, so the environment is free from noise and gas pollution. Breathing the clean air, enjoying the ever-present green trees and lovely flowers, all people here feel like they are in heaven. With classical and romantic European-style buildings, the island truly deserves to be called an "Architecture Museum".

The Island Ring Road, which circles the island, allows you to fully enjoy all the sights of this small, charming island. Among the many scenic spots on the island, the most attractive ones are Sunlight Rock and the Shuzhuang Garden.

Located in the south-central part of the island, Sunlight Rock is the island's highest point — 92.7 meters above sea level. Though it may not rank with high mountain peaks, it appears great when seen from far away. The name comes from a sun-shaped formation of granite. When the sun rises, the morning light illuminates the granite in Sunlight Temple and the rock is bathed in sunlight.

At the foot of Sunlight Rock stands the Memorial Hall of Zheng Chenggong. During the later Ming Dynasty, the troops of national hero Zheng Chenggong were here. He led his army to drive away the Dutch colonists and recovered Taiwan. Going up the steep rock path, visitors will see many works left by poets in history. Continuing on, you will see the training grounds of Zheng Chenggong's troops. Near the field is a huge rock bridging two cliffs, forming a natural entrance to a cave. This is called "Old Summer Cave" where you can feel a pleasant cool breeze. It's the perfect viewing spot to enjoy the scenery of Gulangyu Island.

First built in 1931 on the south side of the island, Shuzhuang Garden was once a private garden. In the style of "Yihong Garden" described in the novel *Red Chamber Dream*, it is like a beautiful flower set upon the seaside. It became a garden park open to the public in 1955. It is divided into two parts — the Garden of Hiding the Sea and the Garden of Making-up Hills. A Chinese traditional garden, Shuzhuang Garden attracts visitors far and near every year.

 Words and Expressions to Learn

reef / riːf / *n.* 礁

granite / ˈɡrænaɪt / *n.* 花岗岩

vehicle / ˈviːɪkl / *n.* 交通工具, 车辆

illuminate / ɪˈluːmɪneɪt / *v.* 照亮

***   ***   ***   ***   ***   ***

Sunlight Rock 日光岩

Old Summer Cave 古避暑洞

the Shuzhuang Garden 菽庄花园

Yihong Garden 怡红院

be bathed in 沐浴在……

Red Chamber Dream《红楼梦》

the Memorial Hall of Zheng Chenggong 郑
　成功纪念馆

Garden of Hiding the Sea 藏海园

Garden of Making-up Hills 补山园

Dutch colonist 荷兰殖民者

Passage 2　The Poyang Lake

Located in Jiujiang City, Jiangxi Province, the Poyang Lake is the largest fresh-water lake in China. Having experienced many geological changes, the Poyang Lake is now wide in the south and narrow in the north, like a huge gourd tied on the waist of the Yangtze River.

For thousands of years, the Poyang Lake has been nurturing the people in Jiangxi Province and attracting visitors with her charm. Looking out over the Poyang Lake, with its blue waves that stretch to the horizon, is much like standing on the shore and looking out over an ocean. On days when the sun shines and the sky is clear, the sky and the water of the lake seem to meet on the horizon. Sailboats on the lake dart back and forth, as if fighting with the billowing clouds. Rafts move along one after another like a big dragon.

Besides the attractions such as Dagu Hill, Nanshan Hill, the Lake-view Pavilion, the Poyang Lake is also famous for aquatic plants, which create a good environment for many rare species of freshwater fish. In addition, many kinds of rare birds are attracted to the lake, making it a good choice for birdwatchers.

The Poyang Lake Bird Protection Area is a habitat for many endangered species of birds. Measuring 224 square meters in area, it offers a mild climate and a habitat rich in aquatic plants and fish with no industrial pollution. In winter days, the Poyang Lake is home to the world's largest population of birds.

Every November, thousands of birds fly in from Siberia, Mongolia, Japan, North Korea, and the northeastern and northwestern regions of China. These migratory birds spend the long winter in the Poyang Lake together with the native birds, leaving gradually as the weather starts to warm in March. The Poyang Lake is considered by many to be the largest bird habitat in the world. Every winter it welcomes 95% of the world's white cranes, and that earns it two of its popular names:"World of White Cranes" and "Kingdom of Rare Birds".

The white crane is one of the world's endangered species. All of its feathers are pure white except for a few black ones on the tips of the wings, which give it another name "black sleeve crane". Its sword-like beak is brownish yellow, and it stands on a pair of long, pink legs. Because they can live 70 years or more, the Chinese call them "immortal cranes" and consider them a symbol of good luck.

Serious birdwatchers use telescopes to get a good look at the birds, which are very shy and will fly away if you get too close. Colorful birds are everywhere, flying close to the surface of the water, high in the sky, or circling and diving for food. The elegant white cranes can be seen flapping their wings and playing with each other. There are so many of them that they can look like a great white wall — a truly incredible sight.

Words and Expressions to Learn

geological / dʒɪəˈlɒdʒɪkəl / *a.* 地质（学）的	billowing / ˈbɪləʊɪŋ / *a.* 汹涌的，翻滚的
gourd / gʊəd / *n.* 葫芦	habitat / ˈhæbɪtæt / *n.* 栖息地
nurture / ˈnɜːtʃə / *v.* 养育	beak / biːk / *n.* 鸟喙
dart / dɑːt / *v.* 急冲，急行	Siberia / saɪˈbɪərɪə / *n.* 西伯利亚

***   ***   ***   ***   ***   ***

fresh-water lake 淡水湖	migratory bird 候鸟
back and forth 来来回回	white crane 白鹤
aquatic plant 水生植物	black sleeve crane 黑袖鹤
endangered species 濒危物种	

Part C Exercises

I. *Make up a brief dialogue about visiting the Poyang Lake according to the information given in Reading Passage 2.*

II. *Answer the following questions according to the dialogue and the passages.*

1. What is the Chinese version of Bai Juyi's poem?
2. What is the Chinese version of Su Dongpo's poem?
3. Why are there so many birds on the Poyang Lake every winter?
4. What is the other name for white cranes?
5. How did Gulangyu Island get its present name?
6. Why is Gulangyu still free from pollution in modern society?
7. What cultural relics can visitors see on Gulangyu Island?

III. *Read the following legend about the origin of the name of Wuyi Mountain in Fujian Province and retell the story to your partner in your own words.*

The name of Wuyi Mountain comes from a story about a legendary person called Qian Keng who lived during Shang Dynasty (16th century — 11th century B.C.), believed to be the eighth generation descendant (后代) of Huangdi, the Yellow Emperor. Because of Qian Keng's great achievements, King Yao gave him the title of lord of Pengcheng (present Xuzhou in Jiangsu) and thus he became known by the surname (姓) Peng. His descendants referred to him as Peng Zu (Ancestor Peng). To get away from wars at that time, Peng Zu took his two sons, Peng Wu and Peng Yi, to a scenic mountain area in northern Fujian. They settled down there, worked the land and lived as farmers. Later, in memory of these first settlers to the region, people name the mountain range after the two sons, Wu and Yi, and thereafter also used the name Wuyi to refer to Peng Zu.

IV. **Fill in the blanks with the proper form of the words given in the brackets.**

1. _____ (locate) in the Panlongshan in the western suburb of Jingdezhen City, the Ceramic History Museum is a 2. _____ (profession) ceramic museum 3. _____ (cover) an area of about 83 hectares, and was built in 1980. The museum has a rich 4. _____ (collect) of over 5,000 articles. The items on display include ceramics from past dynasties, 5. _____ (history) information about ceramics, precious collections of 6. _____ (paint) and calligraphies, among which many are of excellent quality. In addition to the wide 7. _____ (vary) of articles in the 8. _____ (exhibit), the beautiful antique architecture of the museum attracts 9. _____ (tour) too. The antique architecture is in two parts: Ming Garden and Qing Garden. The two gardens are 10. _____ (composition) of ancient kiln-workshops, ancient kilns. Near the Qing Garden are a group of kiln-workshops in which the ceramics are manufactured. Tourists cannot only watch the manufacturing process and appreciate the elaborate techniques, but also experience the process themselves. Visitors can buy any beautiful ceramic works they like.

V. **Translate the following sentences into Chinese.**

1. 井冈山是中国革命圣地 (sacred place) 之一。
2. 1927年8月1日，中国共产党在江西省省会南昌领导了著名的南昌起义 (uprising)。
3. 庐山的云雾茶在宋代是给朝廷的贡品 (tribute)。
4. 景德镇号称 "瓷都"，早在唐代就开始生产瓷器。
5. 江西省被称为 "鱼米之乡"，也因茶叶、甘蔗 (sugar cane)、水果等闻名。

VI. **Topics for discussion**

1. In order to protect Gulangyu Island from pollution, Fujian government decided to limit the number of visitors during the peak seasons. What do you think of this?

2. Poyang Lake was reported to have suffered severe draught, which has damaged its ecological system. What do you think are the causes of it? What can be done to restore everything?

UNIT **4** Lesson 20
Henan

Part **A** *Conversation*

Dialogue   Visiting Shaolin Temple

(G: Guide   T: Tourist)

T: Wow, finally, the famous Shaolin Temple!

G: Yes. It is called "the Number One Temple under Heaven".

T: Shaolin Kung Fu was developed here, right?

G: Yes. Shaolin Temple is famous for Buddhism and Shaolin Kung Fu. Look, this is the Shanmen Hall. Look up. See the tablet? The words are "Shaolinsi", meaning Shaolin Temple. They were written by Emperor Kangxi of Qing Dynasty.

T: That means the temple was very important in Qing Dynasty, right?

G: Yes. And here is the Hall of Heavenly Kings. Look! These are the Four Heavenly Kings.

T: Oh, they look solemn and scary.

G: They are said to be responsible for checking on people's behaviors, helping the troubled, and blessing the good.

T: Look! They have different facial expressions!

G: And this is the Mahavira Hall. Important celebrations and regular prayers are held here.

T: Oh, who are the statues along the walls?

G: They are the famous 18 Buddhist Arhats. Every one of them is a Kung Fu master. Look at the floor! Can you find something special?

T: Let me see! Oh, the pits! So many of them!

G: They are the footprints left by monks when they practiced Shaolin Kung Fu .

T: Oh, my goodness! They must have trained a lot here.

G: You bet! This is the Pagoda Forest, a graveyard for Buddhist masters through the ages.

T: So many pagodas. Why do they have different layers and shapes?

G: Well, different layers and shapes show the Buddhist masters' status and achievement during his lifetime.

T: Oh, I see. Look! What is that cave for?

G: That is called Dharma Cave. It is said Dharma used to sit in this cave facing the walls meditating patiently for nine years and finally he reached the immortal spiritual state and created the Buddhist Zen.

T: Can we go inside and have a look?

G: Sure. Let's go. There used to be a Meditating Stone in the cave. It is said Dharma's shadow was reflected upon the stone and embedded on it because of his long time meditation facing the wall. Unfortunately the stone was ruined.

T: Oh, what a pity!

G: This is the Shaolin Temple Training Center. Shaolin monks have been practicing kungfu for more than 1,500 years.

T: Wow! Who invented the whole system?

G: I guess nobody knows the answer. But I do know a lot of foreigners are learning Chinese Kung Fu now.

 Words and Expressions to Learn ·

tablet / 'tæblət / n. 匾
solemn / 'sɒləm / a. 庄严的
scary / 'skeərɪ / a. 可怕的
bless / bles / v. 保佑
pit / pɪt / n. 坑

meditate / 'medɪteɪt / v. 沉思默想
immortal / ɪ'mɔːtl / a. 不朽的, 永生的
reflect / rɪ'flekt / v. 映射, 倒映
embed / ɪm'bed / v. 嵌入

✳✳✳　　✳✳✳　　✳✳✳　　✳✳✳　　✳✳✳　　✳✳✳

the Shanmen Hall 山门殿
the Hall of Heavenly Kings 天王殿

the Mahavira Hall 方丈殿
18 Buddhist Arhats 十八罗汉

My goodness! 天哪！

the Pagoda Forest 塔林

Dharma 达摩

Buddhist Zen 佛教禅宗

Part  B Reading

Passage 1 Songshan Mountain

Songshan Mountain lies in Dengfeng city, in the heart of Henan Province and about 80 kilometers east of its capital, Zhengzhou. Songshan Mountain, which is also known as Zhongyue (the Middle Mountain), is one of the Five Famous Mountains of China.

Songshan Mountain Range has fine natural scenery. Its 72 mountains, grouped around the peaks of Mount Shaoshi and Mount Taishi, extend for about 70 kilometers from east to west. Besides these mountains, there are many valleys, caves, pools and waterfalls, each of which provides visitors with a unique and wonderful experience. The landscape is so unique that it has been given the title of "International Geological Park" by UNESCO.

The history of Songshan Mountain is as rich and interesting as its landscape. It is not far from Luoyang, the ancient capital city of nine different dynasties, making it an essential place for emperors to offer sacrifices to their ancestors and the gods. This has left many sites of historic and cultural interest in this area. The beauty of the area's scenery also led many famous scholars, monks and Taoists to this area to give lectures, explain Buddhist sutras and develop the teachings of different religions. Practitioners of the three faiths of Buddhism, Taoism and Confucianism absorbed ideas from each other, which led to these three beliefs growing closer together.

Songshan Mountain is the birthplace of China Zen Buddhism, and is the home of many wondrous temples, including Shaolin Temple, the largest pagoda forest in China Ta Lin (meaning pagoda forest) and the most ancient pagoda in China, Songyue Temple pagoda. A visitor can also visit the oldest cypress, as well as the earliest star observation platform in China.

What makes Songshan Mountain different from the rest of the Five Mountains is its rich and extensive cultural history. For this reason, a visit to Songshan Mountain will be greatly rewarding for scholars of religion, physical training, archaeology, geology, art, and architecture, as well as for travelers with a passion for beauty and history.

 Words and Expressions to Learn

archaeology / ˌɑːkɪˈɒlədʒɪ / *n.* 考古学

geology / dʒɪˈɒlədʒɪ / *n.* 地质学

✱✱✱   ✱✱✱   ✱✱✱   ✱✱✱   ✱✱✱   ✱✱✱

International Geological Park 国际地质公园

UNESCO 联合国教科文组织(the United

Nations Educational, Scientific and Cultural Organization) 的简称

Passage 2   The Yin Ruins

In 1899, in Xiaotun Village of Anyang city, Henan Province, villagers found many tortoise shells and bones carved with letters and symbols, which led to the discovery of the Yin Ruins, an ancient city with a long history and splendid culture. Since then this place has attracted worldwide attention among archeologists, because those letters and symbols have proved to be the earliest words of human beings, the Oracles.

About 3,300 years ago, an emperor of Shang Dynasty moved the capital of the country to Yin, which is today's Anyang city, and since then Yin has been the capital city for more than 250 years. Today the Yin Ruins has proved to be the earliest remains of an ancient capital city in written record.

Covering an area of 24 square kilometers, the Yin Ruins had a palace district, civil residence district, tomb district and workshop district, divided into two parts by the Heng River in the city. This clearly shows us a powerful country and a well-equipped ancient city.

The large-scale excavation in the Yin Ruins has been continued since last century. Besides the 150,000 pieces of oracles, many bronze wares have been discovered, and among them, Simuwuding, a 4-legged bronze cooking vessel, is the biggest and heaviest bronze object ever found worldwide. Apart from oracles and bronze wares, people have also excavated a lot of pottery wares and jade pieces. The excavation is still going on and great discoveries come forth from time to time. A famous archeologist has said, there are more treasures to be found in the Yin Ruins.

Because of its great value in not only the Chinese culture but also in the whole human civilization, the Yin Ruins topped the 100 Greatest Archeological Discoveries of last century in China and it is now working on being included in the World Cultural and Natural Heritage List of the United Nations Educational, Scientific and Cultural Organization (UNESCO).

 Words and Expressions to Learn ·

archeologist / ɑːkɪˈɒlədʒɪst / *n.* 考古学家   vessel / ˈvesəl / *n.* 器皿

***   ***   ***   ***   ***   ***

the Yin Ruins 殷墟   bronze ware 青铜器
tortoise shells 龟壳   Simuwuding 司母戊方鼎
the Oracles 甲骨文   pottery ware 陶器
the large-scale excavation 大规模的发掘

Part  *Exercises* · · · · · · · · · · · · ·

I. *Collect enough information about traveling in Henan and make up a brief dialogue.*

II. *Decide whether the following statements are true or false according to the passages.*

1. Important celebrations and prayers are held in the Hall of Heavenly Kings of Shaolin Temple.
2. The whole system of Shaolin Kung Fu was invented by the famous 18 Buddhist Arhats.
3. Zen Buddhism was developed in the area of Songshan Mountain.
4. Songshan Mountain is different from the other famous mountains in China in that it has an extensive cultural history.
5. Simuwuding, the heaviest bronze object in the whole world, was discovered in the Yin Ruins.
6. The earliest remains of an ancient capital city in written record was discovered in Luoyang.

III. *Fill in the blanks with suitable prepositions or conjunctives.*

1. _____ the year 64 of Eastern Han Dynasty, Emperor Ming sent a delegation to study Buddhism in the western world. After three years, two eminent Indian monks came back 2. _____ the delegation. They brought 3. _____ them a white horse carrying Buddhist sutras and Buddhist figures 4. _____ its back. This was the first time that Buddhism appeared in China.

To express his thanks 5. _____ the two monks and their white horse, the emperor ordered the building of a monastery 6. _____ he named it the White Horse Temple the following year. The two monks translated sutras in the temple until they completed the Chinese sutra 'Forty-two Chapter Sutra' and therefore, the temple is honored 7. _____ the 'Cradle of Buddhism in China'.

The temple, which is located about seven miles away 8. _____ the city of Louyang, is covered with green ancient trees and appears solemn and tranquil. The temple boasts great antique architecture which has remained intact 9. _____ over 1,900 years. Everything in the temple is kept 10. _____ they were when it was first built.

IV. *Translate the following dialogue into English.*

— 这个五一节你有什么计划吗？
— 我想去河南旅游。
— 真的吗？河南的名胜很多呀。有殷墟、龙门石窟(Longmen Grottoes)、少林寺等等。
— 除了名胜，洛阳的牡丹(peony)也很有名。
— 是啊。人常说"洛阳牡丹甲天下"嘛。从1983年开始，每年都举行洛阳牡丹节。
— 我一定去看看"花中之王"。对了，你知道河南有什么特产(specialty)吗？我想买一点带给家人和朋友。
— 有很多。我去年到河南旅游时，买了些河南泌阳出产的花菇(cracked mushroom)，很不错。

V. *Translate the following passage into Chinese.*

Longmen Grottoes (龙门石窟) are located about eight miles south of Luoyang. Craftsmen began working on Buddhist grottoes here in 494 when an emperor of the Northern Wei moved the capital from what is now known as Datong in Shanxi Province to Luoyang. They are therefore an extension of Yungang Grottoes in Datong. The work at Longmen continued all the way through several dynasties. In more than 1,300 caves, there are 40 small pagodas, and almost 100,000 Buddha statues ranging in size from one inch to

57 feet. These caves and the stone sculptures have the same historical significance with the caves at Yungang and Dunhuang in Buddhist culture of China.

VI. Topic for discussion

In recent years, the Shaolin Temple Monks are frequently going abroad giving Kung Fu performances to people of other countries. What is your comment on this?

UNIT 4

Lesson 21
Hubei and Hunan

Part A Conversation

Dialogue | **A visit to Phoenix Ancient Town**

(G: guide; T: tourist)

G: Here we are, the famous Fenghuang Ancient Town, or you may call it Phoenix Ancient Town.

T: Oh, I can't believe my eyes. This place is beautiful, simply beautiful!

G: You said it. This town ranks among the most beautiful towns in China. It has a recorded history of about 1,300 years.

T: That's really a long history. It is even older than our country.

G: Have you noticed most of the houses are wooden structures and are built on stilts?

T: I guess it must have something to do with the damp weather here.

G: That's a very good guess. Another reason is related to the region's terrain. It slopes down from northwest to southeast.

T: Hmm, I have noticed that. The houses seem to be arranged in layers.

G: You are right. The highest elevation of the town is 1,117 meters while the lowest elevation is 170 meters.

T: Wow! That is a big slope. Oh, I like the bridges here. They are so elegant, just like in some Chinese paintings I saw.

G: Yes, the elegant bridges and mysterious towers and pagodas are typical of the town.

T: Elegant and mysterious. Yes, they are the best words to describe the town.

G: Actually, the best moment to appreciate the town's mysterious beauty is in the early morning or after a rain.

T: Why so?

G: Because in early morning or after a rain, light mist sets in around the bridges over the water and stilted houses, the area simply becomes a mirror of traditional Chinese paintings.

T: Oh, yeah. I can imagine that. A stroll on the flagstone streets is really a treat.

G: Visiting a Miao village is also a must. You will find a large array of silver ornaments, homemade tie-dyes, and unique local snacks there.

T: Great. I have watched some documentaries about the Miao people and their silver ornaments. They are fabulous! What are we waiting for? Let's go!

G: Wait! Before that, we will go boating on the Tuo River and you can enjoy the undulating mountain ranges, deep valleys along its banks.

T: Oh, I can't wait. Let's go!

 Words and Expressions to Learn ···

stilt / stɪlt / n. 高跷,支撑物

damp / dæmp / a. 潮湿的,湿度大的

terrain / te'reɪn / n. 地势,地形

elevation / ˌelɪ'veɪʃən / n. 海拔,高度

primitive / 'prɪmɪtɪv / a. 质朴的,自然的

appreciate / ə'priːʃɪeɪt / v. 欣赏

flagstone / 'flægstəun / n. 石板,扁石

treat / triːt / n. 享受,难得的乐事

ornament / 'ɔːnəmənt / n. 饰品,装饰物

homemade / 'həum'meɪd / a. 家里做的,自制的

tie-dye / 'taɪdaɪ / n. 扎染织物

documentary / ˌdɒkju'mentərɪ / n. 纪录片,纪实节目

fabulous / 'fæbjuləs / a. 惊人的,难以置信的

undulating / 'ʌndjuleɪtɪŋ / a. 连绵起伏的,呈波浪形的

***　　***　　***　　***　　***　　***

Phoenix Ancient Town 凤凰古城

rank among 位于……之列

a recorded history 有文字记载的历史

have something to do with 与……有关

set in around 开始笼罩

Part **B**　Reading

Passage 1　Mawangdui Han Tombs

Located in the eastern suburb of Changsha City, the world famous Mawangdui Han Tombs are one of the most fascinating attractions in Hunan Province and an open book to the glorious Western Han Dynasty. All three tombs were excavated between 1972 and 1974. According to research this place was a family graveyard from at least two thousand years ago. The tombs are very grand and complicated as well. Number 1 and Number 3 Tombs were in excellent condition when excavated and Number 1 Tomb is the largest among the three. Number 1 and Number 2 Tombs have been refilled. Number 3 Tomb has been preserved and covered with a ceiling for the benefit of the visitors.

More than 3,000 relics have been found in the three tombs, such as silk products, silk books, silk paintings, lacquer wares, potteries, bamboo slips used for writing, weapons, herbs, and so on. The number of lacquer wares is the largest, including ancient cooking utensils, boxes, kettles, plates and folding screens, and the like. Red or black colors were painted on them. Most of the potteries contain food. The mouths of the containers were sealed with grass and mud and with bamboo brands bearing the name of the food tied on the containers' necks. There are wooden tomb figurines both clothed and unclothed according to their different social status based on the strict ranking system of Western Han Dynasty. The silk clothes from Number 1 Tomb are in a variety of styles and of fine workmanship. One of the most outstanding items is a silk coat which is as light as mist and as fine as gossamer. It is 1.28 meters in length with a pair of long sleeves, but weighs only 49 grams. The coffin excavated from Number 1 Tomb is decorated with strange images of animals and gods on its lacquered surface and has a relatively high artistic value.

A map excavated from Number 2 Tomb provides another surprise. Its drawing technique is very advanced, place marks being very similar to a modern map. It was praised as "a striking discovery" when exhibited in America, Japan, Poland and many other countries. Silk books, with more than one hundred thousand Chinese characters, deal with ancient philosophy, history, science, technology, medicine and many other subjects.

The excavation of Number 1 Tomb at Mawangdui has a great effect on world archeological history. The reason is that the body of this tomb's owner — a noble lady and other articles buried with the dead were perfectly preserved for more than 2,000 years. When removed from the tomb, the body was complete and still moist and soft. Some of her joints could move; her organs and surrounding tissues were still in perfect condition, and the skin still flexible; she looked as if she had been buried yesterday. This is extremely rare to see both at home and abroad. Meanwhile it is also a scientific miracle in antisepsis, shocking the whole world and attracting the attention of both scholars and visitors. Try to think: when facing a lady who is more than 2,000 years old, how will you feel?

The sarcophagus of Number 1 Tomb was covered by a colorful silk painting. It is the best preserved painting of its kind from Han Dynasty with the highest artistic value in China. It is in the shape of the English letter "T", so people also call it "T" silk painting. In fact, this kind of silk painting was called "long narrow flag" in ancient times and used for funerals. It was held by the person who headed the funeral procession and then put over the coffin when burying the dead. This particular silk painting from Number 1 Tomb can be divided into three parts. The upper part is about heaven, the middle part is about earth and the lower part is about afterlife. Heaven means the final home of the dead. Earth shows the wealth and nobility of the dead when alive. World after death displays the happiness of the dead in the afterworld. The whole painting is symmetrical and colorful, reflecting the advanced painting skills in Western Han Dynasty. All the mysteries, strange animals and mysterious signs in the painting present us with a romantic world with its own sense of symbolism. As yet no one has been able to explain its real meaning.

All the relics are displayed in Hunan Provincial Museum.

 Words and Expressions to Learn ·

suburb / ˈsʌbəb / n. 郊区　　　　　　　　excavate / ˈekskəveɪt / v. 挖掘,开凿

figurine / ˌfɪɡəˈriːn / n. 小雕像

gossamer / ˈɡɒsəmə / n. 蛛丝，游丝

coffin / ˈkɒfɪn / n. 棺木，棺材

moist / mɔɪst / a. 潮湿的

joint / dʒɔɪnt / n. 关节

tissue / ˈtɪʃuː / n. (身体)组织

flexible / ˈfleksɪbl / a. 有弹性

antisepsis / ˌæntɪˈsepsɪs / n. 抗菌，防腐

sarcophagus / sɑːˈkɒfəɡəs / n. 石棺，大理石棺

procession / prəˈseʃən / n. 队列，队伍

symmetrical / sɪˈmetrɪkəl / a. 对称的

***　　***　　***　　***　　***　　***

Mawangdui Han Tombs 马王堆汉墓(位于湖南长沙)

for the benefit of 为了方便……，为了……的利益

lacquer ware 漆器

bamboo slips 竹简

and the like 如此等等

social status 社会地位

deal with 论述，谈论，有关

as yet 迄今为止

Passage 2　The Shennongjia Forest Zone

The Shennongjia Forest Zone in eastern Hubei Province has an area of 3,253 square kilometers, and contains four towns, four villages, one national forest park and one national nature reserve area. Because of its marvelous natural scenery, rare plants and animals and famous legends such as the mysterious "Wild Man" said to be found in the mountains, the Shennongjia Forest Zone has attracted many tourists every year, including a lot of researchers and scientists.

Shennongjia was named after a very famous Chinese chief in prehistoric time, Shennong, also known as Yandi. He was believed to be one of the two ancestors of Chinese people (the other was Huangdi, the Yellow Emperor). He invented crockery, discovered herbal medicine by personally tasting herbs and taught his people farming work. It is said that while Shennong tasted herbs here, he suffered poisoning more than seventy times! However in the end, he managed to discover many useful herbs. To commemorate his great work, people named this area after him.

Shennongding Peak, the highest mountain of Shennongjia, is 3,105.4 meters above sea level. The lowest point, the Shizhu River in southeastern Shennongjia Forest Zone, is only 398 meters above sea level. Visitors can experience four seasons at different altitudes. Flowers blossom at every corner; firs, spruces, dove trees, and many rare trees can be seen everywhere. Virgin forests, clear streams and grand waterfalls beckon visitors to indulge in the wild nature. Peculiar caves often amaze visitors. There is the Swallow Cave with thousands of swallows living in it, the Tide Cave that floods three times a day, the Icy Cave that is always icy in summer, the Fish Cave that is home to lots of fish at time of thunder. Wild animals, some of which are rare species like the golden haired monkey, spotted deer and so on, are also frequently seen.

The most peculiar species found in Shennongjia are certainly the "white animals." The first albino animal spotted in Shennongjia was a white bear, which looks like a giant panda in white skin. White monkeys, white roes, white deer, white squirrels, white snakes, white crows and even white toads have also been discovered. Aside from the rare animals, Shennongjia is a natural garden for herbal medicines as well. More than two thousand kinds of precious herbs can be easily found in the Shennongjia Forest Zone.

The Wild Man of Shennongjia is a mysterious figure as famous as Nessie and UFOs. The records of the Wild Man appear many times in ancient Chinese books, and since the 1970s, many people in Shennongjia have declared that they had seen the Wild Man. They are said to look like apes, about two meters tall, covered with red or brown hair and can move very fast while standing erect. There have been many researches about them in Shennongjia, which have come up with some evidence of the creature, such as their footprints and hairs. It is believed by many that the Wild Man is an ancient species just like the giant panda and the golden haired monkey. Recently, some hikers and visitors also announced their sightings of the Wild Man. But to this day, no one has yet been caught.

Without doubt, the Shennongjia Forest Zone is an attraction teeming with virgin scenery and folk legends, awaiting the enjoyment and excitement of tourists and researchers alike.

 Words and Expressions to Learn ....

prehistoric / ˌpriːhɪˈstɒrɪk / *a.* 史前的，有历史
    记载以前的
crockery / ˈkrɒkərɪ / *n.* 陶器，瓦器
spruce / spruːs / *n.* 云杉
beckon / ˈbekən / *v.* 召唤，示意

indulge / ɪnˈdʌldʒ / *v.* 放纵，享受，沉溺
albino / ælˈbiːnəʊ / *n.* 患白化病的人或动物
roe / rəʊ / *n.* 雌马鹿
erect / ɪˈrekt / *a.* 直立的，垂直的

the Shennongjia Forest Zone 神农架森林保 　护区(位于湖北省)	Tide Cave 潮汐洞
	Icy Cave 冰洞
Yandi 炎帝	aside from 除了
Shennongding Peak 神农顶	Nessie 尼斯湖怪
the Shizhu River 石柱河	come up with 提出,得出
dove trees 珙桐树	teeming with 充满
Swallow Cave 燕子洞	

Part **C** Exercises

I. *Make up a dialogue between a guide and a tourist about touring the Shennongjia Forest Zone according to the information in Reading Passage 2.*

II. *Answer the following questions according to the dialogue and the passages.*

1. What is unusual about the silk coat taken from No.1 Tomb of the Mawangdui Han Tombs?

2. Why does the map from No.2 Tomb surprise the visitors?

3. Why do we say the excavation of No.1 Tomb has great effect on world archeological history?

4. What is the significance of the silk painting from the Mawangdui Han Tombs?

5. Why have so many tourists home and abroad been attracted to Shennongjia?

6. How did Shennongjia get its name?

7. What is the most peculiar fact about animals in the Shennongjia Forest Zone?

8. What has helped to add mystery to the Shennongjia Forest Zone?

III. *Fill in the blanks with the proper form of the words given in brackets.*

　　1. _____ (see) from a distance, the Yueyang Pavilion seems like a giant bird in 2. _____ (fly). The red building with its yellow glazed roof tiles is a splendid and colorful sight. Views here are spectacular. You will see the pavilion 3. _____ (glow) in the sunshine together with the drifting clouds with their 4. _____ (reflect) on the glimmering surface of the Dongting Lake. You will also see the white sails of passing boats contrasting with the blue sky. Couplets (对联) and 5. _____ (carve) screens are hung on the wall inside the building 6. _____ (provide) the visitors with information about the history of this pavilion.

　　The age of the pavilion is disputed. However, it is 7. _____ (general) believed that the pavilion was built more than 1,700 years ago. The pavilion was used to serve military (军事的) purposes with the name of "Baling Tower". It was not until the Tang Dynasty that it was 8. _____ (name) as the Yueyang Pavilion. The Yueyang Pavilion was damaged in the chaos of wars and was 9. _____ (build) in the Song Dynasty. Since then, it has become a tourist attraction and a place of 10. _____ (inspire) for both poets and writers. The pavilion was made very famous during the Northern Song Dynasty by the works of Fan Zhongyan who was a great politician and writer.

IV. Translate the Chinese passage into English.

据传说,在武昌,曾经有一处酒店,店主是一位姓辛的年轻人。一天一位道长来到酒店,为答谢店家让他免费喝酒,他用橘子皮在酒店的墙上画了一只仙鹤,并且命它一听到拍手声就下来跳舞。成千上万的人来到酒店观看这一奇迹,所以酒店总是挤满了客人。十年之后,那位道长再次造访酒店。他吹了一曲笛子,仙鹤从墙上飞下来。那道长便骑着仙鹤飞走了。为了纪念这一奇遇,辛家人便建了一座塔楼并命名为黄鹤楼。

黄鹤楼在历史上屡毁屡建,直到一百年前最后一次被烧为灰烬。现在的是一个全新的重建的塔楼。从1981年动工,共花费了四年时间。新的黄鹤楼被视为武汉的标志。

V. Topics for discussion.

1. Do you believe that there are "Wild Men" living in the Shennongjia Forest Zone? Why?
2. Many scenic spots were polluted because of the huge number of tourists. Do you have any suggestions as to the protection of those beautiful places?

UNIT 4

Lesson 22
Guangdong, Guangxi and Hainan

Part **A** Conversation

Dialogue   A Trip to Luhuitou

(G:Guide   T: Tourist)

G: Good morning!

T: Good morning! Where are we going today?

G: How about Luhuitou?

T: Does the name mean anything?

G: A good question! There is indeed a beautiful folk tale about the place.

T: I guess so. I would like to know that story. Is it romance again?

G: Wow, you know Chinese folk stories so well! As you said, it is romance again.

T: A young man and a young lady?

G: Not exactly! As the story goes, once upon a time, there was a young man of the Li Minority. He chased a deer all the way from Wuzhi Mountain to the present location of Luhuitou.

T: Did the young hunter catch up with the deer at last?

G: Well, he almost did. The deer ran to the seashore and there was no place to escape.

T: Oh, no, then what?

G: Don't forget it is romance! When the young man looked at the deer, he began to feel sympathetic to her.

T: Her? Then it's a doe.

G: Yes. The young man lowered his bow and arrow. The doe suddenly changed into a beautiful Li minority girl.

T: Oh, I see. The two fell in love at the first sight, right?

G: Haha, you are now an old hand at Chinese folk tales! Look, this is the Haikubulan Stone.

T: What does Haikubulan mean? Is there another story?

G: Actually, it is part of the story I've just told you. Haikubulan means the stone would not fall apart even if the sea dried up. So the stone stands for their undying love.

T: How romantic!

G: Did you see that character over there? Let's go and take a look.

T: Wow, it is the Chinese character for "love".

G: This is a witness of their love.

T: Well, I have found the Li Minority people are very different.

G: The Li Minority is one of the 55 minority groups in China. They mostly live on Hainan Island.

T: I guess they must have their unique food, clothes and things to play with.

G: Yes. Because they are separated from the mainland, they live quite a different life here. Not only are their foods and clothes different, but also their way of life.

T: For example?

G: In Hainan, women do most of the work.

T: What about men?

G: Haven't you noticed the many teahouses in here? They drink tea from early morning to late night!

T: Really? What a way of life!

G: But, don't worry. Now more and more tourists are crowding into this island, people here are beginning to change!

T: That's good news!

 Words and Expressions to Learn ·

chase / tʃeɪs / v. 追赶
seashore / ˈsiːʃɔː / n. 海岸, 海滨
doe / dəʊ / n. 母鹿

arrow / ˈærəʊ / n. 箭
undying / ʌnˈdaɪɪŋ / a. 不朽的, 永恒的
witness / ˈwɪtnəs / n. 证人

***　　***　　***　　***　　***　　***

Luhuitou 鹿回头

Li Minority 黎族

Wuzhi Mountain 五指山

feel sympathetic to 同情

at the first sight 首次见面

be an old hand at 是……方面的老手，很擅

长……

Haikubulan Stone 海枯不烂石

Chinese character 汉字

Part B Reading

Passage 1   Shenzhen Chinese Folk Culture Village

China is a big and united family made up of many ethnic groups. Geographically speaking, they live in different parts of China and it is impossible to experience each ethnic group's architecture, their festivals and taste their snacks during one single visit. But the Chinese Folk Cultural Village in Shenzhen will help solve this problem. The village has an area of more than 200,000 square meters with 24 peculiar cottages which are built at a ratio of 1 : 1 and are welcoming all visitors.

In the village, you will have a better chance to experience the colorful Chinese folk cultures.

The stone village of the Buyi ethnic group, distributed mainly in the Sichuan and Guizhou Provinces, is a wonderful stone world. The simple furniture such as tables, stoves and basins are all made of stone. The Mosuo people pile solid wooden stocks into a house which was earthquake-proof. What really interests tourists is that this group is the world's only matriarchal community in existence today. The Dai ethnic group lives in Yunnan Province where there is plenty of bamboo. Because of this, all the girders, tiles and roofs of their homes are made entirely of bamboo. You may call it "a bamboo garden". Actually, this kind of building is a two-storied attic in the air. Dozens of wooden stocks support the whole attic and the floor is covered with bamboo. Here is the Mongol ethnic group which is generally known as "a group on horse-back" because of their nomadic living habits. Mongols live in the yurts which are not only cool in summer and warm in winter but also easy to set up or take apart. No matter which group you are visiting, young boys and girls will warmly welcome your arrival.

If you come at the right time, you will be able to experience some unique festivals of the minorities. In the Water-splashing Festival of the Dai people, people splash water on each other. They hope to get rid of evil and bad luck from the last year and expect happiness and good luck in the coming year. Come prepared to get thoroughly wet. In addition, the dragon-boat contest each spring is still the most important event in Dai people's lunar calendar. In contrast, the Torch Festival is the most traditional event of the Yi ethnic group and held in the sixth month of the Chinese lunar calendar. Tourists will see the Yi people in bright-colored clothes carrying torches as they walk around their houses and farmlands. Usually, chickens or ducks will be sacrificed to ancestors. Maybe you will be invited to take part in the celebrations when the villagers happily sing and dance around their bonfires. A breathtaking and memorable Knife Bar Festival of the Lisu ethnic group is celebrated in the second month of the Chinese lunar calendar. This two-part festival starts on the first day with the "jumping into the fire sea". Several barefooted men jump in and out of a burning fire. The performance on the second day is as dangerous as that on the first day. It is called "climbing the mountain of knives" because brave men will climb a ladder formed by two wooden poles with 32 sharp long knives as the rungs. When barefooted heroes reach the top of the ladder, they let off firecrackers to declare their success. This traditional festival commemorates a hero who bravely helped the Lisu people resist foreign invaders during Ming Dynasty.

In the Chinese Folk Culture Village, additional attractions are folk dances, local snacks and handicrafts. You will be able to choose many souvenirs from the variety of different designs. The tasty snacks may leave you wanting more of these delicious foods. All in all, after strolling through this village, you will have a greater understanding of some of the Chinese cultural groups.

 Words and Expressions to Learn · · · · · · · · · · · · · · · · · ·

cottage / ˈkɒtɪdʒ / n. 小屋，村舍
stock / stɒk / n. 木柱，树干
matriarchal / ˌmeɪtrɪˈɑːkəl / a. 母系的
girder / ˈɡɜːdə / n. 大梁
attic / ˈætɪk / n. 阁楼

yurt / jʊət / n. 蒙古包，毡包
bonfire / ˈbɒnfaɪə / n. 篝火
barefooted / ˈbeəfʊtɪd / a. 赤脚的
rung / rʌŋ / n. 梯级，横档
souvenir / ˌsuːvəˈnɪə / n. 旅游纪念品

***　　***　　***　　***　　***　　***

Shenzhen Chinese Folk Culture Village 深圳中国民族文化村

at a ratio of 以……比例

Buyi ethnic group 布依族

Mosuo people 摩梭人

Dai ethnic group 傣族

Mongol ethnic group 蒙古族

set up 搭建

take apart 拆卸

the Water-splashing Festival 泼水节

lunar calendar 阴历

in contrast 相比之下

the Torch Festival 火把节

the Yi ethnic group 彝族

Knife Bar Festival 刀杆节

the Lisu ethnic group 傈僳族

Passage 2   Guilin

Guilin is a living canvas of China's charming scenery, romantic landscape and is a spiritual land of peace!

When you see Guilin, you will totally understand what has inspired thousands of Chinese artists over the ages to draw such beautiful paintings! "I often sent pictures of the hills of Guilin which I painted to friends back home, but few believed what they saw." The writer of this was Song Dynasty scholar Fan Chengda and his comments show that the scenery of Guilin has been attracting and astonishing visitors for many centuries. Guilin is the very essence of the classical Chinese landscape paintings with fantastically shaped peaks with pines and delicate pavilions, partly shrouded in the mist.

Guilin is said to have been founded in 214 BC. At that time, one of the earliest projects in ancient China (along with the Great Wall) was the Ling Canal. It was built by order of the first Chinese emperor, Qin Shi Huang. It still connects central and south China through the Yangtze, Li and Pearl Rivers.

Since the construction of the Ling Canal in Qin Dynasty, Guilin has developed into a cultural exchange center between the south and the north. The legendary scenery has attracted many famous Tang Dynasty poets to Guilin. The poems and essays they wrote added more charm to the timeless mountains and rivers, forming the unique culture of Guilin.

Seated on the bank of the Li River, Guilin was a quiet, sleepy town until the end of the 1970s, when tourism suddenly developed. It was like a Shangri-La being discovered by the outside world. Guilin has the most spectacular Karst region in the world. These magical limestone rock formations, with the green surroundings make Guilin a true paradise. The symbolic landscape in Guilin is a buffalo leisurely working in the rice paddies, with little boys on their back against the misty but graceful green mountains as background.

Guilin has a very mild and pleasant weather. Sweet Osmanthus is the city flower of Guilin. The name of the city Guilin actually means Forest of Sweet Osmanthus trees. In autumn, the air is filled with the sweet smell of Osmanthus trees all over the city. The city tree of Guilin is banyan tree, which you will see everywhere in the city like an on-going bonsai show!

Guilin is a very peaceful place with 12 different minority peoples living together, and enjoying this land of natural miracles! The colorful village life, the unique customs and festivals of the different minority peoples only add more energy and flavor to Guilin. They are actually another main reason to visit Guilin!

A great highlight of any Guilin tour is the cruise down the Li River. The hills beyond hills with their reflections in the crystal water give you the feeling of being in a fairyland. The green bamboo waves at you in the breeze all the way along the river. Buffaloes contentedly munching the grass; ducks swimming along the river; fishermen fishing on the bamboo rafts with their cormorants resting peacefully next to them, it is truly a masterpiece of nature. You will be enchanted by those amazingly shaped mountains, whether shrouded in mist or under the blue sky, during the early morning or in the sunset. Lost in the quiet voice of nature, you will always feel like you were reborn into a new world! At the end of the cruise, you will arrive at a small but quite international town: Yangshuo! Started as a fishing village, Yangshuo has become a very interesting town with a mixed culture of its international residents!

Guilin — truly a place that you should never miss seeing at least once in your lifetime!

 Words and Expressions to Learn . . . .

canvas / ˈkænvəs / *n.* 油画，画布

essence / ˈesəns / *n.* 精髓，本质

inspire / ɪnˈspaɪə / *v.* 启发，给以灵感

shroud / ʃraʊd / *v.* 笼罩，遮蔽

Karst / kɑːst / n. 喀斯特

limestone / ˈlaɪmstəʊn / n. 石灰岩

buffalo / ˈbʌfələʊ / n. 水牛

paddy / ˈpædɪ / n. 稻田

banyan / ˈbænjæn / n. 榕树

bonsai / ˈbɒnsaɪ / n. 盆景, 盆栽

miracle / ˈmɪrəkl / n. 奇迹

munch / ˈmʌntʃ / v. 用力咀嚼

cormorant / ˈkɔːmərənt / n. 鸬鹚

enchant / ɪnˈtʃɑːnt / v. 使陶醉, 使入迷

***   ***   ***   ***   ***   ***

Fan Chengda 范成大 (南宋诗人)

the Ling Canal 灵渠

by order of 奉……之命

Shangri-La 香格里拉, 世外桃源

Sweet Osmanthus 桂花

Part C Exercises

I. Make up a brief dialogue between you and your friend about visiting Guilin according to the information given in Reading Passage 2.

II. Answer the following questions according to the dialogue and the two passages.

1. What problem can the Shenzhen Chinese Folk Culture Village solve?

2. Why do the Mongol people live in yurts?

3. What brought about the rapid development of Guilin in history?

4. What is the symbolic scenery of Guilin?

5. Besides the enchanting natural scenery, what is the other reason to visit Guilin?

III. Complete the following passage by translating the Chinese into English.

    1. _____ (不同于) other provinces, Hainan is the smallest province in China. Although scenery in Hainan 2. _____ (缺乏长城的壮观) and the mystery of the Terracotta Warriors, its 3. _____ (自然美) has gained a good reputation among the visitors and has been widely known 4. _____ (在国内外). People call it 5. _____ (东方夏威夷).

    Hainan is located 6. _____ (中国最南端), and occupies an area of 7. _____ (35000 平方公里). Due to the mild climate and favorable environment, Hainan 8. _____ (被看作是) a long life island. The young often travel to Hainan seeking 9. _____ (回归自然) and the old would rather live there to enjoy their lives. Hainan now has a population of 7.11 million, among which about one million are 10. _____ (少数民族).

IV. *Fill in each of the blanks in the following passage with a suitable preposition.*

Similar 1. _____ Tianyahaijiao, Nantianyizhu has a legend too. Long ago, the sea 2. _____ Hainan was so stormy that many fishermen lost their lives. The sorrow of their relatives accumulated and finally reached Heaven. Two angels of Wangmu, Goddess of Heaven were very sympathetic 3. _____ them and therefore decided to do something for the fishermen. They sneaked out 4. _____ Heaven from the South Heaven Gate and came to South China Sea. They stopped the storm and helped the fishermen to navigate their way. 5. _____ a result, their life is greatly improved. Realizing the angels were missing, Wangmu sent God of Thunder to bring them back. The angels refused to go back and resisted. They together changed 6. _____ a giant stone so that they could continue to navigate the fishermen. The God of Thunder angrily smashed the stone 7. _____ two pieces. One of the pieces split 8. _____ three near Li'an, while the other landed next 9. _____ Tianyahaijiao, planted 10. _____ the beach. Only at the end of the 19th century was the pillar engraved the four Chinese characters, reading "Nantianyizhu" (the Pillar of Southern Heaven).

V. *Translate the English passage into Chinese and the Chinese passage into English.*

1. West Street is the oldest street in Yangshuo with a history of more than 1,400 years. Situated at the center of Yangshuo County, West Street has become, since the 1980's, a window to Eastern and Western cultures and each year it attracts about 100,000 foreigners who come to savor its unique mix of cultures. At times, foreigners outnumber Chinese, so West Street is called "foreigners' street", or "the global village". Besides the local accent of Yangshuo, English has become the language for daily use. Chinese visitors at the West Street may think they are in a foreign country, while foreigners come here to search for the ancient civilization of China. However, whether you are Chinese or a foreigner, West Street is a terrific place to take a rest, both physically and psychologically. West Street will drive all of your pressures and burdens away, and give you a calmer view of life. It shows different faces at different times: calm and peaceful in the morning, while trendy and modern in the evening. Traveling to West Street is an experience any visitor should not miss.

2. 亚龙湾位于海南省最南端，距热带海滨旅游城市三亚25公里，平均水温终年保持在舒适的摄氏25.5度。这里风景迷人，有连绵的山丘，宁静的海湾，清澈的蓝色大海，银色沙滩。这里的沙滩有夏威夷的任何沙滩的三倍长。这里拥有几处保护良好的珊瑚礁，各种颜色不同，形状各异的热带鱼类生活其中。蓝色的海水清澈透明，游客可以观察到水面下十米深处的一切景象。

VI. *Topic for discussion*

It is often reported visitors to Hainan and other tourist attractions are sometimes cheated and overcharged. Analyze in groups the causes and suggest solutions to this problem.

Section Six   Southwest China

UNIT **4** Lesson 23
Sichuan and Guizhou

Part **A** *Conversation*

| Dialogue | Visiting Jiuzhaigou Valley |

(G: Guide   T: Tourist)

G: Let's get on the sightseeing bus. It will take us to Shuzheng Group Lakes.

T: Let me look at the map on the ticket. Yeah, here it is. Shuzheng Group Lakes.

G: Jiuzhaigou Valley is called "fairyland" for its primitive and natural beauty. There are about 114 lakes. We have a beautiful fairy tale about these lakes. It says that a long time ago, a god named Dage ground a magic mirror with wind and cloud and gave it to his beloved goddess Wonuosemo. When Wonuosemo was looking into the mirror, a devil came and tried to grab the mirror. Frightened, she dropped the mirror and it broke into pieces, fell to the human world, and became these 114 glittering lakes.

T: That's a good tale. How did it get the name "Jiuzhaigou" then?

G: "Jiu" means "nine", "zhai" means "village" and "Gou" means "valley". There are nine Tibetan villages in the valley. Here we are, the Shuzheng Group Lakes. You can see this is a lake group.

T: Amazing! This is really a lake group.

G: There are about 40 of them and all of them are connected.

T: And there are even trees growing in the lakes!

G: Look at the water.

T: Wow, it's so clear, so pure. This is the most beautiful water I've ever seen.

G: OK, let's walk to Panda Lake. It is not far from here.

T: Panda Lake? Are we going to see pandas there?

G: There are no pandas now, but in the past, pandas used to eat arrow bamboos and drink water there.

T: Look! So many fish in the water!

G: It's said these fish have no scales. Shh. Can you hear something?

T: Yes... Look! A waterfall!

G: This is the famous Nuorilang Waterfall. It is 180 meters wide and 30 meters high.

This is one of China's largest calcified falls. Just imagine what it looks like in winter!

A white curtain of ice hanging from the top of the cliff!

T: I should come again in winter!

G: Here is the Multi-color Lake, the most beautiful lake here.

T: It is incredible. How come it has such beautiful colors? Light green, milky white,

bright yellow, pale blue, and ...

G: It is hard to name every color. Many organisms live in the water and there are also

many plants growing in the pond. All these things contain different pigments.

T: It is really amazing. Wait, I'll take pictures.

G: This is the Long Lake. Also it's the largest one in Jiuzhaigou.

T: Oh, it's much colder here.

G: That's because it's about 3,000 meters above sea level here.

T: No wonder.

G: It is much colder here also because the water in the lake comes from the melted

snow on the surrounding mountains. The lake has no exit.

T: No exit? Then where will the water go in the rainy seasons?

G: Well, the water either evaporates or seeps into the earth when there's too much. So

the water never overflows or dries up.

T: What a magical lake!

 Words and Expressions to Learn ···

sightseeing / ˈsaɪtsiːɪŋ / n. 观光, 游览

glittering / ˈɡlɪtərɪŋ / a. 闪闪发亮的

scale / skeɪl / n. 鳞片

organism / ˈɔːɡənɪzəm / n. 有机物

pigment / ˈpɪɡmənt / n. 色素

evaporate / ɪˈvæpəreɪt / v. 蒸发

seep / siːp / v. 渗入

✳✳✳   ✳✳✳   ✳✳✳   ✳✳✳   ✳✳✳   ✳✳✳

Shuzheng Group Lakes 树正群海	Nuorilang Waterfall 诺日朗瀑布
grind a magic mirror 磨一面魔镜	Multi-color Lake 五色海
arrow bamboo 箭竹	

Part **B** Reading

Passage 1   Huanglong Scenic and Historic Interest Area

The "World Wonder" and "Fairyland on Earth" are names enjoyed by Huanglong Scenic and Historic Interest Area which is well known for its colorful lakes, snow mountains, valleys and virgin forests. It was included in the UNESCO world heritage list in 1992.

Huanglong Scenic and Historic Interest Area is located in Songpan County, in the northwest part of Sichuan Province and consists of Huanglong and Muni Valley. Huanglong's major scenery is concentrated in the 3.6-kilometer-long Huanglong Valley that includes snow-covered peaks and the easternmost glaciers in China. Along the valley are numerous colorful ponds of different sizes and shapes, whose water has a shining golden color due to the gold-colored limestone deposits at their bottom, so in sunlight, a golden dragon seems to rush out of the forest. Thus it was named Huanglong (Yellow Dragon) Valley.

Upon entering the scenic area, a group of beautiful ponds with crystal clear water will immediately catch your eyes. These are the Yingbin Colored Ponds. In spring, the luxuriant trees, blooming flowers, butterflies and birdsong add even more to their beauty. From the ponds, you can see the reflection of trees, mountains, clouds and sky, which is a real feast to the eyes. Along the valley, you will see many attractions including Feipuliuhui, Xishen Cave, Penjing Ponds, Huanglong Temple, Huanglong Cave, Shitazhenhai and Zhuanhua Pond, etc. In Huanglong Cave, there are three sitting Buddha figures whose bodies are covered with calc-sinter crystals. In winter, forests, bamboo shoots and waterfalls of ice form a magical scene. Shitazhenhai is the most beautiful attraction in Huanglong. The calcium carbonate deposits give different hues to the water, which is truly breathtaking. Zhuanhua Pond is crystal clear and the spring water never stops welling up. If you throw flowers or leaves into the pond, they will swirl with the flow of the water.

Muni Valley includes Erdao Lake and Zhaga Waterfall which is the biggest calcified waterfall in China. Located in the northern part of Muni Valley, Erdao Lake is the largest in the area and around the lake are many underground limestone caves which connect Erdao Lake with other lakes in the area. The color of Erdao Lake changes with seasons, wonderfully matching the lake with the surrounding colored limestone. Standing by the lake, you may find the lake very peaceful and calm, however, there is a strong and active undercurrent. Erdao Lake holds attractions such as Swan Lake, Baihua Lake, etc. Beside Baihua Lake, there is a mysterious cave which holds magnificent naturally-formed stalactites. Zhaga Waterfall Scenic Area stretches for about 5 kilometers, and boasts many attractions. At the bottom of Zhaga Waterfall, there is a round stone onto which the waterfall cascades. In the sunlight, the spattering water is like jade, showing wonderful colors. This is the Jianyutai. Feicui Spring is one of the ten most famous springs in China due to the water's medicinal value, and many have recovered from diseases after drinking or bathing in its water. The local population considers Feicui Spring holy and allows no damage.

Huanglong Scenic and Historic Interest Area gained its fame for its magical landscape of limestone formations, as well as its forest and rare animals, such as the giant panda and Sichuan golden snub-nosed monkey.

Huanglong's beauty is beyond words; you need to see it with your own eyes to truly appreciate this "Fairy Land on Earth".

 Words and Expressions to Learn ·

easternmost / ˈiːstənməʊst / *a.* 最东端
deposit / dɪˈpɒzɪt / *n.* 沉积，沉淀物
feast / fiːst / *n.* 宴会，大餐
swirl / swɜːl / *v.* 打旋，旋转

calcified / ˈkælsɪfaɪd / *a.* 钙化的，石灰质化的
undercurrent / ˈʌndəkʌrənt / *n.* 暗流，潜流
stalactite / ˈstæləktaɪt / *n.* 钟乳石
cascade / kæsˈkeɪd / *v.* 大量倾泻

***   ***   ***   ***   ***   ***

Songpan County 松潘县

Muni Valley 牟尼沟

due to 由于	Erdao Lake 二道海
Yingbin Colored Ponds 迎宾彩池	Zhaga Waterfall 扎嘎瀑布
Feipuliuhu 飞瀑流辉	Swan Lake 天鹅湖
Xishen Cave 洗身洞	Baihua Lake 百花海
Penjing Ponds 盆景池	Jianyutai 溅玉台
Shitazhenhai 石塔镇海	Feicui Spring 翡翠泉
Zhuanhua Pond 转花池	Sichuan golden snub-nosed monkey 四川 金丝猴
calc-sinter crystals 钙华晶体	
calcium carbonate 碳酸钙	beyond words 难以言表

Passage 2   The Nine-Dragon Cave

The Nine-Dragon Cave Scenic Spot is situated at the northern end of Mount Liulong, 17 kilometers southeast of Tongren City, Guizhou Province. It is a famous scenic spot in Guizhou and covers an area of 245 square kilometers.

This area has a pleasant climate with upright hills, verdant forests and crystal creeks, and comprises natural and cultural attractions such as Guanyin Hill, Lianhua Temple, Jinjiang River Valley, the Nine-Dragon Cave, and some other caves. Among them, the most celebrated is the Nine-Dragon Cave. The cave is situated on the slope of the Guanyin Hill on the right bank of the Malong Creek (Scolding Dragon Creek). It is a large natural Karst Cave about 70 meters wide and 30 to 50 meters high. The widest part is about 100 meters. Consisting of seven caves and twelve scenic spots, it has two levels connected by small caves.

As legend goes, six yellow dragons once lived on the hill. One day, they invited three black dragons from the Jinjiang River to meet them in the cave. Fascinated by the scenery in the cave, the nine dragons were reluctant to leave and decided to live there. Each wanted to occupy the cave as its own and thus ended up quarrelling with each other till daybreak. It was then too late to get back and so they decided to climb onto the huge colorful stalactite pillars. Hence, the name Nine Dragon Cave came into being. As the nine dragons kept quarrelling, people could not get peace, so they scolded them in front of a brook at the foot of the hill. Thus Scolding Dragon Brook got its name.

Nine-Dragon Cave was proved to be 2,258 meters long with a total area of about

70,000 square meters. There are 7 big halls inside the cave. Three big halls have been opened to tourists with 12 scenic spots. The first is a somewhat flat-roofed hall with appealing scenery like a waterfall cave, a dragon with a ball in its mouth, a lion with a tower on its back, a long sword piercing towards the sky and a white elephant. The second is also flat-roofed, with exquisite stone curtain designs. One can also see a dancing fairy, a golden cockerel, jade pillars and silver flowers. The third hall is the real gem of the Nine-Dragon Cave. With a round roof, it can hold about ten thousand people. In the hall stand six huge pillars, each about 30 meters in height. One of them has a height of 39.88 meters with a circumference of 16.4 meters. It is the highest stone post in a cave in China. It is the second highest in the world. A proud peacock, a golden whelk, a roaring lion, a lobster coming out of its hiding and dragons climbing on the pillars are only some of the features you will wonder at. In addition, there is also an underground river in the cave, which is warm in winter and cool in summer. It traverses the bottom of the cave, passes by the cliff in front of the cave and then rushes down as a flying waterfall. Anyway, if you do come to Guizhou, the Nine Dragon Cave is a place you should never miss.

 Words and Expressions to Learn · · · · · · · · · · · · · · · ·

verdant / ˈvɜːdənt / *a.* 青翠的, 郁郁葱葱的
crystal / ˈkrɪstl / *a.* 清澈的, 透明的
celebrated / ˈselɪbreɪtɪd / *a.* 著名的, 驰名的
reluctant / rɪˈlʌktənt / *a.* 不情愿的
occupy / ˈɒkjʊpaɪ / *v.* 占有, 占用
appealing / əˈpiːlɪŋ / *a.* 迷人的, 吸引人的
pierce / pɪəs / *v.* 刺, 戳

exquisite / ˈekskwɪzɪt / *a.* 精美的, 赏心悦目的
cockerel / ˈkɒkərəl / *n.* 小公鸡
circumference / səˈkʌmfərəns / *n.* 周长
whelk / welk / *n.* 峨螺
lobster / ˈlɒbstə / *n.* 龙虾
traverse / ˈtrævəs / *v.* 横贯, 穿过

***   ***   ***   ***   ***   ***

The Nine-Dragon Cave Scenic Spot (贵州) 九
　龙洞景区
Mount Liulong 六龙山
Guanyin Hill 观音山
Lianhua Temple 莲花寺

Jinjiang River Valley 锦江河谷
Malong Creek 骂龙溪
end up 最终, 以……告终
come into being 形成

Part C Exercises

I. *Make up a dialogue between a guide and a tourist about touring Mt. Emei according to the information in following passage.*

Mt. Emei is well-known for its enjoyable natural scenery, extensive Buddhist culture, abundant species and unique landform. Thus it gets such titles as "Kingdom of Plants", "Geological Museum", "Animals' Paradise" and "Buddhist Celestial Mountain".

Going into the mountain, you can see continuous ranges of peaks with tall trees on top of them. Water flows swiftly. Birds are singing and pretty butterflies are dancing. In spring, all the creatures are burgeoning (发芽，迅速生长) and the whole mountain is in a fresh green coat; in summer, beautiful flowers are blooming noisily in competition; in autumn, the entire Mt. Emei is decorated by red leaves; in winter, it is covered with snow like a pure bride in white wedding dress.

Mt. Emei is covered with green vegetation all the year round. Its plentiful rainfall, peculiar landform, varied climate and complicated structures of the soil provide a perfect environment for a great number of species. Here you can admire rare trees, many different flowers and herbs. These plants not only endow the mountain with beauty but also create a natural fairyland for the animals here. Among all the animals there are many rare species.

Golden Summit with its highest peak is 3,099 meters above sea level. The four great spectacles of Golden Summit and also of Mt. Emei are sunrise, sea of clouds, Buddha rays and saint lamps. They are the essence of beauty and mysterious charm of Mt. Emei.

II. *Answer the following questions according to the dialogue and the passages.*

1. How did the Nine-Dragon Cave and Malong Creek get their names?
2. What features of the Nine-Dragon Cave do the figures 2,258, 30-50, 70, 39.88 and 10,000 describe?
3. Which lake is the most beautiful one in Jiuzhaigou Valley? What is it famous for?
4. Is there anything special about the water in the Long Lake of Jiuzhaigou?
5. What is Huanglong Scenic and Historic Interest Area famous for?
6. How did Huanglong Valley get its name?
7. Why do the local people value Feicui Spring so much?

III. Translate the English passage into Chinese and the Chinese one into English.

1. The Huangguoshu waterfall cluster consists of 18 cataracts. The Grand Fall is the largest one in Asia, about 74 meters high and 81 meters wide. Hidden behind the waterfall is a 134-meter long water-curtain cave with fantastic stalactites (钟乳石). The cave consists of five halls, six windows, three springs and six tunnels. In the flood season with plenty of rainfall, the waterfall pours into the Rhinoceros Pool (犀牛潭) with the force of a thousand horses galloping. Seen from the cave, the fall looks like a huge curtain hanging in front of it. Some people say it looks like the Milky Way pouring down from Heaven, making the cliff tremble. Stretching your hand out of the window, you can touch the flying water. While in the dry season, water would separate into several streams falling down from the overhanging cliffs like a fairy maiden's soft hair, charming and graceful. Through the six windows, you can view the falls from different angles. On a sunny day the sight is especially beautiful as a rainbow arches over the falls with misty clouds floating slowly over the valley. On the hill opposite is a pavilion where visitors can enjoy the whole view of the powerful pouring down of the Grand Fall.

2. 在通常情况下, 大熊猫总是很温顺, 就像一位害羞的淑女。当遇到陌生人它常用手掌盖住脸, 或者低下头把脸藏起来。因此, 大熊猫也被叫作 "熊猫小姐"。它很少主动袭击其他动物或者人类。如果它碰巧在野外遇到人, 它总是尽量避免正面接触。然而, 当一头熊猫当上了妈妈, 情况就不一样了。熊猫妈妈很容易被激怒。它会用牙齿和爪子来保护自己的小宝宝。就算是有人为了照料的目的看看它的宝宝, 它也会这样。有时候熊猫喜欢打扮自己, 做出些使自己舒服的动作。比如, 它常常像猫那样先拉伸自己的腹部, 然后再拱起脊背来放松自己。此外, 它睡醒后会舒展前肢打个呵欠。如果熊猫身上被水浸透了, 或者当它淌过(wade across)一条河后, 它会像狗那样把水从身上甩掉。

IV. Topic for discussion

Many famous scenic spots such as Jiuzhaigou are limiting the number of visitors in order to protect them from damage. What do you think of it? Do you have better suggestions to protect the environment in these beautiful but fragile (脆弱) spots?

UNIT 4

Lesson 24
Yunnan and Tibet

Part A *Conversation*

Dialogue   To Zhongdian — Shangri-La

(T: Tourist   G: Guide)

G: Have you ever read a novel *Lost Horizon*?

T: Of course. It is a novel written by James Hilton, a British writer and was published in 1933, if I remember correctly. But why are you asking?

G: Because I'm taking you to the place described in the novel.

T: You mean ... Shangri-La?

G: Yes. Isn't it exciting!

T: But Shangri-La doesn't exist in reality. In the novel, James Hilton said his readers would not find Shangri-La on any map.

G: But he also said Shangri-La was located in a long valley with rounded, sad-looking and snow-capped mountains on either side.

T: Yes, I remember that. He described Shangri-La as a paradise on Earth, with towering snow mountains, torrents of rivers, deep gorges, verdant grasslands, thick forests, and charming lakes and so on.

G: That is exactly you will find in Zhongdian.

T: Zhongdian? I thought you said Shangri-La.

G: Zhongdian is the old name of the place. Since the mid-1990s more and more visitors have come to believe Zhongdian looks exactly like Shangri-La in *Lost Horizon*. In the summer of 2002, Zhongdian requested to change its name to Shangri-La and our government approved.

T: Oh, I see.

G: Shangri-La is actually a word of Tibetan origin, and the word means "a place of beauty and peace".

T: Really? I didn't know that.

G: And what's more, in 1944, an American transport plane did crash in the town of Zhongdian and what the pilot saw convinced him of the existence of Shangri-La.

T: Hmm, that's interesting.

G: Hilton said there were snow mountains in Shangri-La, and we have Meili, Baimang and Haba standing like giants with snowcaps. Meili Snow Mountain is the most famous one. Its highest peak is 6,740 meters above sea level. The mountain is praised as "the most beautiful mountain in the world", which is always veiled in mist like a shy girl.

T: Oh, I'm eager to see this shy girl with my own eyes.

G: Besides, Meili Snow Mountain is also regarded as a holy mountain by the Tibetan Buddhists. To tell you the truth, although many mountaineers have successfully climbed to the top of Qomolangma, the highest peak of Meili Snow Mountain is not yet visited by a human soul.

T: How come?

G: Because the peak is protected by vertical cliffs and the weather there is extremely changeable and dangerous.

T: I see. Besides the snow mountains, what else is there to prove Zhongdian is Shangri-La?

G: The rivers. Zhongdian is cut across by the Jinsha River, the Lancang River and the Nu River.

T: I've heard of them. They are all very large rivers. They all flow through Zhongdian?

G: Yes. And what is unusual is that these three great rivers run side by side for several hundred kilometers but never converge. The shortest distance between the Lancang River and the Jinsha River is only 66 kilometers and less than 19 kilometers between the Lancang River and the Nu River.

T: Amazing!

G: And interestingly, they finally flow into different oceans thousands of kilometers apart.

T: What a miracle!

G: And that is why the area has been listed as the 29th project of the World Cultural and Natural Heritage in China, called Three Parallel Rivers in Yunnan Protected Area.Altogether 16 ethnic groups live in this area and each of them has unique culture, tradition, life style and religion, but they live together peacefully.

T: It seems the trip to Shangri-La will be another highlight of my vacation in China.

G: Definitely. Wait a few more minutes and we will get to this paradise and then you can see with your own eyes.

T: Oh, I can't wait!

 Words and Expressions to Learn ·······················

towering / ˈtaʊərɪŋ / *a.* 高大的,高耸的
torrent / ˈtɒrənt / *n.* 急流

converge / kənˈvɜːdʒ / *v.* 会聚,汇流

***   ***   ***   ***   ***   ***

Zhongdian 中甸
Lost Horizon《消失的地平线》
James Hilton 詹姆斯·希尔顿
a paradise on Earth 人间天堂

Meili, Baimang and Haba 梅里,白芒和哈巴雪山
Three Parallel Rivers in Yunnan Protected Area 云南三江并流保护区

Part **B** Reading ··

 **Tibet Travel Overview**

Tibet, nestling in the Roof of the World, produces a sense of mystery for many in the world. Making a trip to this remote region will help to lift the veil and provide insights into ancient and modern Tibet.

Tibet, located in southwest China, has an area of 1.2 million square kilometers, equal to that of Germany, Spain and France put together. Its 2.32 million people, composed mainly of the Tibetans, live at an average height of over 4,000 meters above sea level. After the North and South Poles, Tibet is often called the "third pole of the

Earth". Unique geography has given birth to unique scenery, while an ancient culture and Buddhism combine to form a unique social system. All these add to the sense of mystery that sets Tibet apart from the rest of the world, creating wonderful conditions for the development of tourism.

The world's highest mountain, Qomolangma seems to reach the sky at 8,848 meters above sea level on the Sino-Nepalese border, and has long been a huge attraction for international mountaineers. But there are numerous peaks each more than 5,000 meters high in the area that remain snowcapped all year round. Famous rivers originate here. There are more than 1,500 lakes in Tibet, all crystal clear. Tibet is also one of the largest forested areas in China with rich wildlife.

Lhasa, the capital of the Tibet Autonomous Region has a history of 1,300 years. Many historical relics representing the cream of the Tibetan culture are well kept. The Potala Palace in Lhasa is the best-preserved palace complex, which is the highest and largest ancient palace in the world. Its many murals, engravings and Buddhist scriptures are held as the symbol of the ancient civilization and culture of the Tibetan people.

The Norbu Lingka is like a green gem by the Lhasa River. It used to be the summer palace for the Dalai Lama of various generations. Built during the period of the 7th Dalai Lama in the mid-18th century, it is an ideal place for worshipping, relaxing and enjoying the best of Tibetan architecture. The famous Barkor Street is lined with small shops offering colorful handicrafts popular with tourists.

Xigaze was an administrative center in the old days. It is also the official home of the Panchen Lama of various generations. Shannan, Zetang and Yarlung, regarded as the birthplace of the Tibetan people, have been made state-level scenic spots. Nyingchi in east Tibet is famous for its natural beauty and natural resources. The northern Tibet grasslands in Ngari possess unique geography and mysterious snow mountains. Ngari is known as the Roof on the Roof of the World, and it is famous for various mountains and lakes considered holy by the Tibetans.

What charms tourists as well is the local customs. The Tibetans are good at singing and dancing. Traditional sports include wrestling, throwing stones, tug-of-war, horse racing and archery. At most times of the year, tourists are highly likely to come across traditional festivals and will be invited to join in. Tourists are free to visit ordinary families, experiencing the lifestyle of the Tibetans.

Tibet used to be the only Chinese region inaccessible by railway. People had to enter Tibet by bus or by air. Now that the Qinghai-Tibet Railway opened to traffic on July 1, 2006, traveling to the roof of the world has become more convenient.

Temperature difference is great in Tibet between day and night. Given long sunshine hour, Tibet is free from freezing cold in winter. Annual temperature averages eight degrees centigrade in southern Tibet and below zero in northern Tibet. Lhasa, located in the central part of Tibet, is not very cold in winter and not very hot in summer. March to October are considered to be the best months for a visit to Tibet.

  Words and Expressions to Learn

nestle / ˈnesl / v. 偎依

veil / veɪl / n. 面纱

originate / əˈrɪdʒɪneɪt / v. 起源于，发端于

engraving / ɪnˈgreɪvɪŋ / n. 版画

gem / dʒem / n. 宝石

administrative / ədˈmɪnɪstrətɪv / a. 行政的，管理的

tug-of-war / ˌtʌgəvˈwɔː / n. 拔河

inaccessible / ˌɪnəkˈsesəbl / a. 难到达的，不可及的

***   ***   ***   ***   ***   ***

set ... apart from 把……与……分开

Qomolangma 珠穆朗玛峰

the Sino-Nepalese border 中尼(泊尔)边境

the Potala Palace 布达拉宫

the Norbu Lingka 罗布林卡，藏语意为 "宝贝公园"，为历代达赖喇嘛的夏宫。

Xigaze 日喀则

the Panchen Lama 班禅喇嘛

Shannan 山南

Zetang 泽当镇

Yarlung 雅龙

Nyingchi 林芝

Ngari 阿里

Passage 2   **Lijiang Ancient Town**

The Ancient Town of Lijiang is 2,400 meters above sea level, and has an area of 3.8 square kilometers. Built in the late Song Dynasty and the early Yuan Dynasty, it has a history of more than 800 years. Since Kublai Khan, the first emperor of the Yuan Dynasty set his reign here, Lijiang began to develop rapidly and became the political, cultural, and educational center in this area. Till now, when walking on the streets of the ancient town, one can still feel the prosperity of it. There are a lot of shops with fancy and excellent collections of handicrafts.

The ancient town is the only ancient city built without a city wall and there is an interesting story telling the reason. Lijiang had been under the reign of the Mu (meaning wood) family for more than 500 years. If the Chinese character "木" (Mu) is put into a frame (representing the city wall), you have the character "困" (Kun) which means siege or difficulty. This would mean that the Mu family and their descendants would always be trapped like a rat in a hole. So, Lijiang Ancient Town was never given a city wall.

The buildings in the town incorporate the best parts of the architectural features of Han, Bai, and Tibet into a special Naxi style. The layout of the town is free-style and flexible, the houses are close to but different from each other, and the lanes are narrow and meandering. Naxi People pay much attention to decoration, and the houses are mostly timber and tile structures with a garden, carvings of people and animals on doors and windows. Living in such a beautiful and comfortable environment is a really pleasant experience.

The ancient Town of Lijiang depends on water for existence and water is just like its blood. Black Dragon Pool (Heilongtan) is the main water source of the town and divides into many streams, which can reach every family and every street in the town. Due to the reticular aqueducts, willow trees grow everywhere and there are about 350 bridges in the little town, some of which were built in Ming and Qing Dynasties. The usage of water here is very scientific. They build three mouths for every well from the upriver to the downriver. The water in the first mouth is for drinking and cooking, the second one is for washing vegetables and fruits, and the last one is used for cleaning and washing. The water not only meets the needs of the people, but also gives the town a sense of gentleness. The town is known as "the Oriental Venice" or "Suzhou in Highland", but it is much more than this. Once you have visited Ancient Town of Lijiang, it will live in your heart for the rest of your life.

The center of the ancient town is the Square Street. Four main streets go from Square Street to the four different directions. Countless lanes leading to all directions form a network and connect every corner of the town. Streets in the ancient town are paved with the local bluestones which are neither muddy in the rainy season nor dusty in the dry season. These stones add a sense of antiquity and mystery to the ancient town. The sluice at the center of the town is opened late in the night and the resulting current of water flushes and washes all the streets to keep the town clean. This practical use of water is unique to the Ancient Town of Lijiang.

 Words and Expressions to Learn ·

siege / siːdʒ / *n.* 围困

antiquity / ænˈtɪkwɪtɪ / *n.* 古老

meandering / mɪˈændərɪŋ / *a.* 迂回曲折的

sluice / sluːs / *n.* 水闸

timber / ˈtɪmbə / *n.* 木材

***   ***   ***   ***   ***   ***

the Ancient Town of Lijiang 丽江古城

reticular aqueduct 网状输水道

the Lijiang Autonomous County of the Naxi Ethnic Minority 丽江纳西族自治州

the Oriental Venice 东方威尼斯

the Square Street 四方街

incorporate ... into 包含,把……合并成

Part C Exercises

I. *Collect information about the Jokhang Temple in Lhasa and make up a dialogue about it.*

II. *Decide whether the following statements are true or false according to the dialogue and the passages.*

1. According to James Hilton, Zhongdian is Shangri-La in his novel *Lost Horizon*.

2. So far nobody has successfully made it to the top of Haba Snow Mountain.

3. Tibet produces a sense of mystery for many people around the world because of its unique geography, unique scenery, and unique culture.

4. Xigaze is the administrative center of Tibet and the official home of Panchen Lamas.

5. The author thinks of the Qinghai-Tibet Railway as the most convenient way to enter Tibet.

6. The Ancient Town of Lijiang used to be a political, cultural and educational center in history.

7. What is unusal about Ancient Town of Lijiang is that there is no city wall surrounding it.

8. Water is the most important thing to Lijiang and the usage of water there is scientific and environment-friendly.

III. *Fill in each of the blanks in the following passage with a suitable preposition.*

Legend 1. _____ this mysterious and beautiful snow mountain — Jade Dragon Snow Mountain goes 2. _____ this: Once upon a time, Jade Dragon and Haba were twins. They lived on panning (淘金) in the Jinsha River until one day an evil spirit usurped (掠夺) the river. The brothers were very brave and had a fierce fight 3. _____ the devil. Haba died in the fight and Jade Dragon drove 4. _____ the devil after wearing out 13 swords. To guard the people and prevent devil 5. _____ returning, Jade Dragon held the 13 swords in hands day and night. As time passed, the brothers had turned 6. _____ the two snow mountains, and the 13 swords had become the 13 peaks. Jade Dragon Snow Mountain is a holy mountain 7. _____ the local Naxi People not only because 8. _____ the legend, but also because long time ago, it was a place for young lovers to sacrifice their young lives 9. _____ honor of true love and to escape 10. _____ arranged marriages (包办婚姻) and feudal ethics (封建道德).

IV. *Fill in the blanks with the proper form of the words given in brackets.*

The Longjiang River is the most beautiful river in the city of Tengchong in Yunnan Province. However, for decades, it had been an obstacle (障碍) to people 1. _____ (travel) to and from Tengchong. Although a concrete bridge 2. _____ (build), it still took 30 minutes 3. _____ (drive) across the river along a mountain road. Now, the situation has completely changed with the completion of the Longjiang Grand Bridge.

After five years of construction, Asia's longest and highest bridge the Longjiang Grand Bridge 4. _____ (finish) closure in advance and passed load test on April 5 of 2016. The 8,100-foot-long suspension bridge over the Longjiang River was open to traffic on May 1, 2016.

The new bridge, 5. _____ (connect) Baoshan and Tengchong, and going straight to Myanmar, 6. _____ (hover) 920 feet above the valley below, reducing the driving time over the canyon to less than one minute. It is the 7. _____ (tall) and longest of its kind built across two mountains in Asia. The 8. _____ (center) span of the bridge measures 3,924 feet (1,096 meters) and is only slightly shorter than that of the famous Golden Gate Bridge in San Francisco.

Not everyone thought that sidewalks on such a highway suspension bridge 9. _____ (be) necessary, but Li Zhengrong insisted on the idea. "We included sidewalks so people can walk along the bridge and fully appreciate the beauty of their hometown as well as share the 10. _____ (convenient) the bridge has brought to their life."

V.   *Complete the following passage by translating the Chinese into English.*

If you have been to Dianchi Lake, 1. _____ (它位于昆明西南部的西山脚下), you'll know what the "Pearl of the Plateau" means. Dianchi Lake, 2. _____ (占地面积为300多平方公里), is the largest lake on the Yunnan-Guizhou Plateau and 3. _____ (中国第六大淡水湖). With its shimmering water, sailboats, and nearby rice fields, 4. _____ (滇池是游客最喜爱的一处景点).

The most beautiful view of Dianchi Lake appears at dawn and sunset, the refraction of the ethereal rays glitter on the water surface 5. _____ (就像成千上万条银鱼在游动、嬉戏). At night, when the breeze is blowing over the water and the world is brimming over with hazy moonlight, 6. _____ (滇池静静地躺着，平静地呼吸着，像睡着了一样).

Western Hill forms a delightful contrast with Dianchi Lake. 7. _____ (沿着湖的西岸伸展开来), the wooded hill looks somewhat like a reclining beauty. People in Kunming call it "Sleeping Beauty Hill." 8. _____ (据传说) in ancient times, there was a young woman whose husband was taken by the local chieftain and sent away as a slave. She thought of her husband day and night and wept so many tears 9. _____ (以至于它们汇成了滇池), while she herself lay down and became Western Hill. 10. _____ (西山是个在迷人的湖畔散步的好地方).

VI.   *Translate the following passage into Chinese.*

When drinking Qingke wine, keep the body straight, hold the cup with both hands, look straight ahead and listen as the host sings a song. After the song, you say a few polite words, hold the cup in the right hand, dip the third finger of the left hand into the wine three times and flip three drops of wine into the air as offerings to Buddha, and then toss off the remainder of the wine. If the host asks you to drink a cup in three gulps, you sip twice, but drain the cup the third time. If you do not want any more, after flipping three drops of wine in the air, just taste your finger and the host will understand. If the guest feels uncomfortable or unable to drink much, he or she should explain it to the host. The lack of oxygen on the high Tibetan Plateau makes it inadvisable to overindulge in alcoholic drinks.

VII. *Topics for discussion.*

1. The Longjiang Grand Bridge was open to traffic on May 1, 2016. Talk about the possible influence, positive and negative, it has on economy, culture, social structure in the area.
2. Mountaineers from all over the world come to conquer Qomolangma, the highest peak in the world and many died or were injured in accidents in the past. Do you think it worthwhile to pursue such a dangerous activity? Why?
3. What do you think of the name change of Zhongdian to Shangri-La? Find some information about the novel *Lost Horizon* and see if you think Zhongdian is the place described in the novel.

UNIT 4 Lesson 25 Hong Kong, Macao and Taiwan

Part A Conversation

Dialogue · A Talk about Hong Kong Movies

(T: Tourist   G: Guide)

T: Hong Kong is pretty much like New York with tall buildings and fancy stores everywhere.

G: Actually, many westerners say they feel at home in Hong Kong. Maybe it has something to do with Hong Kong's special history.

T: I know something about it. It was once a British colony, right?

G: To be exact, before the year of 1997. Then it came back to China.
And, what else did you know about Hong Kong before you came here?

T: Um, let me see. The Victoria Peak, the Disney Park, the Chinese University of Hong Kong, and Hong Kong movies!

G: Hong Kong movies?

T: Yes, Hong Kong movies! I like them very much. To be frank with you, I often watch Hong Kong movies to kill time!

G: Really? For a quarter of the last century, Hong Kong had, after Hollywood and Bollywood, the third largest movie industry in the world. Today Hong Kong still produces hundreds of movies a year.

T: That is a lot!

G: And, a lot of people, especially, young people like them. By the way, can you name some Hong Kong movie stars you like?

T: Many of them! But Andy Lau is my favorite!

G: He is also one of my favorites.

T: I like the heroes he acted in the movies.

G: Me, too. Hong Kong is famous for its gunplay, swordplay and art movies.

T: But sometimes there is too much violence in some of the movies and that is not good for the young people.

G: In fact, Andy Lau is more famous for his art movies than for his swordplay and gunplay ones. Over the years, Lau has his strong position as not only a superstar and Heavenly King, but also as the most hard-working actor in Hong Kong. His hard work has won the respect and admiration of fans and critics alike.

T: Oh, please wait! You said Heavenly King? What's that?

G: That is a Chinese term to honor his great success in the field of entertainment. You know that in little more than twenty years' time, Lau has made over a hundred films! And many of them are still very popular.

T: He is very productive!

G: And he has been a very successful singer, too.

T: Wow! I didn't know that!

G: His tapes and videos are available everywhere in Hong Kong.

T: Then I should buy some tomorrow.

G: I am sure you will leave Hong Kong with a huge bag!

T: Like Santa Claus, ha-ha!

 Words and Expressions to Learn ·

colony / ˈkɒlənɪ / *n.* 殖民地
gunplay / ˈɡʌnpleɪ / *n.* 枪战 (片)
swordplay / ˈsɔːdpleɪ / *n.* 武打 (片)
Hollywood / ˈhɒlɪwʊd / *n.* 好莱坞 (美国闻名

于世的电影工业基地)
violence / ˈvaɪələns / 暴力
critic / ˈcrɪtɪk / *n.* 评论家
productive / prəˈdʌktɪv / *a.* 多产的

***　　***　　***　　***　　***　　***

feel at home 感到自在
have something to do with 与……有关
Victoria Peak 太平山顶
to be frank 坦率地说
kill time 消磨时光

Bollywood / ˈbɒlɪwʊd / *n.* 宝莱坞 (印度孟买
广受欢迎的电影工业基地的别名)
Andy Lau 刘德华, 香港知名艺人
Heavenly King 天王
Santa Claus 圣诞老人

Part B Reading

Passage 1   A-Ma Temple in Macao

The A-Ma Temple is the oldest temple in Macao, which has a history of over 500 years.

As legend has it, A-Ma was a lady from Putian, Fujian Province. On the ninth day of the ninth lunar month of the year 987, when she reached the age of 27, she said to her family, "I feel very peaceful and quiet in my mind, but I don't want to live in the human world any more. I would like to climb the mountain to realize my wish …" Her family thought that she simply wanted to climb the mountain and enjoy the scenery — but they didn't know that she would never return to them. So she climbed Mount Meifeng, and when she reached the top, beautiful clouds appeared in the sky and strange music was heard. She jumped onto the clouds and went away with the wind. It was said that later people often saw her appear in the sky over the sea. Wearing red clothes, she would fly here and there, appearing wherever there was danger to protect boats and people. In recognition of her super powers and great religious attainment, local people started to call her "Mazu".

The worship of Mazu as a goddess spread very quickly in the coastal areas as well as to some inland provinces, and many temples were built to honor her. She was called the protector of the common people, who continued to simply call her Mazu. Later, with the development of sea transportation, Mazu worship was brought overseas by sailors. Especially during Ming and Qing Dynasties, the worship of Mazu spread to wherever Chinese went. Now, Mazu temples are found where Chinese people live all over the world.

The whole A-Ma Temple in Macao is a typical Chinese folk architecture, with the temple eaves pointing to the sky. The temple includes four buildings: the main hall, the stone hall, the great mercy hall and the hall of the Goddess of Mercy. At the gate, there are stone lions guarding the temple.

The A-Ma Temple was built on a mountainside. There are paths winding upwards the hill. Along the mountainside, there are many poems on the stones in all forms.

Inside the courtyard, there is a relief stone sculpture of a Chinese sailing-ship. Here goes another legend that A-Ma sailed out to sea from her native land by this ship. After dealing with strong wind and waves, she reached Macao safely. It is said that she could tell things in the future and after her death, she appeared on the sea and helped businessmen and fishermen to deal with difficulties and turn danger into safety. People built the temple here in memory of her. On March 23 on lunar calendar every year, the birthday of A-Ma, and during the Spring Festival, the temple is crowded with worshippers, praying for good luck.

 Words and Expressions to Learn ·

Portuguese / ˌpɔːtʃəˈgiːz / *n. & a.* 葡萄牙人
(的), 葡萄牙语(的)
origin / ˈɒrɪdʒɪn / *n.* 来源
attainment / əˈteɪnmənt / *n.* 造诣

Mazu / ˈmɑːzuː / *n.* 妈祖
worship / ˈwɜːʃɪp / *n.* 崇拜
coastal / ˈkəʊstəl / *a.* 沿海的
mercy / ˈmɜːsɪ / *n.* 仁慈

***   ***   ***   ***   ***   ***

A-Ma Temple 阿妈庙 (又称妈阁庙)
in recognition of 为表彰, 承认……

relief stone sculpture 浮雕石刻

Passage 2 The Sun Moon Lake

The Sun Moon Lake lies to the north of Yu Mountain and to the south of Nenggao Mountain, Nantou County in Taiwan Province. It is the biggest natural lake in Taiwan and is formed by the stream water in the basin between Yu Mountain and Ali Mountain. The local people used to call the lake Dragon Lake, Pearl Pool and Shuishe Great Lake. The surface of the lake is 760 meters above sea level, and the average depth of the water is 30 meters. Inside the lake there is a small island which looks like a pearl on the surface of the water, hence the name "Pearl Islet". After the Anti-Japanese war, it was renamed "Guanghua Islet" in celebration of recovering Taiwan. To the northeast of the islet, the lake is in a shape as round as the sun, so it is called the Sun Lake while the lake in the south-west looks like the crescent moon, so it is called the Moon Lake. So the whole lake came to be named as the Sun Moon Lake.

Actually, the mountains around are a most important part of the beauty of the Sun Moon Lake. Range upon range of hills are green and full of life. On the mountain alongside the Sun Moon Lake, many places of interest were built. There are Wenwu Temple, Peacock Garden, Temple of Butterfly, Xuanguang Temple, Xuanzang Temple and Hanbi Tower, etc. Pavilions, terraces and towers are wonderful spots to enjoy the sights. Among the natural scenery all around, temples and ancient pagodas are here and there, which adds more air of great quietness and calmness to the beauty of the lake. The most attractive spots are Xuanzang Temple and Wenwu Temple. Xuanzang Temple is at the foot of Blue Dragon Mountain. Inside the Xuanzang Temple, statue of the great monk Xuanzang of Tang Dynasty is enshrined. The board which reads "National Master of Law," is hung inside the temple. At the back of the temple, there is a staircase of about 1,300 stone steps, leading upwards to the Xuanzang Hall. The Temple, standing tall, brilliant and grand, is full of national characteristics. Wenwu Temple is built alongside the mountain, full of power and grandeur. The building has red eaves gutter and green tiles, high towers and superb pavilions. The statue of Confucius is enshrined in Wen Temple while in Wu Temple, the statue of Guan Yu, a famous General in Han Dynasty, is enshrined. Besides, the statues of Holy Farmer King, Wenchang King and Jade Emperor are worshipped here too.

Early in the morning, the whole lake is bathed in a thin mist. Mountain peaks, temple roofs and singing birds are secretly hidden around. When evening comes, the lake is like a blue pearl lying quietly and beautifully among the mountain ranges, which has helped songwriters and poets produce their most successful works. In a word, all year round, the Sun Moon Lake is always a scenic spot attracting travelers at home and abroad.

 Words and Expressions to Learn ·

crescent / ˈkresənt / n. 新月   staircase / ˈsteəkeɪs / n. 楼梯
terrace / ˈterəs / n. 台地，梯田   grandeur / ˈɡrændʒə / n. 伟大，壮观
enshrine / ɪnˈʃraɪn / v. 作为神龛保存   mist / mɪst / n. 薄雾

＊＊＊   ＊＊＊   ＊＊＊   ＊＊＊   ＊＊＊   ＊＊＊

Yu Mountain 玉山   Nenggao Mountain 能高山

Shuishe Great Lake 水社大湖	Xuanzang Temple 玄奘庙
Guanghua Islet 光华岛	Hanbi Tower 涵碧楼
in celebration of 庆祝	Blue Dragon Mountain 青龙山
Wenwu Temple 文武庙	eaves gutter 檐槽
Peacock Garden 孔雀园	Holy Farmer King 神农氏
Temple of Butterfly 蝴蝶庙	Wenchang King 文昌帝
Xuanguang Temple 玄光寺	Jade Emperor 玉皇大帝

Part  Exercises

I. *Make up a dialogue between a tourist and a guide about a tour of the Sun Moon Lake according to Reading Passage 2.*

II. *Decide whether the following statements are true or false according to the passages.*

1. A-Ma Temple is found all over the world where Chinese people live.
2. Mazu is a goddess who is said to protect people on the sea.
3. The A-Ma Temple was built before the arrival of the Portuguese settlers.
4. The Sun Moon Lake is still called Dragon Lake by the local people.
5. The Sun Moon Lake has got its present name from the islet in it.
6. The mountains and scenic spots around the Sun Moon Lake contribute greatly to its beauty.
7. The Sun Moon Lake was dug to hold the stream water from Yu Mountain and Ali Mountain.
8. The statues of Confucius and Xuanzang were enshrined in Wenwu Temple.

III. *Translate the following sentences into English.*

1. 刘德华是香港著名的电影明星。
2. 坦率地说,我并不喜欢在假期里外出旅游。
3. 近几年沿海地区的发展令人兴奋。
4. 你周末通常怎么打发时间?
5. 为了庆祝球队的胜利,他们开始大声歌唱。

IV. *Translate the following passage into Chinese.*

Taiwan Island is rich in more than 110 kinds of minerals (矿物) with coal, oil, natural gas, gold, silver, copper (铜) and sulphur (硫) as its main resources. It is also extremely rich in terrestrial heat (地热), a great variety of plants and forest occupies 52% of the land area of the whole island, holding the first place in all China. It is rich in water resources too and the output of Taiwan's coral (珊瑚) occupies about 80% of the world total production, winning the fame of "The Kingdom of Coral". Taiwan is also one of the main regions which export butterflies in the world.

V. *Topics for discussion.*

1. What do you know about the history of Hong Kong and Macau?
2. Talk with your classmates about some other scenic spots in Taiwan Province.

UNIT 4

Lesson 26
Great Rivers and the Silk Road

Part **A** *Conversation*

Dialogue | **Visiting the Three Gorges Dam Project**

(G: Guide   T: Tourist)

G: OK, here we are, the Yangtze Three Gorges Dam, the largest hydroelectric power plant in the world, the largest construction project ever organized in the world.

T: Ah! It is really a grand project! Is it true that it has taken 17 years to complete?

G: Yes. When completed in the year 2009, the water level behind the dam reached 175 meters.

T: Why did China build such a huge dam? Environmentalists argue damming can damage the balance of nature in the area.

G: The decision is not an easy one for our government. It was based on long and prudent feasibility studies. Every coin has two sides, you know. In the case of the dam, it can bring far more benefits than damage.

T: What benefits will it bring, then?

G: The first and the most important one is flood control. Our country has suffered great losses in both life and property caused by floods. The wet season begins in April in South China, which brings heavy rain to the middle and lower reaches of the Yangtze. By July, the wet weather reaches the Sichuan Basin and the mountainous terrain causes widespread rainfall to the upper reaches of the river. Therefore, as the water level caused by the earlier wet season starts to subside, the "Sichuan waters" begin to threaten again.

T: In this case the dam definitely relieves the people of the sorrow caused by floods.

G: Yes. The pool behind the dam has a flood control capacity of 22.15 billion cubic meters.

This is enough to control the greatest floods experienced in the past 100 years.

T: That would be a great achievement.

G: And with the help of the flood diversion structure, the Three Gorges Dam Project protects both banks of the Yangtze River from the kind of destruction that has occurred over the past 1,000 years.

T: Wow! Then the dam is a guardian angel to the Yangtze River.

G: The angel also protects more than 1.6 billion hectares farmland and 15 million people's lives and property in the down river area.

T: What other benefits has the dam brought along?

G: Hydroelectricity, of course.

T: Oh, I forgot that.

G: The project is the world's biggest hydropower plant. It is expected to generate about 84.7 billion kilowatt hours every year.

T: That's a lot.

G: Yes. And as we all know, hydropower plants are much cleaner than coal-burning power plants, and so the dam project, in a sense, helps reduce environmental pollution.

T: Hmm, sounds reasonable. Then has the dam affected navigation?

G: Sure. But for better, not worse. The 600-kilometer long waterway in the upper reaches of the river is greatly improved and it is possible for 10,000-ton ships to sail directly upstream to Chongqing.

T: Really? Does it cost more for using the dam?

G: Actually no. The cost is cut by 35%–37% instead. The reservoir helps greatly improve navigation conditions both upstream and downstream in dry seasons.

T: Amazing! But the dam has definitely affected tourism, hasn't it?

G: Yes. Our government has taken measures to preserve and move the historical and cultural relics found along the banks of the river. But many scenic spots have been adversely affected. The most dramatic section of the river including the Three Gorges has eventually been drowned by the completion of the dam.

T: What a pity! If the Three Gorges were gone, what is there left to see?

G: Hey, don't be so pessimistic! The heart should be inside the body and I think this might be a better way to preserve the Gorges and their relics. Who knows, maybe one day, people will be organized to dive into the river to visit these wonders again!

T: You are very creative! And I like your idea.

G: Besides, the Gorges has not disappeared. They simply have a new look, just like you change your hairstyle once in a while. The new Three Gorges plus the world's largest Dam Project will attract as many, if not more people to the Yangtze.

T: I believe so. And I will be one of them to come again.

G: You are always welcome.

 ## Words and Expressions to Learn

prudent / ˈpruːdənt / *a.* 谨慎的，慎重的
terrain / təˈreɪn / *n.* 地形
subside / səbˈsaɪd / *v.* 减弱，平息
accurate / ˈækjʊrət / *a.* 准确的
relieve / rɪˈliːv / *v.* 减轻，缓解
capacity / kəˈpæsɪtɪ / *n.* 能力，容量

diversion / daɪˈvɜːʃən / *n.* 改道
generate / ˈdʒenəreɪt / *v.* 产生，发（电）
navigation / nævɪˈɡeɪʃən / *n.* 航运
reservoir / ˈrezəvwɑː / *n.* 水库，蓄水池
adversely / ˈædvɜːslɪ / *ad.* 不利地，负面地
pessimistic / pesɪˈmɪstɪk / *a.* 悲观的

***　　***　　***　　***　　***　　***

hydroelectric power plant 水电站
feasibility studies 可行性研究
in the case of 就……而言
cubic meters 立方米

a guardian angel 守护天使
kilowatt hour（电力计量单位）度，千瓦时
take measures 采取措施

Part **B** Reading

 ## Passage 1　Hukou Waterfall

The Yellow River is the mother river of the Chinese nation. In its basin, there is a tourist attraction that visitors should not miss — Hukou Waterfall, a glistening pearl in the middle reaches of the Yellow River. It is located in Yichuan County in Shaanxi Province. It is the only magnificent yellow waterfall in the world and the second biggest waterfall in China after the Huangguoshu Waterfalls.

When the mighty Yellow River flows through mountains to Hukou, the billowy stream narrows suddenly, the gentle water gains speed as if rushed forward till it finally cascades over the waterfall, falling 30 meters into a deep riverbed like a herd of galloping horses, as if water being poured from a kettle, hence its name "Hukou" or "Kettle Spout". The thundering sound can be heard from quite a distance. The tremendous mass of water strikes the rocks, creating piles of foam and huge water poles. It is an amazing view with mist all around. Its rumbling sound, its grand vigor can make you exclaim that Mother Nature is really incredible.

The power of the yellow water of Hukou Waterfall is tremendous when falling down to the pond, so it is hard for you to get close to the main waterfall. Looking from a distance, you can still enjoy the vast and gorgeous yellow ocean of mist-covered water. The big waves and foam, like angry beasts, are running and roaring. The beauty and vigor of the waterfall are indeed beyond words.

There are many wonders at Hukou Waterfall, such as smoke from the river, boats on land, rainbows in the sunshine, and so on. At Hukou the water falls to the deep pond from a high place, stirring the mist which rises high into the air like surging heavy smoke coming out of the river. You can see various shapes of rainbows formed by the rising mist and refracted sunshine from different angles. Sometimes rainbows are arched, cutting into the river from the sky like a dragon playing with the water; sometimes they are colored ribbons lying across the river; sometimes they become colorful masses which change second by second. Because of the torrential water in Hukou, all the boats from the upper reaches must be pulled out of the river onto the bank when they arrive. These boats will have to detour around this section, carried by a group of boatmen or shipped by truck before they can be put in the river again.

The view of Hukou Waterfall changes with the seasons. In spring the frozen ground thaws and the stalactites of snow fall into the pond like mountains falling down and cracking up the earth. In summer and autumn there is much rainfall. With the rains, the river rushes and the yellow waves seem to reach the sky. In winter Hukou Waterfall gives the visitors another new look. On the surface of the silvery ice waterfall, water flows down. Little silver icicles hang on the cliffs around the waterfall. It presents you a distinctive natural landscape of the northern region of China.

Hukou Waterfall has for years attracted visitors from all over the world. You can have a better understanding of natural wonder if you come here in person. Hukou Waterfall will give you a warm welcome with its thrilling sound, rolling golden waves, changing scenery and majestic vigor.

 Words and Expressions to Learn ·

glistening / ˈglɪsənɪŋ / *a.* 闪耀的，闪闪发
光的
billowy / ˈbɪləʊɪ / *a.* 波涛翻滚的
rumbling / ˈrʌmblɪŋ / *a.* 轰隆隆的
vigor / ˈvɪgə / *n.* 活力，精神
surging / ˈsɜːdʒɪŋ / *a.* 汹涌澎湃的

refract / rɪˈfrækt / *v.* 使折射
torrential / təˈrenʃəl / *a.* 奔流的，急流的
detour / ˈdiːtʊə / *v.* 迂回，绕行
thaw / θɔː / *v.* 融化，解冻
icicle / ˈaɪsɪkl / *n.* 冰柱，垂冰

Passage 2　The Silk Road

The Silk Road was an ancient network of trade routes including both the land and the sea routes connecting Asia and Europe, with the land route generally considered the ancestor to the Silk Road.

"Silk Road" is in fact a relatively recent term. For a long time in the history, these ancient roads had no particular name until the mid-nineteenth century, when the German geologist *Baron Ferdinand von Richthofen* named the trade and communication network *Die Seidenstrasse* (the Silk Road). The Silk Road got its name because of the lucrative trade of silk carried out along its length, beginning during Han Dynasty (206 BC– 220 AD). Han Dynasty expanded Central Asian sections of the trade routes largely through missions and explorations of the imperial envoy, Zhang Qian, who is regarded as the pioneer of the Silk Road.

Trade on the Silk Road played a significant role in the development of the civilizations of China, ancient Korea, Japan, the Indian subcontinent, Persia, Europe, the Horn of Africa and Arabia. It opened up political and economic relations among these civilizations. Though silk was certainly the major trade item exported from China, many other goods like seashells and Hetian jade, knowledge about science, arts and literature, as well as crafts and technologies were also shared across the Silk Road. Most famous technical advances spread worldwide through the Silk Road included paper making and printing technologies. Similarly, irrigation systems across Central Asia share features due to the communication and interactions between travelers from different cultures and societies.

Maritime trade was an extremely important branch of this global trade network. Most famously used for the transportation of spices, the maritime trade routes have also been known as the Spice Routes, supplying markets across the world with cinnamon, pepper, ginger, cloves and nutmeg as well as a wide range of other goods. Textiles, woodwork, precious stones, metalwork, incense, timber, and saffron were all traded by the merchants travelling these routes, which stretched over 15,000 kilometers, from the west coast of Japan, to the Mediterranean.

Perhaps the most lasting legacy of the Silk Road lies in bringing cultures and peoples in contact with each other. The constant movement and mixing of populations also brought about the transmission of knowledge, ideas, cultures and beliefs, which had a profound impact on the history and civilizations of the Eurasian peoples.

Today, many historic buildings and monuments still stand along the Silk Road. The legacy of this remarkable network is still reflected in the many distinct but interconnected cultures, languages, customs and religions that have developed over millennia. From their early, exploratory origins, the Silk Road has developed into a driving force in the formation of diverse societies across Eurasia and far beyond. In June 2014, UNESCO designated the Chang'an–Tianshan corridor of the Silk Road as a World Heritage Site.

In 2013, the Chinese government proposed a "One Belt One Road" Initiative. Based on the ancient Silk Road, the world's longest and most promising economic development zone is emerging. The new Silk Road is sure to display its vigor and dynamism to advance economic cooperation and cultural communication among Eurasian countries.

Words and Expressions to Learn

geologist / dʒɪˈɒlədʒɪst / *n.* 地质学家

lucrative / ˈluːkrətɪv / *a.* 赚钱的

mission / ˈmɪʃən / *n.* 使命，任务

interaction / ˌɪntərˈækʃən / *n.* 相互影响

maritime / ˈmærɪtaɪm / *a.* 海上的，海运的

cinnamon / ˈsɪnəmən / *n.* 肉桂，桂皮

clove / kləʊv / *n.* 丁香

nutmeg / ˈnʌtmeg / *n.* 肉豆蔻

saffron / ˈsæfrən / *n.* 藏红花

transmission / trænzˈmɪʃən / *n.* 传播

diverse / daɪˈvɜːs / *a.* 多样性的

designate / ˈdezɪɡneɪt / *v.* 指定，标示

dynamism / ˈdaɪnəmɪzəm / *n.* 动力

***   ***   ***   ***   ***   ***

Baron Ferdinand von Richthofen 德国著名
地理学家和地质学家斐迪南·冯.李希霍
芬男爵

the Indian Subcontinent 印度次大陆

the Mediterreanean 地中海

"One Belt One Road" Initiative "一带一路"
倡议

Part C Exercises

I. *Prepare a dialogue between a guide and a tourist about the Silk Road according to Read Passage 2.*

II. *Answer the following questions according to the dialogue and the passages.*

1. When was the Three Gorges Dam Project completed?

2. What is the biggest benefit the Dam has brought to China?

3. How can the Dam Project help environmental protection?

4. How does the Dam help better navigation conditions along the Yangtze River?

5. What world records does the project hold?

6. What feature is unique to Hukou Waterfall?

7. How did the waterfall get the name of Hukou or Kettle Spout?

8. Why was the Silk Road named so?

9. What were the most important technical advances spread worldwide through the Silk Road?

10. Why was the maritime branch of the Silk Road also called the Spice Routes?

III. *Read the passage about the Grand Canal and decide whether the statements are true or false.*

The Grand Canal, about 1,200 miles (1,764 kilometers) long, is the longest and greatest man-made waterway in ancient China, much longer than the Suez and Panama Canals. With 27 sections and 58 historical sites, it was placed on the UNESCO's World Heritage List in 2014. Running from Hangzhou, Zhejiang Province in the south to Beijing in the north and connecting different river systems, it has contributed greatly to the Chinese economy from ancient times till present day. Now more than 2,000 years old, some parts of the canal are still in use, mainly functioning as a water-diversion conduit.

The canal we see today was built section by section in different areas and dynasties before it was linked together in Sui Dynasty. In 604 AD, Emperor Yangdi of Sui Dynasty toured Luoyang. The following year, he moved the capital to Luoyang and ordered a large-scale expansion of the canal. Due to the primitive building techniques, it took over six years to complete the project. About half the peasant builders (about 3,000,000) died of hard labor and hunger. This project was thought to have been a waste of manpower and money, which resulted in the downfall of the Sui Dynasty.

As a major transportation hub, the Grand Canal connected five large river systems of the Yangtze, the Yellow, the Huaihe, the Haihe, and the Qiantang Rivers and flowed through Beijing, Tianjin, Hebei, Shandong, Jiangsu and Zhejiang. As a result, it provided a good way to transport foods and goods from the south to the north. Just as importantly, it greatly improved the administration and defense of China and strengthened economic and cultural connections between the north and the south.

Boating on the old Canal is one of the best ways to get a panoramic view of the landscape of typical river towns in southern China, which include ancient buildings, stone bridges of traditional designs and historical relics. Besides the ever changing scenery along the banks of the canal, travelers will surely get much fun and delight from the colorful local cultures and various food and snacks along the way.

Like the Great Wall, the Grand Canal is noted as one of the most magnificent and wondrous constructions in ancient China, which can offer people a profound look into China's fascinating historical past.

1. The Grand Canal is 1,764 miles long, much longer than the Suez and Panama Canals.

2. The Grand Canal is the longest and greatest waterway in China.

3. Though more than 2,000 years old, the Grand Canal is still functioning well as it used to.

4. The Grand Canal was built during the Yangdi period in Sui Dynasty.

5. The Grand Canal is completely a waste of manpower and money and led to the downfall of Sui Dynasty.

6. The Grand Canal connected five river systems and flowed through six cities and provinces.

7. Boating on the Canal is a good way to enjoy the ever changing landscape and colorful local cultures.

8. The Grand Canal is the most magnificent and wondrous construction in ancient China.

IV. *Fill in each of the blanks with the proper form of the word given in brackets or a suitable preposition.*

1. _____ (general) speaking, the Yellow River is divided into three sections. 2. _____ (run) 3,472 kilometers 3. _____ mountains and arid regions, swamps and grasslands, the vigorous upper reaches of the Yellow River starts in Qinghai Province to Hekouzhen in Inner Mongolia. This magnificent river flows quietly, like a shy girl in this section, irrigating the farmlands and 4. _____ (nurture) the people. In the middle reaches, it flows 1,206 kilometers to Taohuayu in Zhengzhou, Henan Province. This part of the 5. _____ (might) Yellow River runs through the vast region of Loess Plateau, cutting the plateau into two parts 6. _____ a sharp sword: the left side of the river is Shanxi Province and the right side is Shaanxi Province. The Yellow River has become the natural geographical demarcation of the two provinces. And at the same time, many branches take a great amount of mud and sand 7. _____ it, so this area is the main silt source of the Yellow River. A famous 8. _____ (engineer) project is located in this section: the Xiaolangdi Multipurpose Dam, which is used 9. _____ flood control, ice jam control, siltation control, 10. _____ (irrigate), and water supply, as well as 11. _____ (generate) hydroelectric power. In the lower reaches, it flows 786 kilometers through the North China Plain, 12. _____ (end) at the delta of Bohai Sea. In this section, 13. _____ (excess) sediment deposits of the river have raised the riverbed several meters 14. _____ the 15. _____ (surround) grounds. Thus, the world famous "River above Ground" emerges.

V. *Complete the following passage by translating the Chinese into English.*

Wu Gorge is 45 kilometers long from west to east, flanked by high peaks 1. _____ (常被云雾笼罩). Wushan, a town that is well known for its extraordinarily beautiful setting, looks both down the Wu Gorge and up the Daning River into the Three Little Gorges. The Three Little Gorges 2. _____ (连绵不断的奇峰夹岸，许多山峰高耸入云).

Looking down the Yangtze River, visitors can see 12 high peaks, which are described by legend as being 12 fairy spirits. The best known is Shennufeng (Goddess) Peak, which is topped by a large rock 3. _____ (好像一座窈窕淑女的雕像

217

俯瞰着河里的船只). The rock is 4. _____ (高约十米,周长六米), and stands atop the 1,020-meter high peak on the north side of the Yangtze River. It is said that this beautiful maiden is actually the embodiment of Yaoji, the youngest daughter of the Heavenly Mother. Yaoji became a protector of the people, 5. _____ (引导航行的船只穿过峡谷,平息长江可怕的洪水).

Later, Wushan became Yaoji's favorite place. She built a small palace there, which she shared with her 11 fairy handmaidens. Eventually, these 12 maidens became the 12 peaks of the Wu Gorge. 6. _____ (黎明和黄昏时分,神女峰笼罩在霞光中), giving it a heavenly appearance.

VI.   Topics for discussion.

1. The Yellow River has become a river above ground in the lower reaches threatening to cause destruction. Do you have any suggestions as to the solution to the problem?
2. There has been a heated discussion about the advantages and disadvantages of the Three Gorges Dam Project. What is your opinion about it? State your reasons.
3. Comment on the "One Belt One Road" Initiative of our government.

UNIT 5
Shopping

UNIT 5 Lesson 27
Pottery and Porcelain

Part A *Conversation*

Dialogue   In a Cloisonné Store

(W: Woman   M: Man   S: Shop Assistant)

S: Welcome to our store. Is there anything I can do for you?

W: You've got a lot of cloisonné vases here, haven't you? We saw many big beautiful ones in the shop window.

S: Yes, we're the largest cloisonné dealer in the city. What kind of cloisonné vases do you like?

W: Well, I'd like to see a medium-sized one, preferably something with a light blue background.

S: How do you like this one? The background is light blue with a traditional Chinese pattern of birds and flowers.

W: Oh, it looks great! How do you like it, dear?

M: Well, I think I like the one with an ancient figure on it. It's very Chinese.

S: The lady on this vase is Xishi, one of the four beauties of ancient China.

W: I like her dress. Look at the lines of the ribbons! So vivid!

M: The colors are bright, too. Do you think the color will fade and the metal wires rust?

S: Please rest assured. They are enameled, and the colors will never fade. The metal wires are made from brass. So the more you brush them, the brighter they will shine.

W: I like it. How much is it?

S: 300 *yuan*, not including the box. The box costs 50 *yuan*. If you buy two vases of this kind we can give you a 15% discount.

W: Really? That's great. I'll take two. This one and the one with birds and flowers.

S: Two vases plus two boxes. That's 610 *yuan* in total.

M: Here is the money. Please pack them well. We might have to mail them back home.

S: No problem.

W: By the way, could you please tell me something about how cloisonné vases are made?

S: I'm no expert at all. But I do know the major processes include making the copper roughcast, forming various patterns on the roughcast with thin copper strips, filling the patterns with enamel of different colors, firing and polishing ...

M: Wow, that's a lot of work.

S: You said it. The actual production is more painstaking and complicated.

W: I can imagine that. Do you only make cloisonné vases?

S: No. Cloisonné articles can be as big as tables and chairs and as small as chopsticks and earrings.

W: Earrings? Could you please show me a pair? I think it would be cool to wear cloisonné earrings.

M: I agree. How about I get a pair for your coming birthday?

W: Oh. Thank you so much, dear!

 Words and Expressions to Learn

cloisonné / klɔɪzə'neɪ / *n.* 景泰蓝
preferably / 'prefərəblɪ / *ad.* 更可取地，更称
   心地
rust / rʌst / *v.* 生绣
enamel / ɪ'næməl / *v.* 给……上釉

brass / brɑːs / *n.* 黄铜
discount / 'dɪskaunt / *n.* 折扣
painstaking / 'peɪnz.teɪkɪŋ / *a.* 精心的，辛
   苦的

*** *** *** *** *** *** *** ***

It's very Chinese. 它很有中国特色。
rest assured 放心

copper roughcast 铜胎

Passage 1   Chinese Porcelain

Porcelain is often called china, or chinaware, because it was first made in China. Porcelain is characterized by whiteness, a delicate appearance, and translucence. It is the hardest ceramic product and can be used for electrical insulators and laboratory equipment. However, porcelain is known primarily as a material for high-quality vases, tableware and other decorative objects.

Porcelain differs from other types of ceramics in its ingredients and in the process by which it is produced. Two common types of ceramics — earthenware and stoneware — are made from a single natural clay, which is then fired. In many cases, the object is coated with a glassy substance called glaze. Firing at a low temperature produces earthenware, a porous material. Earthenware can be made waterproof by glazing. Firing at a high temperature produces stoneware, a hard, heavy material. Stoneware is nonporous without glazing. Porcelain is basically made from a mixture of two ingredients — kaolin and petuntse. Kaolin is pure white clay that forms when the mineral feldspar breaks down. Petuntse is a type of feldspar found only in China. It is ground to fine powder and mixed with kaolin. This mixture is fired at high temperatures and the petuntse melts together and forms a nonporous, natural glass. The kaolin, which is highly resistant to heat, does not melt and therefore allows the item to hold its shape.

A piece of porcelain is shaped on a potter's wheel or in a mold. After this stage, the porcelain worker may decorate it. Painting the porcelain surface may be done in several ways. A deep blue made from the metal cobalt is the most dependable color used for under-glazing. Paints that are applied over the glaze are commonly called enamels. Enamel colors require a second firing to stay permanent. Chinese decorators separate each color with a dark outline, but European artists blend colors together with no separating line. In addition, Europeans use decorations purely for their artistic value, but Chinese decorations are symbolic. For example, a pomegranate design symbolizes a wish for many offspring because a pomegranate has many seeds.

For centuries, the Chinese have made the world's finest porcelain. Collectors regard many porcelain bowls and vases produced during Ming Dynasty and Qing Dynasty as artistic treasures. Painting over the glaze with enamel colors also became a common decorating technique at that time. During Qing Dynasty, the Chinese developed a great variety of patterns and colors and exported porcelain objects to Europe in increasing numbers. In 1500s, the secret of making porcelain spread to Korea and to Japan. Workers in these countries also created beautiful porcelain objects.

 Words and Expressions to Learn

characterize / ˈkærɪktəraɪz / v. 特点是……
translucence / trænzˈluːsəns / n. 半透明度
ceramic / sɪˈræmɪk / a. 陶瓷的 (ceramics n. 陶瓷)
insulator / ˈɪnsjʊleɪtə / n. 绝缘材料
earthenware / ˈɜːθənweə / n. 土陶
stoneware / ˈstəʊnweə / n. 粗陶
glaze / ɡleɪz / n. 釉
porous / ˈpɔːrəs / a. 多孔的
waterproof / ˈwɔːtəpruːf / a. 防水的

kaolin / ˈkeɪəlɪn / n. 高岭土，瓷土
petuntse / pɪˈtʌntsɪ / n. (烧制瓷器用的) 瓷土
feldspar / ˈfeldspɑː / n. 长石
mold / məʊld / n. 模具
cobalt / ˈkəʊbɒlt / n. (金属) 钴
permanent / ˈpɜːmənənt / a. 永久性的
symbolic / sɪmˈbɒlɪk / a. 象征的
pomegranate / ˈpɒmɪɡrænɪt / n. 石榴

***   ***   ***   ***   ***   ***

be ground to fine powder 被磨成很细的粉末

Passage 2   Snuff Bottles

Snuff bottles are not native to China but were reportedly introduced from the West by Matteo Ricci, an Italian priest who worked in Beijing in the early 17th century. Yet the art of interior painting in snuff bottles was born and developed in China and unique to the country, which involves skills such as painting, calligraphy, carving, handicrafts, ceramics, glassware, enamel, etc. This is why the Chinese snuff bottle has been well-known all over the world for years.

A popular story tells how the art originated. In Qing Dynasty, an official who was addicted to snuff stopped on his way at a small temple for a rest. When he took out his crystal snuff bottle to take a sniff, he found it was already empty. He then scraped off the little powder that had stuck on the interior wall of the bottle by means of a slender bamboo stick, thus leaving lines on the inside, visible through the transparent crystal. A young monk saw him at this and got the idea of making pictures inside the bottle. Thus a new art was born.

The "painting brush" of the snuff bottle artist today is not very different from what the official in the story used at the beginning. It is a slender bamboo stick, not much thicker but much longer than a match, with the tip shaped like a hook. Dipped in colored ink and thrust inside the bottle, the hooked tip is employed to paint on the interior, following the will of the painter. The art became perfected and flourished towards the end of Qing Dynasty at the turn of the century. Curio dealers began to offer good prices to collect them for a profit.

Snuff bottles are small in size, no more than 6 to 7 centimeters high and 4 to 5 centimeters wide, yet the accomplished artist can produce, on the limited space of the internal surfaces, any subject on the whole gamut of traditional Chinese painting — human portraits, landscapes, flowers and birds and calligraphy. Liu Shouben, a famous master in this field, succeeded in painting all the 108 heroes and heroines of the classical novel *Water Margin*, each with his or her characteristic expression, all inside one single bottle!

In the beginning because of the smooth surface of glass, craftsmen could only paint simple pictures like grasshoppers, Chinese cabbages, simple landscapes with a few touches, and simple figures, etc. Later, craftsmen learned to fill the bottle with iron sand and emery, then shake it and rub it and make it just like Xuan paper. They could then paint the bottle in great detail.

Snuff bottles are made of a wide variety of materials such as ivory, jade, pearl as well as gold, silver and so on, but glass has remained the most popular substance to use and most surviving snuff bottles from the past are of this material.

 Words and Expressions to Learn ·

transparent / trænsˈpærənt / *a.* 透明的   accomplished / əˈkɒmplɪʃd / *a.* 有造诣的

gamut / ˈɡæmət / n. 整个范围，全部

emery / ˈeməri / n. 刚玉

grasshopper / ˈɡrɑːʃɒpə / n. 蚱蜢

ivory / ˈaɪvəri / n. 象牙

***   ***   ***   ***   ***   ***

snuff bottle 鼻烟壶

Matteo Ricci 利玛窦 (1552—1610 年，意大利天主教耶稣会传教士，明末来中国传教，后到北京，结识学者徐光启，介绍西方自然科学，与徐光启合译《几何原本》，著有《天学实义》等)

interior painting 内画

be addicted to 对……上瘾

a slender bamboo stick 很细的竹签

following the will of the painter 依照画家的意愿

curio dealer 古董商

the 108 heroes and heroines of the classical novel *Water Margin* 《水浒传》中的 108 个好汉

Xuan paper 宣纸

Part C Exercises

I. *Make up a brief dialogue between a guide and a tourist about tri-colored glazed pottery（唐三彩）after reading the following passage.*

The tri-colored glazed pottery of Tang Dynasty was developed 1,300 years ago. This art form drew on the skills of Chinese painting and sculpture and employed techniques of clay-strip forming and incising（雕刻）. The lines produced from this process were rugged and powerful. Glazes of different colors were painted on and while chemical reactions took place in the process of firing in the kiln（窑）, they dripped naturally so that the colors mingled with each other and formed smooth tones.

The tri-colored glazed pottery flourished during a rather short period of time (the 8th century) of the dynasty, when pottery articles of this kind were used by the aristocracy（贵族）as funerary objects. Those in existence today are limited in number and are considered to be rare treasures, valued for their brilliant colors and life-like shapes.

Excavated tri-colored Tang pottery articles are usually horses, camels, female figurines, dragon-head mugs, figurines of musicians and acrobats, and pillows. Of these, the tri-colored camels have won the greatest admiration. They are presented as bearing loads of silk or carrying musicians on their backs — their heads are raised as if neighing（嘶鸣）; the red-bearded, blue-eyed drivers, clad in tunics（穿着束腰外衣）with tight sleeves and hats with upturned brims, represent true-to-life images of men from Central Asia of that time, as they trudged along the Silk Road.

II. Answer the following questions according to the passages.

1. In what way does porcelain differ from other types of ceramics?
2. In what way are the decorations of European porcelain different from decorations of Chinese porcelain?
3. Why have Chinese snuff bottles been well-known all over the world for years?
4. What has made Chinese snuff bottles unique?
5. What material is most common for snuff bottles?

III. Decide whether the following statements are true or false according to the passages.

1. To make a piece of porcelain, two firings are required.
2. Porcelain is basically made from a mixture of two ingredients — kaolin and cobalt.
3. Snuff bottles were introduced to China by a French priest.
4. Inside painting was invented by a minor local official who loved snuff very much.
5. Snuff bottles can be made of different materials.

IV. Translate the following dialogue between a tourist and a shop assistant into English.

— 欢迎光临。请问我能为您做点什么?
— 您能告诉我为什么这里有这么多装着花、树根和小石头的盆子(pot)吗?
— 噢,这些叫盆景(potted landscapes)。在中国,一个盆景常被比作一幅三维(3-dimensional)画。
— 您是说它从任何一个角度(angle)都可以形成一幅画吗?
— 是的。请看这个盆景。这棵从山上采来的小树已经有几百年了。园艺工人(gardener)把它的根放到这个花盆里,用了三年的时间把它塑造(shape)成现在的样子。
— 真是不可思议! 你看,它有这么多的枝条,而且开了这么多漂亮的花。
— 中国人认为在欣赏盆景时性情(temperament)也会受到影响。
— 是吗?那我买一个送给我的妻子作为生日礼物吧。我肯定她会喜欢的。

V. Translate the following passage into Chinese.

Chinese chinaware has been exported for far longer than is usually assumed. Originating in Shang Dynasty (17th century – 1046 BC), chinaware has been a distinctive handicraft of

China. The workmanship peaked in Tang Dynasty and this product began to sell to other countries in Asia and Europe. It was among the most popular goods traded through the Silk Road and was favored by European nobilities. Slowly, the word "China", which refers to chinaware in general, became a term to name this ancient country, where the earliest and best chinaware was made.

VI.   *Topic for discussion*

Though porcelain was first made in China, the best quality tableware china on market is usually made in other countries. Why? What can be done to improve porcelain made in our country?

UNIT 5
Lesson 28
Chinese Painting and Calligraphy

Part A Conversation

Dialogue | **At a Stationery Counter**

(T: Tourist   S: Shop Assistant)

S: Good afternoon, Sir. What can I do for you?

T: Good afternoon. I'd like to buy something typically Chinese. Could you offer some suggestions?

S: My pleasure, Sir. Well, have you ever heard of "the Four Treasures of the Study"?

T: Four treasures of the study? What are they?

S: Look here, Sir. They are Xuan paper, writing brush, ink slab and ink stick. Aren't they typical souvenirs from China?

T: Right you are. I have heard they are used in painting and calligraphy. But I'm afraid I can't write with a writing brush, you know.

S: It doesn't matter. You can learn how to use it. In China many children are trained to write with it when they are very young.

T: Maybe I'm too old to learn. Never have I dreamed to use a writing brush someday.

S: You know, one is never too old to learn. And I'm sure you can get a lot of fun out of it.

T: Ah, you're very persuasive. Are these writing brushes all the same?

S: No. Basically we have three kinds of brushes. They are made of white goat hair, black rabbit hair and yellow weasel hair.

T: Look at this one over here. Is the handle made of jade?

S: Yes, you are right. Usually the handle is made of bamboo or wood, but some especially sold as souvenirs can be made of lacquer, porcelain and even precious materials like jade and ivory.

T: Please show me this one of jade. Although I don't know how to use it, it can be a very good decoration in my study.

S: Sure. You also need an ink slab to go with it. It will add more Chinese flavor to your study.

T: A good suggestion. But is the ink slab expensive?

S: That depends. We have ink slabs made of stone, jade, porcelain, lacquer and copper.

T: I'm sure the stone ones are the cheapest. Just show me a good stone ink slab, please.

S: What about this one? It has a carving of phoenix on its cover.

T: It's pretty. I'll take it.

S: And do you need an ink stick and some Xuan paper?

T: I'm afraid I wouldn't have a chance to use them. And I don't want to give an exhibition of the Four Treasures of the Study in my home. I guess I'll skip them.

S: You are a very sensible buyer.

 Words and Expressions to Learn ·····························

stationery / ˈsteɪʃənərɪ / *n.* 文具　　　　　weasel / ˈwiːzəl / *n.* 黄鼠狼
persuasive / pəˈsweɪsɪv / *a.* 有说服力的　　sensible / ˈsensɪbl / *a.* 明智的

＊＊＊　＊＊＊　＊＊＊　　　＊＊＊　＊＊＊　＊＊＊

the Four Treasures of the Study 文房四宝　　ink slab 砚
writing brush 毛笔　　　　　　　　　　　ink stick 墨

Part B Reading

| Passage 1 | Chinese Seals |

Nowadays, seals are still widely used, and the art of seal-engraving has become more, not less, popular than ever before. More noteworthy is that many foreigners are now able to appreciate this art form, which for a long time has been considered uniquely Chinese.

Seal-cutting is traditionally listed along with painting, calligraphy and poetry as one of the "four arts" expected of an accomplished scholar and a unique part of the Chinese cultural heritage. A seal stamp in red is not only the signature on a work of calligraphy or painting but an indispensable part.

The art of seal-cutting dates back about 3,700 years to Yin Dynasty and has its origin in the cutting of oracle on tortoise shells. It flourished in Qin Dynasty 22 centuries ago, when people engraved their names on utensils and documents (of bamboo and wood) to show ownership or authorship. Out of this grew the cutting of personal names on small blocks of horn, jade or wood, namely the seals as we know today.

As in other countries, seals may be used by official departments as well as individuals. From as early as the Warring States Period an official seal would be given as a symbol of power by the head of a state to a man whom he appointed to a high office. The seal, in other words, stood for power. Private seals are likewise used to stamp personal names on various papers for purposes of proof or as a symbol of good faith.

Seals reflect the development of written Chinese. The earliest ones, those of Qin and Han Dynasties, bear the curly script (zhuan), which explains why the art of seal-cutting is also called zhuanke and also why the zhuan script is also known in English as "seal characters". As time went on, the other script styles appeared one after another on Chinese seals which may now be cut in any style.

The materials for seals vary with different types of owners. Average persons normally have wood, stone or horn seals, whereas noted public figures would probably prefer seals made of more valuable materials. Today, stone is the most widely used material in seal engraving. Among all the stones, Shoushan stones, which come from Shoushan County, Fuzhou City, are the most famous. The most valuable for engravers is Tianhuang Stone, a kind of Shoushan stone. It is said that the emperors of Qing Dynasty used to put a piece of Tianhuang on the table for wealth and good luck when they held a ceremony to worship heaven. Another less precious stone is called "chicken's blood" stone, which comes from Changhua County in Zhejiang Province. The "chicken's blood" stone contains cinnabar which makes it look like blood splashed on the stone in free patterns.

Seals cut as works of art should excel in three aspects — calligraphy, composition and the graver's handwork. The artist must be good at writing various styles of the Chinese script. He should know how to arrange within a limited space a number of characters to achieve a graceful effect. He should also be familiar with the various materials — stone, brass or ivory — so that he may apply the cutting knife with perfect skills.

 Words and Expressions to Learn ·····························

indispensable / ˌɪndɪˈspensəbl / *a.* 必不可少的　　excel / ɪkˈsel / *v.* 突出
horn / hɔːn / *n.* (动物等的) 角　　　　　　　　　composition / ˌkɒmpəˈzɪʃən / *n.* 构成
cinnabar / ˈsɪnəbɑː / *n.* 朱砂

***　　***　　***　　***　　***　　***

tortoise shell 龟壳

Passage 2　Traditional Chinese Painting

Though Chinese painting has much in common with Western painting from an aesthetic point of view, as an important part of the country's cultural heritage, it still possesses its unique national character. Chinese traditional painting seldom follows the convention of central focus perspective or realistic portrayal, but gives the painter freedom on artistic conception, structural composition and method of expression so as to better express his own feelings. Chinese painting has absorbed the best of many forms of art, like poetry, calligraphy, painting, and seal engraving.

One of its main features is that it is painted on Xuan paper (or silk) with the Chinese brush, Chinese ink, mineral and vegetable pigments. Xuan paper is most suitable for Chinese painting. It can allow the writing brush wet with Chinese ink and held in a trained hand, to move freely on it, making strokes vary. These soon turn out to be human figures, plants and flowers, birds, fish and insects, full of interest and life. To work on this art needs continual exercise, a good control of the brush, and a feel and knowledge of the qualities of Xuan paper and Chinese ink.

Before setting a brush to paper, the painter must have a well-composed draft in his mind, drawing on his imagination and store of experience. Once he starts to paint, he will normally have to complete the work at one go, and there is no possibility of any change of wrong strokes.

Chinese often consider a good painting a good poem, and vice versa. Hence the expression "painting in poetry and poetry in painting". In the past, many great artists were also great poets and calligraphers. The inscriptions and seals on the paintings can not only help us understand the painter's ideas and emotions, but also provide decorative beauty to the painting.

According to subject matter, classical Chinese painting can be divided into three categories: landscapes, figures and birds-and-flowers. Throughout the course of Chinese painting, images of emperors, philosophers, and court ladies provide role models from the past; landscapes and bird-and-flower paintings demonstrate the central place of nature in Chinese thought. Religious paintings reflect both the Daoist philosophy native to China and Buddhism.

In terms of technique, Chinese paintings are divided into two major categories: free hand brushwork (xieyi) and detailed brushwork (gongbi). The former is characterized by simple and bold strokes intended to represent the likeness of the objects, while the latter by fine brushwork and close attention to detail. Employing different techniques, the two schools try to achieve the same end, the creation of beauty.

It is difficult to tell how long the art of painting has existed in China. Pots of 5,000–6,000 years ago were painted in color with patterns of plants and animals, reflecting various aspects of daily life of the past. These may be considered the beginning of Chinese painting.

In 1949 from a tomb of the Warring States Period was unearthed a painting on silk of human figures, dragons and phoenixes. The earliest work on silk ever discovered in China, it measures about 30 centimeters long and 20 centimeters wide.

From this and other early paintings on silk it may be easily seen that the ancients were already familiar with the art of writing or painting with the brush, for every stroke is perfect.

Paintings on paper appeared much later than those on silk for the simple reason that silk was invented long before the invention of paper.

In 1964, when a tomb dating to Jin Dynasty was discovered in Turpan, Xinjiang, a colored painting on paper was discovered. It shows, on top, the sun, the moon and the Big Dipper and, below, the owner with a fan in his hand. A vivid portrayal of a feudal land-owner, measuring 106.5 centimeters long and 47 centimeters wide, it is the only known painting on paper with such a long history in China.

While traditional Chinese painting still occupies an important place in the life of modern Chinese, many painters now desire to express their experience of new times. By combining new methods of expression with traditional Chinese painting techniques, they are opening up a vast, new world of artistic expression.

 Words and Expressions to Learn ·

convention / kən'venʃən / *n.* 常规，习俗
stroke / strəʊk / *n.* (写字、绘画的) 一笔，一划

bold / bəʊld / *a.* 醒目的
phoenix / 'fiːnɪks / *n.* 凤凰

***　　***　　***　　　***　　***　　***

central focus perspective 中心焦点的视图
realistic portrayal 写实
artistic conception 艺术概念
structural composition 构图
a well-composed draft 想好的草图
at one go 一下子，一口气

and vice versa 反过来也如此
the Daoist philosophy native to China 产生
于中国的道教哲学
the Big Dipper 北斗七星
a feudal land-owner 封建地主

 Exercises ·

I. *Make up a dialogue about Chinese calligraphy between a tourist and a guide after reading the following passage.*

> Calligraphy, literally "beautiful writing", is one of the four traditional arts dating back to the earliest days of Chinese history. For the Chinese, calligraphy is not just a method of

communication but also a means of expressing the dynamic forces of the natural world.

A Chinese calligrapher's tools, like those of a painter, are comprised of four basic items that are commonly referred to as "the four treasures of the study". They are the brush, ink, ink stone, and paper.

Concerned with both the present and a long time past, calligraphy is at once the most rigorously convention-bound and the most fiercely individualistic of the graphic arts. It was once an important critical standard for the Chinese literati in the imperial era and now prevails (盛行) not only in China but also worldwide as a unique branch of art. Unlike other visual art techniques, all calligraphy strokes are permanent and inflexible, demanding careful planning and confident execution (技巧，手法). While one has to conform to the defined structure of words, the expression can be extremely creative.

To become an artist or expert in calligraphy, one has to practice word by word and stroke by stroke until the spirit of the practice gets into one's mind. The Chinese brush calligraphy can temper a person into a state in which one can apply sub-consciousness absorbed from daily practice to control the concentration (浓度) of ink and the compatibility (和谐) of font (字体) and size of each piece or word.

By controlling the concentration of ink, the thickness and absorption of the paper, and the flexibility of the brush, the artist is free to produce an infinite variety of styles and forms. In Chinese calligraphy, diffusing ink blots and dry brush strokes are viewed as a natural impromptu (即兴的) expression rather than a fault. Western calligraphy often pursues font-like uniformity and homogeneity (同质，均匀) of characters in one size is a must. To Chinese artists, calligraphy is a mental exercise that coordinates the mind and the body to choose the best styles in expressing the content of the passage. It is a most relaxing yet highly disciplined exercise for one's physical and spiritual well-being. Therefore, historically, many calligraphy artists were well-known for their longevity.

II. Answer the following questions about the passages.

1. To which dynasty does the art of seal-cutting date back?
2. Why is the art of seal-cutting also called zhuanke?
3. Which stones used for carving seals are the most famous?
4. What are the two styles of traditional Chinese painting in terms of techniques?
5. What categories are Chinese paintings divided into in terms of subject matter?

III.   *Complete the dialogue by translating the Chinese into English.*

S: Welcome to Yangliuqing New Year's Painting shop. What can I do for you?

T: I'm just looking. These paintings are very interesting.

S: They are called "New Year's Paintings". Look at these figures on them. 1. _____

_____ (大多数是孩子在采摘果实，这代表着来年丰收).

T: 2. _____ (这就是希望把好运带回家，是吧)?

S: Yes, you are right. People also 3. _____ (通过绘画来讲述民间故事和

传说).

T: It's really a good way to remember what happened in the past. Okay, I'll take some.

S: 4. _____ (您喜欢哪几幅)?

T: The one with a boy and a girl bowing to each other and the one with a kid carrying a fish.

S: Good choice. The first is called "gongxifacai", which means "wishing you a good fortune in the

next year". The second is "jiqingyouyu" to bless you a prosperous new year.

T: Very good. I'll take these two. How much?

S: It's thirty *yuan* for each.

T: 5. _____ (请为我包好).

S: Sure.

IV.   *Translate the following sentences into English.*

1. 要练习书法，需要文房四宝。
2. 刻印章是中国的一种传统艺术。
3. 我们有一位很有经验的刻章师可以为您刻章。
4. 油画和国画的一个主要不同就是前者是通过颜色创作，而后者是通过线条来创作。
5. 国画中的现实主义是一种主观的表达。

V.   *Translate the following passage into Chinese.*

Chinese calligraphy and Chinese painting are closely related because lines are used
in both. Chinese people have turned simple lines into a highly developed form of art.
Lines are used not only to draw contours (轮廓) but also to express the artist's concepts
and feelings. For different subjects and different purposes a variety of lines are used.
They may be straight or curved, hard or soft, thick or thin, pale or dark, and the ink may
be dry or running. The use of lines is one of the elements that give Chinese painting its
unique qualities.

VI. *Topic for discussion*

Years ago, the Shanghai education bureau decided to start teaching writing-brush(毛笔) calligraphy to elementary school students. What is your view on this?

UNIT **5** Lesson 29
Chinese Embroidery

Part **A** *Conversation*

Dialogue   Buying Suzhou Embroidery

(T: Tourist   G: Guide   S: Shop Assistant)

G: Look, this is Suzhou embroidery.

T: How amazing that they can embroider beautiful pictures on such thin silk. How long has Suzhou embroidery been around?

G: More than two thousand years.

T: No wonder the girls in Suzhou wear such beautiful clothes!

G: Suzhou embroidery is not limited to clothing. In the past, there were also embroidered maps.

T: Really? I thought Suzhou is known mainly for its gardens.

G: Suzhou is also known as the hometown of silk! In the past, Suzhou embroidery was always the royal family's favorite.

S: Hello. Is there anything I can do for you?

T: I want to buy something for my father for the coming Father's Day. And ... some gifts for my friends back home.

S: What about this tie for your father? It looks pretty sharp.

T: Hmm, it'll make my father look too serious!

S: How about this one? It has bamboo and panda patterns on it. Very Chinese.

T: Oh, I'm sure this one's perfect for him. I'll take it.

S: Look at these. They are called double-sided embroidery. They can make good gifts for friends.

T: What is double-sided embroidery anyway?

S: Usually a piece of embroidery is one-sided. It means you can see the pattern of a cat, a bird, a flower or a beauty only on one side. The other side tends to be a little messy, or at least you can't make out the design.

T: Then with double-sided embroidery we can see the same design on both sides?

S: Exactly.

G: Double-sided embroidery is a technique unique to Suzhou.

T: Let me have a look. They are really nice. Look at this cat trying to catch a butterfly. It looks alive.

G: Yes. And you can't find any loose end of thread on either side.

T: That's really amazing. How do they make it?

G: Your question has beaten me.

T: Could you please tell us something about the skills, Sir?

S: I don't know much, either. But I do know it is extremely intense work to finish a piece. The embroiders have to split a single piece of silk thread into 12 to 48 thinner threads and then stitch layer after layer using threads of different colors to reach the final wonderful effect.

T: 12 to 48 thinner threads? Incredible! Then the threads will be invisible to the eye.

G: That's why the artists have to take a break every ten to fifteen minutes.

T: Wow. That's really hard work.

S: And now we have got a new invention.

T: What is it?

S: A new kind of double-sided embroidery with different designs on both sides.

T: Different designs on both sides? I can't believe it!

S: Look over here!

T: A dragon and a phoenix on the same embroidery! I'll take it. How much is it?

S: I'm afraid it is a bit expensive. It's 15,000 *yuan*.

T: That's really expensive. Can I have a discount?

S: 15,000 *yuan* is the price after the discount.

T: OK, I'll take it. It's well worth the money, I believe.

G: You really have an expert eye for Chinese arts.

T: I'm flattered.

Words and Expressions to Learn

Suzhou embroidery 苏绣	Your question has beaten me. 你的问题把
double-sided embroidery 双面绣	我难住了。

Part **B** Reading

 **Passage 1**   **Major Styles of Chinese Embroidery**

Chinese embroidery has four major traditional styles: Su, Shu, Xiang and Yue.

Su Embroidery

Su is the short name for Suzhou. A typical southern water town, Suzhou and everything from it reflect tranquility and elegance. So does Su Embroidery. Embroidery with fish on one side and kitty on the other side is a representative of this style. Favored with the advantageous climate, Suzhou with its surrounding areas is suitable for silkworms and mulberry trees. As early as Song Dynasty, Su Embroidery was already well known for its elegance and vividness. In history, Su Embroidery dominated the royal wardrobe and walls. Even today, Su Embroidery occupies a large share of the embroidery market in China as well as in the world.

Shu Embroidery

Originated from Shu, the short name for Sichuan, Shu Embroidery, influenced by its geographic environment and local customs, is characterized by a refined and brisk style. The earliest record of Shu Embroidery was during Western Han Dynasty. At that time, embroidery was a luxury enjoyed only by the royal family and was strictly controlled by the government. During Han Dynasty and the Three Kingdoms, Shu Embroidery and Shu Brocade were exchanged for horses and used to settle debts. In Qing Dynasty, Shu Embroidery entered the market and an industry was formed. Government supports promoted the development of the industry. Shu Embroidery has become more elegant and covered a wider range. From the paintings by masters, to patterns by designers, to landscape, flowers and birds, dragons and phoenixes, tiles and ancient coins, it seems anything could be the topic of Shu Embroidery.

Xiang Embroidery

Xiang Embroidery, an art from Hunan, is a witness of the ancient Hunan and Hubei culture. Xiang Embroidery was a gift to the royal family during the Spring and Autumn Period. Through over two thousand years of development, Xiang Embroidery became a special branch of the local art. Xiang Embroidery has been gaining popularity day by day. Besides the common topics seen in other styles of embroidery, Xiang Embroidery absorbs elements from calligraphy and painting. The uniqueness of Xiang Embroidery is that it is patterned after a painting draft, but is not limited by it. Perhaps because of this technique, in Xiang Embroidery, a flower seems to send off fragrance, a bird seems to sing, a tiger seems to run, and a person seems to breathe.

Yue Embroidery

Yue Embroidery includes Guangzhou Embroidery and Chaozhou Embroidery. People generally agree that Yue Embroidery started from Tang Dynasty. Portrait and flowers and birds are the most popular themes of Yue Embroidery as the subtropical climate favors the area with birds and plants. In addition, Yue Embroidery uses rich colors for strong contrast. Since Cantonese are very superstitious, red and green, and auspicious patterns are widely used. The most famous piece of Yue Embroidery is Hundreds of Birds Worshiping the Phoenix.

 Words and Expressions to Learn · · · · · · · · · · · · · · · ·

representative / ˌreprɪˈzentətɪv / *n.* 代表，典型
wardrobe / ˈwɔːdrəʊb / *n.* 衣橱
refined / rɪˈfaɪnd / *a.* 精致的

brisk / brɪsk / *a.* 活泼的
auspicious / ɔːˈspɪʃəs / *a.* 吉祥的

*** *** ***   *** *** ***

Shu Brocade 蜀锦
settle debts 解决债务问题
subtropical climate 亚热带气候

Hundreds of Birds Worshiping the Phoenix
百鸟朝凤

Passage 2 | **History of Chinese Silk**

It is well known that silk was discovered in China as one of the best materials for clothing — it has a look and feeling of richness that no other materials can match. However, very few people know when or where or how it was discovered. Actually, it can date back to the 30th century BC when Huang Di (the Yellow Emperor) came into power. There are many legends about the discovery of silk; some of them are both romantic and mysterious.

One legend has it that once there lived a father with his daughter, who had a magic horse, which could not only fly in the sky but also understand human language. One day, the father went out on business and did not come back for quite some time. The daughter made a promise: If the horse could find her father, she would marry him. Finally her father came back with the horse, but the father was shocked at his daughter's promise. Unwilling to let his daughter marry a horse, he killed the horse. And then miracle happened! The horse's skin carried the girl and flew away. They flew and flew and at last, they stopped on a tree, and the moment the girl touched the tree, she turned into a silkworm. Every day, she spit long and thin silks to show her endless missing of her father.

Another less romantic but more convincing explanation is that some ancient Chinese women discovered silk by chance. When they were picking fruits from the trees, they found a special kind of fruit, white but too hard to eat, so they boiled the fruit in hot water but they still could hardly eat it. At last, they lost their patience and began to beat them with sticks. In this way, silks and silkworms were discovered. And the white hard fruit are cocoons!

Still another legend goes like this: The Silkworm Goddess appeared to the Yellow Emperor, the legendary ancestor of the Chinese people, after he had defeated his enemy Chi You. She presented him with silk as a sign of respect. The Yellow Emperor had the silk made into cloth and then into silk clothes, which he found extremely soft and comfortable. Leizu, the Yellow Emperor's wife, searched until she found some worms capable of producing silk from their mouths. She raised these silkworms by feeding them mulberry leaves. Later generations came to worship Leizu as the Silkworm Goddess.

It takes an average of 25 to 28 days for a silkworm, which is no bigger than an ant, to grow old enough to make a cocoon. Then the farmers will put them onto piles of straws, and then the silkworm will attach itself to the straw with its legs and begin to produce silk to make a cocoon.

The next step is unwinding the cocoons. First the cocoons are heated to kill the pupae, otherwise, the pupae will turn into moths, and moths will make a hole in the cocoons which will be useless. Then the farmers find the loose end of the cocoon, carry it to a small wheel, and then unwind it. At last, two workers measure them into a certain length, twist them into strands, which are called raw silk. Then they are dyed and made into cloth. It takes 111 cocoons to make a man's tie.

During the Warring States Period, the development of productivity made silk more popular and it was no longer a luxury just for the rich and noble. The embroidery and dyeing skills were all improved, and the silk designs had a sense of free and bold air. Later, professional designers created a lot of new patterns and improved the machines. The silk products unearthed from Mawangdui Han Tombs are a proof of the advanced skill and artistry.

 Words and Expressions to Learn ·

convincing / kən'vɪnsɪŋ / *a.* 让人信服的
average / 'ævərɪdʒ / *n.* 平均（数）
cocoon / kə'kuːn / *n.* 蚕茧
unwind / 'ʌn'waɪnd / *v.* 展开，抽出

pupae / 'pjuːpiː / *n.* 蛹 (pupa 的复数)
strand / strænd / *n.* (绳、线等的) 股，缕
productivity / ˌprɒdʌk'tɪvɪtɪ / *n.* 生产力

 *Exercises* · · · · · · · ·

I.   *Make up a dialogue between a tourist and a guide about Chinese embroidery.*

II. *Answer the following questions according to the passages.*

1. What are the four major styles of Chinese embroidery?
2. What's the uniqueness of Xiang Embroidery?
3. What's the most famous piece of Yue Embroidery?
4. How long does it take a silkworm to grow old enough to make a cocoon?
5. When did silk products become popular?

III. *Complete the dialogue by translating the Chinese into English.*

T: These cloth shoes are nice.

G: You have a pretty good eye. These are "thousand layer sole shoes". 1. _____ _____ (这是一个有几百年历史的名牌).

T: These shoes are of superb quality.

G: 2. _____ (它们都是手工做的).

T: (To the shop assistant.)3. _____ (这些鞋有八号半的吗)?

S: Eight and a half? That's American size. It is size 43 in China. Which color do you want? 4. _____ (这些鞋卖得很好的。有多少货卖多少货). Some people buy five or six pairs at a time.

T: I'll take two pairs of them. Hey, can you give us a better price for two pairs?

S: (Laughs.)Sorry. 5. _____ (我们店不讲价). These shoes are not only comfortable and well made. They're a famous brand!

T: What brand is it?

S: Neiliansheng. 6. _____ (过去朝廷的官员喜欢买这个牌子的鞋).

T: Why?

S: It has a lucky sounding name. "Neiliansheng" 7. _____ (听起来像步步高升的意思).

T: Looks like I made the right choice.

G: 8. _____ (让我们去看看那边的绣花鞋吧。我敢肯定你会觉得它们很有中国味).

S: Have a look at these shoes please. These embroidered shoes are not just pretty. They're light and comfortable to wear.

T: The flowers are so pretty. 9. _____ (绣花鞋必须得和中国式的衣服一同穿才好看吗)?

G: Not necessarily. 10. _____ (我觉得和牛仔配起来也很好).

T: Then I'll take a pair.

IV. *Translate the following Chinese passage into English and the English one into Chinese.*

1. 产于四川的蜀锦起源于汉代，在魏晋隋唐时期达到顶峰。红色是其主要颜色。云锦在南北朝时期就开始出现于建康（即现在的南京），在元代得到极大发展。因为大量使用金线银线而得名。在元明清时期，云锦一直是贡品(tribute)。壮锦是由广西壮族人民创造的。它的特点是色彩艳丽，图案中经常出现象征吉祥(auspiciousness)的凤凰。

2. "A silkworm spits out all its silk till its death and a candle won't stop its tears until it is fully burnt." This Tang poem accurately describes the property of the silkworm. Despite

scientific and technological development, a silkworm can only produce 1,000 meters (3,280 feet) of silk in its lifespan of 28 days. The rarity of the raw material is the deciding factor of both the value and the mystery of silk.

V. *Topics for discussion.*

Embroidery and many other traditional arts and crafts are dying out in China. What do you think are the reasons? And what can we do to prevent them from dying out?

UNIT 5 Lesson 30 Chinese Clothing and Ornamentation

Part A　Conversation

Dialogue　At a Jeweler's

(T: Tourist　G: Guide　S: Shop Assistant)

T: I want to buy my mom a silver for her birthday. She's going to be sixty next month.

G: Let's try Laofengxiang Jeweler's, the most well-known jewelry shop in Shanghai.

T: Okay.

S: Hello. Is there anything I can do for you?

T: I'd like to buy my mother a silver bracelet for her 60th birthday. I'd like one in a traditional Chinese style.

S: Well, here's one with a very traditional design. Do you want to have a look?

T: Sure. What does the pattern mean? Is it sort of a bird?

G: Yes. It's a phoenix, the queen of birds in Chinese legends. The design is most suitable for middle-aged women.

T: I see. Yes, very beautiful. But will you show me some other designs?

S: No problem. This one has a lotus flower, the symbol of purity. And this is a dragon, an imaginary animal, a symbol of auspiciousness.

T: OK. I prefer the lotus flower. It looks like a lily, and lily is my mother's favorite flower. Can I try it on?

G: Yes. Let me help you.

T: Oh, it's a bit too tight.

S: This is the largest one we have. But don't worry. We can make it larger for you if you decide to buy it. Just a minute, please.

(A moment later.)

T: It's all right now. Mom wears almost the same size as me.

S: Ma'am, why not buy some bracelets for yourself? We have a set of seven cloisonné bracelets, with different designs and colors. You can wear a different one each day of the week. And the price is reasonable, too. Here they are, the "weekly bracelets".

T: That sounds interesting! If I buy two sets, will you give me a discount?

S: I'll give you 10% off for the silver bracelet, and 15% off for the weekly bracelets if you take two sets.

T: OK. Could you please wrap up the silver and this set? They are presents. Don't bother with the other set. It is for myself.

S: What else do you need, ma'am?

T: Please show me some necklaces. I'd like to buy two for my nieces.

S: May I ask how old they are?

T: One is thirteen and the other is sixteen.

G: For teenage girls, I suggest this pair of crystal pendants on leather lace. Come and look.

T: A moon and a star. So delicate. But I don't like the yellow color.

S: No problem. This pair also comes in blue, green and purple. Here they are!

T: So pretty. I really don't know which to choose.

G: I think teenage girls usually like purple things.

T: OK, I'll take the purple pair. I'm sure they will hug me a dozen times for this gift.

 Words and Expressions to Learn ·

bracelet / ˈbreɪslət / *n.* 镯子　　　　　　leather / ˈleðə / *n.* 皮革
pendant / ˈpendənt / *n.* 吊坠

***　　***　　***　　***　　***　　***

Laofengxiang Jeweler's 老凤祥银楼　　　jewelry shop 珠宝店

Part B Reading

Passage 1 Chinese Qipao

Qipao, the classic dress for Chinese women, combines elegance with fashion. Qipao is one of the most versatile costumes in the world. It can be long or short, with full, medium, short or even no sleeves at all — to suit different occasions, weather and personal tastes.

Qipao can display the temperament, and refined manner of a mature woman perfectly. The collar of qipao is high and tight fitting, not just for preventing coldness but also for beauty. The collar of qipao generally takes the shape of a semicircle, its right and left sides being symmetrical, making the soft and slender neck of a woman more attractive. The collar of qipao should be well made, especially the buttonhole loop on the collar, which serves as the finishing touch.

For convenient movement and display of the slender legs of women, qipao generally has two big slits at either side of the lower hem. The slits of qipao expose a woman's legs indistinctly when she walks. Today you can get qipao with different lengths and kinds of slits (one slit on the side or front as well as two slits).

Qipao usually is made of materials like silk, brocade, satin or velour. Nearly all colors can be used. Often qipao gets a certain pattern, such as Chinese Dragons, different kinds of flowers, butterflies or other typical Chinese icons for prosperity and wealth.

Qipao comes from China's Manchu nationality. There is a legend about its origin. A young fisherwoman living by the Jingbo Lake was not only beautiful, but also clever and skillful. When fishing, she often felt hindered by her long and loose fitting dress. Then an idea struck her: why not make a more practical dress for work? She got down to sewing and produced a long gown with slits, which enabled her to tuck in the front piece of her dress, thus making her job much easier. As a fisherwoman, she never dreamed that a fortune would befall her. The young emperor who ruled China at that time had a dream one night. In the dream, his dead father told him that a lovely fisherwoman in qipao by the Jingpo Lake would become his queen. After awakening from his dream, the emperor sent his men to look for the girl. Sure enough, there she was! So she became the queen, bringing the long gown with her. And soon qipao became popular.

We do not know whether the story is true or not. But one thing is certain. qipao came from the Manchus who grew out of the ancient Nüzhen tribes. In the early 17th century, Nurhachi unified various Nüzhen tribes and set up the Eight Banners System. Over the years, a collarless, tube-shaped gown was developed, which was worn by both men and women. That is the embryo of qipao. The dress is called qipao in Chinese or translated as "banner dress".

Qipao became popular among ladies of the royal family in Qing Dynasty. At that time, qipao fit loosely and were so long that they would reach the insteps. Usually, they were made of silk and the whole dress was embroidered, with broad lace trimmed at the collar, sleeves and edges. In the 1920s, qipao became popular throughout China but underwent a change. The cuffs grew narrower and were usually trimmed with thin lace. The dress was shortened as well. This new adaptation allowed the beauty of female body to be fully displayed. In the 1930s, wearing qipao became a fashion among women throughout China. Various styles existed during this period. Some were short; some were long, with low, high or even no collars at all. Starting from the 1940s, qipao became closer-fitting. In summer, women wore sleeveless dresses. Qipao of this period was seldom adorned with patterns. Qipao had become standard female attire by the 1960s. Following Western fashion, the tailors raised the lower hem, even to above the knee. Today, more and more women in China have come to appreciate its beauty. In fact, many people have suggested that qipao should become the national dress for women in China. This shows that qipao remains a vibrant part of Chinese culture.

Wearing a qipao nowadays has become something of a fashion home and abroad. Many foreign women are eager to get themselves a qipao should they visit China. Qipao is no longer a garment particular to Chinese women, but is adding to the vocabulary of beauty for women all over the world.

Words and Expressions to Learn

versatile / 'vɜːsətaɪl / *a.* 多种用途的，多功能的

temperament / 'tempərəmənt / *n.* 气质，禀性

semicircle / 'semɪsɜːkl / *n.* 半圆形

loop / luːp / *n.* 环形，圈

slit / slɪt / *n.* 开衩，狭缝

velour / və'lʊə / *n.* 丝绒

icon / 'aɪkɒn / *n.* 画像，图像

tuck / tʌk / *v.* 将(某物)缩拢起来塞入狭小空间，收拢

befall / bɪ'fɔːl / *v.* 降临到(某人)头上，发生

unify / 'jʊnɪfaɪ / *v.* 统一

embryo / 'embrɪəʊ / *n.* 雏形

instep / 'ɪnstep / *n.* 脚背

cuff / kʌf / *n.* 袖口

attire / ə'taɪə / *n.* 服装，衣着

***　　***　　***　　***　　***　　***

Manchu nationality 满族

Nüzhen tribe 女真族

Nurhachi 努尔哈赤(即清太祖)

the Eight Banners System 八旗制度

Passage 2　**Jade, the Stone of China**

Many countries have jade culture, but none of them has as long a history as China does. China's jade culture has undergone a long process of development from the New Stone Age 10,000 years ago to the present.

The earliest jadeware found in China was a piece of serpentine stoneware unearthed in Liaoning Province dating back to the New Stone Age, more than 12,000 years ago. The second was a small hanging jade article excavated in the site of Hemudu in Zhejiang Province dating back more than 7,000 years. Jadeware in that period was mainly used for personal decoration. A large number of exquisite jade objects were produced 4,000 years ago. Jadeware at that time was mainly used for witchcraft and as a symbol of power.

During Shang Dynasty, craftsmen used metal tools and made new progress in jadeware models and sculpture. Round jade articles increased in number and jadeware was often given as gifts.

Jade-carving techniques developed fast in the Spring and Autumn and Warring States Periods. The Spring and Autumn Period was known for its well-carved and exquisite jadeware. The delicate patterns of dragon and phoenix on the jade decorations are still treasured today.

In the periods of Qin and Han Dynasties, jadeware became more practical. At that time, people began to believe in the power of jadeware to give people a long life. They thought they would live forever if they had jadeware. Therefore, the practice of burying the dead with jadeware became common. Invaluable jade figures and clothes of jade pieces sewn with gold threads have been found in tombs dating back to Han Dynasty.

During the periods of the Three Kingdoms to Song and Yuan Dynasties, there was no great development in jade-carving techniques. This changed in Ming Dynasty when many famous craftsmen emerged. White jade vessels with gold holders and white jade bowls with gold covers, which were unearthed in the Ming Tombs, reflected the dynasty's highest level in jade carving. Jadeware carving techniques peaked in Qing Dynasty with the support of Emperor Qianlong.

The patterns of jadeware have rich meanings to Chinese people. Bats and gourds were often used as a basis for more than 100 patterns because the Chinese words for bat and gourd sound like "good fortune" in the Chinese language.

Jade in China is varied and can be divided into two categories: hard and soft. Good materials are important, but the value of a jade object depends on the skills and reputation of craftsmen, the dates of carving, peculiar modeling and the owner's status. Certainly, different people will have various views on the value of the same jade object. It is a special skill to exploit the natural color of a piece of jade to create an effective design. So the most expensive ones are not those of one single color, but those of multiple colors, the carving skillfully enhancing the different colors in an object.

For a long time, wearing jade ornaments was in fashion especially in Qing Dynasty. Those who did not wear them were considered improperly dressed, and houses without jade decorations were not considered homes. For poor and ordinary people who could not afford real jade, they would put up a few couplets that said something like "the hall shines with gold and jade." For women, jade bracelets took up most space in their jewelry boxes. Jade bracelets received as engagement and wedding gifts were as precious as today's diamond wedding rings. The Chinese describe a good marriage as a "gold and jade marriage."

There is an old Chinese saying, "Gold has a price, but jade does not. " In traditional Chinese literature, gold and jade are often mentioned together and are seen as symbols of wealth. Even today the price of high quality jade is no less than a piece of gold of the same weight.

 Words and Expressions to Learn

serpentine / 'sɜːpəntaɪn / a. 蛇状的，盘旋的

witchcraft / 'wɪtʃkrɑːft / n. 巫术

engagement / ɪnˈɡeɪdʒmənt / n. 订婚

The hall shines with gold and jade. 金玉满堂

gold and jade marriage 金玉良缘

Gold has a price, but jade does not. 黄金有价玉无价。

Part C　Exercises

I. *Make up a dialogue between a tourist and a guide about qipao according to Reading Passage 1.*

II. *Answer the following questions according to the passages.*

1. What is a qipao like? Describe it in your own words.
2. How does the collar of a Qipao display the beauty of a woman?
3. Why did ancient people bury the dead with jadeware?
4. When did jadeware technique peak?
5. What patterns are often used in Chinese jadeware?
6. What factors decide the value of a jadeware?

III. *Complete the following dialogue among a tourist (T), a guide (G) and a shop assistant (S) by translating the Chinese into English.*

T: This T-shirt is nice. I like clothes 1. ＿＿＿＿＿＿＿＿＿＿ (上面有汉字的).

G: I like them too. The ones with smaller characters are even better.

T: Exactly. Which color is the best?

G: I think the dark green one is good. (To the shop assistant.) Please show us that T-shirt.

S: 2. _____ (您需要什么尺码)?

T: Large.

S: This one is large. 3. _____ (穿上试试大小怎么样)?

T: It's OK, not too large, not too small, just right. What other colors do you have?

S: We have black and red ones, too.

T: Then give me a black one, please.

S: Sorry. 4. _____ (黑色的只有中号的).

T: Oh, 5. _____ (真遗憾)!

S: Then, how about this style? 6. _____ (我想这一款也很合适你).

T: I don't like its collar.

G: Look. These pants look nice. Feel nice, too. 7. _____ (穿上去一定很舒适).

S: 8. _____ (您的眼光真好). This is pure linen. Have a look at the cut of the pants. It's very slimming.

IV. Translate the following passage into Chinese.

Batik cloth can be made into garments, scarves, bags, tablecloths, bedspreads, curtains, and other decorative items. However, because the raw material for batik is pure cotton cloth, care must be taken in maintenance to prevent moisture and erosion. If it is bought for collection, regular exposure to the sun is requested. Batik may be washed with water at any time, but do remember not to bleach (漂 白) it or machine-wash it in case of damage to the edges. Ironing may be permissible after washing. Batik shall be kept in clean and tidy environment. If used and maintained properly, batik can make your house or office unique and inviting.

V. Translate the following passage into English.

相传春秋时,楚人卞和在荆山(今湖北南漳县)发现一块玉璞,遂将此璞献给楚厉王。然而经玉工辨认,璞被判定为石头,厉王以为卞和欺君,下令断卞和左脚,并将他赶走。武王即位,卞和又将璞玉献上,玉工仍然认为是石头,可怜卞和又因欺君之罪被砍去右足。及楚文王即位,卞和怀揣璞玉在荆山下痛哭了三天三夜,以致双眼溢血。文王听说后觉得很奇怪,派人问他:"天下被削足的人很多,为什么只有你如此悲伤?"卞和感叹道:"我并不是因为被削足而伤心,而是因为宝石被看作石头,忠贞之士被当作欺君之臣啊!"文王直接命人剖璞,结果得到了一块美玉。美玉被命名为"和氏之璧",这就是后世传说的和氏璧。过了四百多年,"和氏璧"广为人知,并落入赵王手中。秦王闻讯,表示愿用十五座城池进行交换。赵王慑于秦国威力,派蔺相如奉璧出使秦国。当蔺相如发现秦王并无诚意,他机智地夺回璧,设法带归赵国。这便是成语"价值连城"和"完璧归赵"的出典。

VI. *Topic for discussion*

What's you view on making qipao our national dress for women?

UNIT 6
Gems of Chinese Culture

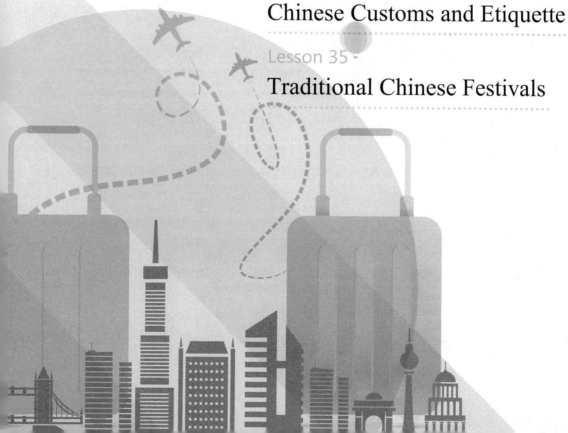

UNIT 6 Lesson 31
Chinese Operas

Part A *Conversation*

Dialogue　Talking about Chinese Operas

(T: Tourist　G: Guide)

T: Miss Li, could you tell me something about Chinese operas?

G: Sure. But why are you so interested in Chinese operas? I mean, most people from other countries find it hard to appreciate Chinese operas.

T: Oh, I used to hear my friends say Chinese operas, especially Beijing Opera, sound like a cat's cry. But the other day, I happened to watch a Chinese film *Farewell to My Concubine.* Have you heard of it?

G: Of course. It used to be very popular.

T: I found myself fascinated by the scenes of the Chinese opera. I like the music, the singing, the body movements, makeup, costumes and everything.

G: Really? The opera in that movie is Beijing Opera. And Beijing Opera is known as China's national opera.

T: Are the other operas as beautiful as Beijing Opera?

G: Beautiful or not, that depends on your taste. But each and every one of them has its own singing and acting styles.

T: Then I want to have a taste of all of them.

G: Are you kidding? There are more than 300 regional operas in our country.

T: What? More than 300? Unbelievable! Then tell me something all the operas have in common.

G: It's really hard to tell. But we can safely say all Chinese operas combine music, art and literature into one performance.

T: I can't agree more. The dialogues are all well written. Though I don't understand every word, I do recognize the smooth flow of the words and perfect rhythm and rhyme.

G: In the Yuan Dynasty, there was a literary genre called zaju, which is actually opera scripts.

T: Hmm, very interesting. And the music is so different, so Chinese.

G: That's because most Chinese operas make use of traditional Chinese musical instruments, like erhu, pipa and so on. Different instruments give the operas unique features.

T: What about the facial makeup? Do all Chinese operas have makeup?

G: Yes, but in different ways. I dare say, Beijing Opera has the most exaggerated facial makeup. Some other operas have very light makeup. But facial makeup in all operas shows the characters' personality, role and fate. People who are familiar with Chinese operas can know the story by simply looking at the facial paintings and the costumes of the characters.

T: Amazing! What about the acting styles? Is there anything in common among all the Chinese operas?

G: Yes. All acting is highly stylized. What appeals to foreigners is probably the marvelous acrobatics. In some plays, performers can make fire come out of their mouths when they act as spirits, or can gallop while squatting to act as a dwarf.

T: For me, squatting is hard enough, not to mention galloping at the same time.

G: It's no easy job for them, either. That's why there is a saying among all opera performers, "One minute's performance on stage takes ten years' practice behind the scene."

T: I can see that in the movie. The little boy suffered a lot before becoming famous.

G: What is shown in the movie is only the tip of an iceberg.

T: Besides Beijing Opera, what other operas do you recommend?

G: Kun Opera. It's a typical ancient opera with a history of 500 years. It is now listed among the World Oral and Intangible Heritage.

T: Really? It will be on my list, too.

Unfortunately, my trip in China is coming to an end, and I'm afraid I won't have enough time to go to so many opera shows.

G: You know what? I've got a good idea.

T: What is it?

G: I'll take you to a bookstore and you can pick up cassette tapes, CDs and VCDs of different Chinese operas and enjoy them anytime you want to.

T: Why didn't I think of that! Let's go!

Words and Expressions to Learn

rhythm / ˈrɪðəm / *n.* 节奏，韵律

rhyme / raɪm / *n.* 押韵

genre / ˈʒɒnrə / *n.* (文学、艺术、音乐等的)体裁，类型，样式

script / skrɪpt / *n.* 剧本

exaggerated / ɪgˈzædʒəreɪtɪd / *a.* 夸张的

stylized / ˈstaɪlaɪzd / *a.* 程式化的，格式化的

acrobatics / ækrəˈbætɪks / *n.* 杂技表演

squat / skwɒt / *v.* 蹲下

dwarf / dwɔ:f / *n.* 小矮人

***   ***   ***   ***   ***   ***

Farewell to My Concubine《霸王别姬》

have in common 共有的(特点等)

I can't agree more. 我非常同意。

appeal to sb. 吸引某人

not to mention 更别说

the World Oral and Intangible Heritage 人

类口述及非物质文化遗产

One minute's performance on stage takes ten years' practice behind the scene. 台上一分钟，台下十年功。

come to an end 结束

Part B Reading

 An Introduction to Beijing Opera

Known as China's national opera, Beijing Opera, which originated in the late 18th century, is a combination of music, dance, art and acrobatics.

Based upon traditional Anhui Opera, it has also adopted repertoire, music and performing techniques from Kun Opera and Qinqiang Opera as well as traditional folk tunes in its development, eventually forming its own highly stylized music and performing techniques. Its repertoire includes historical plays. Many historical events are adapted into Beijing Opera plays, which in the past were an important primer on history and moral principles for the people.

In ancient times, Beijing Opera was performed mostly on open-air stages in markets, streets or teahouses. The band had to play loudly and the performers had to develop a piercing style of singing, in order to be heard over the crowds. The costumes were a collection of sharply contrasting colors because the stages were dimly lit by oil lamps.

Two bands, playing string and percussion instruments, accompany the singing, which follows a fixed pattern but has a variety of tunes and rhythms. The jinghu is the backbone of the bands. The dialogues and monologues are recited in Beijing dialect, and some of the words are pronounced in a special way, unique to the opera.

The actors and actresses, in addition to singing, use well-established movements, such as smoothing a beard, adjusting a hat, jerking a sleeve or raising a foot, to express certain emotions and meanings. The hands and body trembling all over indicates extreme anger and the flicking of a sleeve expresses disgust. If an actor throws his hand above his head and flicks his sleeves back, he is astonished or surprised. An actor or actress displays embarrassment by covering his or her face with one sleeve. Some of the movements are less easily understood. An actor grasps his sleeves with a quick movement and then promptly puts his hands behind his back in a decisive manner to show that he is bracing himself for some danger to come. Sometimes a movement can go on for as long as 20 seconds. For example, while an actor is trying to make a plan, his fingers and hands flutter nervously at his sides, and when the plan is finally made, he just strikes his fist against the palm of the other hand with a loud smack. When worried, the actor will rub his hands together for several seconds. Beijing Opera's acrobatic fighting, whether between two parties or in a crowd, is a skillful combination of martial arts and acting.

There are four main roles in Beijing Opera: sheng, dan, jing and chou. Each role has its fixed singing and acting styles.

"Sheng" is the leading male actor and is divided into "laosheng", who wears beard and represents an old man, "xiaosheng", who represents a young man, "wusheng", who is a military man or a fighter, and "wawasheng" who plays a kid. These roles usually wear no facial paintings. "Hongsheng", another category of "sheng" whose face is painted red, mainly plays "Guan Yu" or "Zhao Kuangyin", the founder of Song Dynasty.

"Dan" refers to the female role. It is divided into many categories. "Laodan" is an old lady while "caidan" a female comedian. "Wudan" usually plays the role of a military or non-military woman capable of martial arts. The most important category, "qingyi" usually plays the role of a respectable and decent lady in elegant costume. "Huadan" represents a lively and clever young girl, usually in short costume.

"Jing", mostly male, is the face-painted role who represents a warrior, hero, statesman, adventurer or demon.

"Chou" refers to a clown who is characterized by a white patch on the nose. Usually white patches of different shapes and sizes mean roles of different characters. They are not definitely rascals, while most of the time they play roles of wit, alert and humor. It is these characters who keep the audience laughing and make up quips at the right moments to ease tension in some serious plays.

The special art of facial painting in Chinese operas has different origins. But no matter what its origin is, the facial painting is worth appreciating for its artistic value. The paintings are presentations of the characters' personalities. For example, a red face usually shows the role's bravery, uprightness and loyalty; a white face symbolizes a sinister role's treachery; a green face describes stubbornness, and lack of self-control. In addition, the pattern of the facial painting reveals the role's information too. In a word, the unique makeup in the opera allows the characters on the stage to reveal themselves voicelessly.

The costumes are based on those of Ming Dynasty, no matter when the story is set. The props can include a cloth wall, tents, whips, paddles, weapons and so on. The props are realistic, and simple so as not to attract the audience from the performance. Exaggeration and symbolism are characteristics of the opera. Holding a whip is enough to indicate an actor galloping on a horse. A few soldiers on the stage may represent a whole army. An actor circling the stage suggests a long journey. Often there are just a table and a few chairs on the stage. The description of many situations depends on the performance of the actors and actresses. Opening a door, walking at night, rowing a boat, eating, drinking and the like are all demonstrated by the stylized movements of the actors and actresses. Performers also use their eyes and facial expressions to help express specific meanings.

Beijing Opera represents an important part of Chinese culture and has become a refined form of art as a result of the hard work of hundreds of artists over the centuries.

 Words and Expressions to Learn

repertoire / ˈrepətwɑː / n. (可演出的全部)剧目，曲目

primer / ˈpraɪmə / n. 初级读本，入门书

piercing / ˈpɪəsɪŋ / a. 刺耳的，尖声的

monologue / ˈmɒnəlɒɡ / n. 独白

jerk / dʒɜːk / v. 急拉，猛一拉

flick / flɪk / v. 颤动，轻拂，轻弹

embarrassment / ɪmˈbærəsmənt / n. 尴尬，窘迫

flutter / ˈflʌtə / v. 晃动，使快速不规则地动

smack / smæk / n. 噼啪声

comedian / kəˈmiːdɪən / n. 喜剧演员，滑稽角色

demon / ˈdiːmən / n. 恶魔

rascal / ˈrɑːskəl / n. 恶棍

alert / əˈlɜːt / n. 警戒

quip / kwɪp / n. 妙语，俏皮话

sinister / ˈsɪnɪstə / a. 阴险的，邪恶的

treachery / ˈtretʃərɪ / n. 欺诈，背信弃义

stubbornness / ˈstʌbənɪs / n. 固执

prop / prɒp / n. (戏剧)道具

***   ***   ***   ***   ***   ***

be adapted into 被改编成

string and percussion instruments 弦乐器和打击乐器

jinghu 京胡

brace oneself for 使防备，使经受锻炼

sheng, dan, jing and chou 生、旦、净、丑

a refined form of art 一种精炼的艺术形式

Passage 2   Huangmei Opera

Huangmei Opera was formed in the 18th century, when Chinese local operas were flourishing. Originally it was a combination of local folk songs, dances and some widely spread ancient operas. Bordering on Anhui Province, Huangmei in Hubei is a county famous for its tea and tea-picking songs, from which Huangmei Opera got its original name, "tea-picking tunes" or "tea-picking opera".

Before 1949, rivers and lakes often flooded, and the victims had to seek refuge in neighboring provinces. Thus Hubei's Huangmei Opera was brought to Anhui by victims of flood and famine. It developed from folk tunes to short operas and complete dramas. Nowadays, the lively short operas are still performed frequently. Even "big plays" are almost always about folk life. The performers manage to infuse simple humor into plays, so that audiences see a realistic way of life.

From the time when Huangmei Opera earned its initial popularity in the countryside, it had a long way to go to become professional performances in the cities. It began as a diversion acted by and for peasants and artisans, usually at festivals and on special occasions.

As time went by, seasonal, semi-professional groups appeared, and they had to perform together with groups specializing in more popular forms like Beijing Opera and Anhui Opera. Not until 1926, 140 years after its appearance, did the Huangmei Opera manage to reach Anqing, then the capital of Anhui Province. It appeared in Shanghai in 1934, but only on the cheap stages of the city's poor quarters, where it was regarded as "bawdy entertainment" and where its unfortunate performers were harried by the local authorities.

Since 1949, with the support of the government, Huangmei Opera has bloomed like a wildflower. In particular, the Anhui Provincial Huangmei Opera Troupe's *The Heavenly Maid and the Mortal* opened a new page in its history. Though the play was a traditional favorite, the troupe revised the script, music and makeup.

The moving plot, beautiful music and excellent singing made the play a household word. It was filmed in 1956, when there were few opera films, and gave 150,000 domestic showings, also traveling to a dozen or so places abroad, so that the little-known wildflower became a masterpiece admired by thousands.

The music of Huangmei Opera is its essential attraction. Three kinds of music are used: coloratura, character songs and basic tunes. The 104 coloratura tunes are taken from folk songs, tea-picking songs and other ditties. A short opera usually has its own features, which may owe most of its popularity to the tune. The music of Huangmei Opera is light and lyrical, so a good performer must be expert in this style. Singing is not only the main approach to characterization but also makes Huangmei Opera different stylistically and musically.

Huangmei Opera is easy to understand and learn, thanks to its lyrical tunes, simple words and literary tradition. Like other Chinese local operas, Huangmei Opera also used local dialect of Huangmei and Anqing, where the opera originated and matured. The language is a mixture of northern and southern dialects and therefore easy for others to imitate while remaining pleasant to native ears. This was conducive to the spread of Huangmei Opera. Its local flavor and folk style are most vividly revealed in its original and lively dialogue, both spoken and sung. Passionate, natural and simple, Huangmei Opera is an enduring drama appreciated by all.

During the First China Shakespeare Festival in 1986, audiences both home and abroad watched with great interest an adaptation of Shakespeare's *Much Ado about Nothing* presented by the Anhui Provincial Huangmei Opera Troupe. Former British Prime Minister Margaret Thatcher sent a message of congratulations to Cao Yu, chairman of the Chinese Dramatists' Association, saying that Shakespeare would have been greatly amused by the imaginative representation.

 Words and Expressions to Learn ···

victim / ˈvɪktɪm / *n.* 受害者

refuge / ˈrefjuːdʒ / *n.* 避难所

famine / ˈfæmɪn / *n.* 饥荒

infuse / ɪnˈfjuːz / *v.* 注入，把……融入

initial / ɪˈnɪʃəl / *a.* 最初的，开始的

diversion / daɪˈvɜːʃən / *n.* 消遣，娱乐

artisan / ˌɑːtɪˈzæn / *n.* 工匠，手艺人

bawdy / ˈbɔːdɪ / *a.* 猥亵的，不入流的

harry / ˈhærɪ / *v.* 使苦恼，不断烦扰

coloratura / ˌkɒlərəˈtjʊərə / *n.* (声乐中的)花腔，华彩

ditty / ˈdɪtɪ / *n.* 短歌，小调

lyrical / ˈlɪrɪkəl / *a.* 抒情诗般的，热情奔放的

adaptation / ˌædəpˈteɪʃən / *n.* 改编

***　　***　　***　　***　　***　　***

border on 与……接壤，毗邻

specialize in 专门从事

The Heavenly Maid and the Mortal《天仙配》

a household word 家喻户晓的人或事物

thanks to 由于，幸亏

be conducive to 有利于，有助于

Shakespeare 莎士比亚

Much Ado about Nothing《无事生非》

Margaret Thatcher 撒彻尔夫人(英国前首相)

the Chinese Dramatists' Association 中国剧作家协会

I. *Make up a dialogue between a tourist and a guide about Huangmei Opera according to Reading Passage 2.*

II. *Complete the following dialogue by translating the Chinese into English.*

(T: Tourist   G: Guide)

T: I really can not bear the singing style of Beijing Opera. 1. _____ (演员们为什么要这么尖声地唱呢)? Can't they sing just like the pop singers?

G: 2. _____ (这 与 它 的 起 源 有 关). In ancient times, the opera was usually performed in the open air, and the band had to play loudly and the performers had to sing that way so that the crowd could hear them.

T: That makes sense. 3. _____ (我猜他们色彩鲜艳的戏装也是用来吸引观众注意力的吧).

G: That's one purpose. Another reason is the dim light on the stage of night performance. 4. _____ (对比强烈的颜色使观众更容易看清演出).

T: Hmm. What confuses me most is the makeup. Some have red faces, some white or even black and green ones. Does the makeup mean anything?

G: Definitely. 5. _____ (不同颜色的面部油彩代表人物的不同性格). For example, red shows bravery, white displays cunning while black means honesty. 6. _____ (总而言之，戏剧里的化妆无声地揭示剧中的人物角色)。

T: That's interesting! And actually, I went to a Beijing Opera show the other night with a friend here. 7. _____ (我发现不同的人物演唱和表演都不一样).

G: You are a very keen observer. Indeed, there are generally four role types in Beijing Opera: sheng, dan, jing and chou.

T: Sheng, dan, jing and chou? What are they?

G: 8. _____ (它们是用来代表不同角色类型的特殊用语). Sheng is the male role, dan is the female, jing is the painted face role, usually male and chou is the clown. 9. _____ (每种角色类型都有自己独特的化妆及固定的演唱和表演风格).

T: I see. It is amazing you know so much about Beijing Opera!

G: Oh, that is because both my parents are "piaoyou" and I have heard enough to still remember this little.

T: "Piaoyou? " What is that?

G: 10. _____ (它是我们中国人用来表示非职业京剧演唱和表演

者的一个词).

T: Now I have learnt enough to show off in front of my friends.

III. *Decide whether the following statements are true or false according to the dialogue and passages.*

1. There are about 800 kinds of local operas in China, each with unique features and regional flavors.

2. Operas were a literary genre instead of a performing art in Yuan Dynasty.

3. Chinese operas combine music, fashion, acting and literature into one art form.

4. The characteristics of Beijing Opera can best be summarized by the words "exaggeration and symbolism".

5. Originally Huangmei Opera was a combination of folk songs and dances in Anhui Province.

6. The early Huangmei Opera plays were about tea-picking and thus got the name "tea-picking tunes".

7. It has been a long, difficult but successful struggle for Huangmei Opera to achieve national fame and even international recognition.

IV. *Match the movements in Beijing Opera listed in Column A with a suitable explanation in Column B.*

1.

A	B
Gestures	Meaning
1. Hands and body trembling all over	a. great surprise
2. Flicking of a sleeve	b. embarrassment
3. Hand above head and flicking sleeves back	c. disgust
4. Covering face with one sleeve	d. extreme anger
5. Grasping sleeves and putting hands behind his back	e. preparing for the coming danger
6. Fingers and hands fluttering at sides	f. worrying about something
7. Rubbing hands	g. a decision or plan made
8. Smashing a fist into the palm of the other hand	h. conceiving a plan

2.

A		B
Role Types		Representation

1. 老生   a. young men

2. 小生   b. kids

3. 武生   c. military men and fighters

4. 娃娃生   d. decent young ladies

5. 红生   e. warriors, heroes or demons with painted face

6. 老旦   f. female comedians

7. 彩旦   g. rascals, roles of wit and humor

8. 武旦   h. old men with beard

9. 青衣   i. Guan Yu or Zhao Kuangyin

10. 花旦   j. clever young girls

11. 净角   k. military women

12. 丑角   l. old ladies

V. Translate the following passage into English.

Kun Opera, also called "Kunshanqiang" or "Kunqu", originated in the Kunshan region of Jiangsu Province. It is one of China's classical operas, with a history of more than 500 years. Kun Opera has a complete system of acting as well as its own distinctive tunes. Its wide-ranging repertoire has many delicate and elegant tunes. The orchestra consists of traditional instruments including the dizi, a horizontal bamboo flute which plays the lead part; xiao, a vertical bamboo flute; sheng, a mouth organ and pipa, a plucked string instrument. Many Chinese local operas are greatly influenced by its tunes and acting styles.

VI. Topics for discussion.

1. Traditional Chinese operas including Beijing Opera are a precious component of Chinese culture, but they are losing favor with the younger generation. Fewer and fewer young people want to learn them or even listen to them. Why is this happening? What can be done to stop Chinese operas from dying out?

2. What local operas do you happen to know? Introduce it/them to your classmates.

UNIT **6** Lesson 32
Chinese Martial Arts

Part **A** *Conversation*

Dialogue   Talking about Chinese Kung Fu

(T: Tourist   G: Guide   Y: Yang, the Guide's Friend)

(At a teahouse.)

G: This is my friend Yang, and this is Mr. Smith from the US.

T: Nice to meet you.

Y: Nice to meet you, too.

G: Yang, Mr. Smith is very interested in Chinese Kung Fu. Could you tell us something about it?

Y: This is a very big topic, but I'll try my best.

T: Thank you. Please tell me who created Kung Fu.

Y: Like many other elements of Chinese cultural heritage, no one knows exactly who created it. And I doubt if its creation should be attributed to one single person.

T: Fair enough. Then what are the basic movements and stances of Chinese Kung Fu?

Y: Generally, there are four techniques believed to apply to all styles of Kung Fu: kicking, striking, throwing and controlling.

T: Kicking is easy to understand. But what are the other three?

Y: Kicking actually also includes tripping. Striking involves all parts of the body — hands, head, elbows, shoulders, and even hips can all attack.

T: That's interesting! Does throwing mean to throw your weapons at the opponent?

Y: Not exactly. Throwing refers to the technique of wrestling, grappling and so on to down an opponent.

T: I see. Controlling is a rather general term. What does it mean here?

Y: It includes joint locks, tendon or muscle stretching, striking on nerve points and the obstruction of breath or blood flow.

T: Wow, that sounds very "lihai". Then what are the standards for judging the performance of a practitioner?

Y: The performance is usually judged by the quality of eight aspects, namely hands, eyes, body techniques, steps, spirit, breath, strength and ability.

T: Could you please explain them a little?

Y: Sure. Briefly the practitioner's hands should move like lightning and can stop dead suddenly; the eyes should be alert and alive following the hands; the body must be agile; steps must be steady with both feet always stuck to the ground.

G: Mind you, it is hard enough to move that fast, not to mention to keep steady.

T: I totally agree. Then the performer should also be high-spirited, hold his breath and make full use of his strength to display his Kung Fu abilities?

Y: Your explanation for spirit is good enough. As to breath, it is called "qi" and it refers to the proper regulation of breath and it will help produce explosive force. Strength in Kung Fu is different from that in weight-lifting.

T: Strength is strength, and how can it be different?

Y: Kung Fu practitioners can focus the body's strength on a small area of application. For example, to exercise a thrusting punch, the ground is the base of power which goes from the feet and is aligned through knees, hips, waist, spine, shoulders and elbows to the hand. This linked support of the entire body enables the performer to "focus" the power of the ground and produce a force greater than he uses brute strength.

T: I see. Then what is ability?

Y: It is a general term for strength, speed, endurance, agility, coordination and technical skills put together.

G: Actually, we have a song which can best sum up a Kung Fu practitioner's stances.

T: Really? Sing for me please.

G: (Sings in Chinese.) 卧似一张弓,站似一棵松,不动不摇坐如钟,走路一阵风。南拳和北腿,少林武当功,太极八卦连环掌,中华有神功。棍扫一大片,枪挑一条线,身轻好似云中燕,豪气冲云天。外练筋骨皮,内练一口气,刚柔并济不低头,心中有天地。

T: That's a beautiful song. Can you teach me later?

G: No problem.

T: Then how long will it take a beginner to become a Kung Fu master?

G: All your life. Many Kung Fu movies and TV series are about the fierce competition among the Kung Fu masters to be number one but there will never be one.

Y: That's very true. As one of your sayings goes, practice makes perfect. But perfection doesn't exist in this world, so practice is an endless process.

T: Very philosophical. Thank you so much for answering all my questions.

Y: And thank you for your tea.

 Words and Expressions to Learn

stance / stɑːns / *n.* 站姿

trip / trɪp / *v.* 绊，绊倒

opponent / əˈpəʊnənt / *n.* 对手

grapple / ˈɡræpl / *v.* 抓牢

tendon / ˈtendən / *n.* 筋，腱

obstruction / əbˈstrʌkʃən / *n.* 阻塞，阻断

agile / ˈædʒaɪl / *a.* 敏捷的，灵活的

regulation / reɡjʊˈleɪʃən / *n.* 控制，调节

explosive / ɪkˈspləʊsɪv / *a.* 爆发性的

align / əˈlaɪn / *v.* 使成一直线

brute / bruːt / *a.* 野蛮的，蛮劲十足的

coordination / kəʊɔːdɪˈneɪʃən / *n.* 协调（力）

philosophical / fɪləˈsɒfɪkəl / *a.* 有哲理的

***   ***   ***   ***   ***   ***

be attributed to 归功于

Fair enough. 说得对。/ 有道理。

get ... wrong 把……弄错了

joint locks 扣住关节以控制他人

strike on nerve points 点穴

stop dead 戛然而止，突然停止

Mind you ... 请注意，说真的……

Part **B** Reading

| Passage 1 | Chinese Kung Fu Overview |

Chinese Kung Fu (Martial Arts or Wushu) is a series of fighting styles, born and developed in China and is now gaining increasing popularity and even stands as a representative for Chinese culture. Over centuries of development, Kung Fu has become a large system containing various schools or sects with over 300 distinct types of boxing. Generally speaking, they can be divided into two basic groups: those using internal energy or Qi as the primary source of power for movement and those using external energy i.e. muscle power.

Chinese Kung Fu learning is becoming more and more popular among people of different ages and nationalities. Now, Kung Fu is learnt and practiced for self-defense as well as its value in body-building and fitness keeping.

Kung Fu training includes basic skills, routines, weapon handling and some fighting stunts, among which the practice of internal and external skills are the most important. All the basic themes taught by different schools are similar: the basic external training of hands, eyes, body, stances, steps and coordination as well as internal training of energy, spirit, breath and strength.

A strong will and persistence are the preconditions for learning. One should follow a master or join a training school to learn systematically. The basic skills of legs, waist, shoulders and stance training need to be practiced daily. After acquiring a solid foundation of the basic skills, one can choose from various sects specific routines of boxing, kicking and weapon skills to improve the combat ability.

Although being fighting styles, Kung Fu advocates virtue and peace, not aggression or violence. This has been the common value upheld by martial artists from generation to generation.

 Words and Expressions to Learn

routine / ruːˈtiːn / n. 固定动作，套路
stunt / stʌnt / n. 绝技，绝招
precondition / ˌpriːkənˈdɪʃən / n. 先决条件，前提
systematically / ˌsɪstəˈmætɪkəlɪ / ad. 系统地

acquire / əˈkwaɪə / v. 获得，学到
combat / ˈkɒmbət / n. 格斗，战斗
advocate / ˈædvəkeɪt / v. 提倡，主张
aggression / əˈgreʃən / n. 侵犯，攻击
uphold / ʌpˈhəʊld / v. 支持，拥护

Passage 2 Tai Chi

Tai chi, or taijiquan, is a wonderful branch of Chinese martial arts with a long history. It is now practiced for both its defense function and its health benefits.

According to the philosophy of Tai Chi, when one meets brute force with brute force, both sides are to be injured. Tai Chi teaches people not to resist an incoming force, but to meet it with softness and follow its motion while remaining in physical contact until the incoming force of attack exhausts itself or is safely redirected. Meeting *yang* with *yin* in combat, or in other aspects of our life, is a primary goal of tai chi training.

With the accelerating pace of our life, Tai Chi has become a good way for people to relieve their pressure and stress. In practice, you need to focus your mind solely on the movements of your limbs and the flow of your breath and energy inside your body. This brings about a state of mental calm and clarity, which can improve people's overall physical functions and health. Nowadays, you can find people, young and old, male and female, amateur and professional, practicing Tai Chi in parks or squares at any time of the day.

Besides its benefits to health, Tai Chi is also an effective way of self-defense. The physical techniques of Tai Chi are characterized by the use of leverage through the joints. Force in Tai Chi lies in coordination and relaxation, rather than muscular tension and it is used to neutralize, yield or initiate attacks. Slow, repetitive practice is the necessary process of learning how the leverage is generated and gently and measurably increases. Tai Chi training involves five elements, *taolu* (solo hand and weapon routines), *neigong* and *qigong* (meditation, breathing and awareness exercises), *tuishou* (response drills) and *sanshou* (self-defense techniques). While Tai Chi is typified by some with slow movements, many styles, including the three most popular: Chen, Yang and Wu, do have secondary forms with faster pace.

The ability to use Tai Chi in self-defense or in combat is the test of a practitioner's understanding of the art. Tai Chi requires proper responses to outside forces — yielding and sticking to an incoming attack rather than meeting it with opposing force. The use of Tai Chi as a martial art is quite challenging and requires a great deal of training.

Defeating the hard with the soft, involving both physical training and mind cultivating, being proper for old and young, Tai Chi is the most popular health training sport in the 21st century. It has spread to more than 150 countries and regions among a population of more than 2 billion. Tai Chi is a physical and mental discipline. Practice

Tai Chi daily and supplement your practice with lessons with a qualified instructor until this slow and controlled repetition has become part of your life, then you will get all and unexpected benefits from this wonderful martial art form.

 Words and Expressions to Learn ·····················

exhaust / ɪgˈzɔːst / v. 排空，耗尽
redirect / ˌriːdɪˈrekt / v. 使改变方向
accelerate / ækˈseləreɪt / v. 加速，加快
clarity / ˈklærətɪ / n. 清晰，清醒
amateur / ˈæmətə / a. 业余的
leverage / ˈliːvərɪdʒ / n. 杠杆作用

neutralize / ˈnjuːtrəlaɪz / v. 使中和，抵消
yield / jiːld / v. 产生
initiate / ɪˈnɪʃɪeɪt / v. 发动，开始
measurably / ˈmeʒərəblɪ / ad. 显著地
secondary / ˈsekəndərɪ / a. 次要的，辅助的
challenging / ˈtʃælɪndʒɪŋ / a. 挑战性的

***　　***　　***　　***　　***　　***

bring about 带来，产生
be characterized by 以……为特征
muscular tension 肌肉收缩，肌肉紧张

be typified with 以……为象征
supplement … with … 用……补充……

Part C Exercises ··········

I. *Make up a brief dialogue between a tourist and a guide about Chinese martial arts according to the passages.*

II. *Answer the following questions according to the passages.*

1. Generally speaking, how do people classify the various Kung Fu schools and sects?
2. What does Kung Fu training emphasize?
3. What are the necessary conditions if a person wants to learn Kung Fu well?
4. Should one choose a specific sect and routine to learn from the beginning? Why?
5. What is the common value held by martial artists?
6. Why do people now practice Tai Chi?
7. What is a main purpose of Tai Chi training?
8. How does Tai Chi help to relieve people's pressure and stress?
9. What are the characteristics of force in Tai Chi?
10. Why do we say Tai Chi is the most popular health training sport in the 21st century?

III. Fill in the blanks with a proper preposition.

In a fight, if one uses hardness to resist violent force then both sides are certain to be injured, at least 1. _____ some degree. Such injury, according to Tai Chi theory, is a natural consequence of meeting brute force 2. _____ brute force. The collision of two like forces, yang with yang, is known 3. _____ "double-weighted" in Tai Chi terminology. Instead, students are taught not to fight or resist an incoming force, but to meet it with softness and "stick" 4. _____ it, following its motion while remaining 5. _____ physical contact until the incoming force 6. _____ attack exhausts itself or can be safely redirected, the result 7. _____ meeting yang with yin. Done correctly, achieving this yin/yang or yang/yin balance in combat (and, 8. _____ extension, other areas of one's life) is known as being "single-weighted" and is a primary goal of Tai Chi training. Laozi provided the archetype (原型，典型) 9. _____ this in the Daodejing when he wrote, "The soft and the pliable will defeat the hard and strong." This soft "neutralization" of an attack can be accomplished very quickly in an actual fight 10. _____ an adept practitioner.

IV. Translate the following passage into Chinese.

Throughout every aspect of nature, there are always two counterparts. When these two counterparts are in balance, the nature is then in perfect harmony. In Chinese culture, the theory of yin and yang pair is used most often to describe this. For every plus there exists a minus, for hotness there exists coldness, for darkness there must be brightness, and for every good there exists evil. Of course, this is an oversimplification of qigong. Its depth and complexity could fill volumes of book, and could take centuries for scholars to fully understand it just by reading it. Therefore, it is definitely something that should be experienced, rather than only read about.

V. Read the passage below and have a discussion about the following topics.

A new study testing Tai Chi for its ability to increase immune function in healthy older adults was performed at UCLA (加利福尼亚大学洛杉矶分校) and the results were reported in the April 2007 edition of *Journal of the American Geriatrics Society*. The study involved 112 adults between the ages of 59 and 86.The researchers divided participants (参加者) into two groups — one receiving health education and the other receiving instruction in Tai Chi for 16 weeks. The researchers were interested in evaluating (评价) whether or not Tai Chi could actually improve immune function. They checked this by vaccinating (接种疫苗) all the participants against shingles (带状疱疹) at the end of the 16-week period. The vaccination allowed researchers a safe way to look at how well the participants mounted an immune response to the challenge of the vaccine.

It turned out that participants who received Tai Chi classes mounted a faster and stronger immune response. This suggests the "readiness" of the immune system was improved by instruction in Tai Chi — a claim that the Chinese have made for years — and now have some hard evidence to back it up. But there was more to the Tai Chi benefit than just immune readiness. The study also evaluated participants on several aspects of mental and physical health. While both the Tai Chi and the Health Education classes improved many measures, the Tai Chi students fared better. They showed improvements on a depression test, general physical functioning, vitality, body pain and general mental health.

This is another fascinating study uncovering the benefits of mental and physical activity on measures of body and brain fitness.

1. Comment on the findings of the study mentioned in the passage and give other evidence and proof if possible.

2. More and more foreigners are coming to our country to learn Chinese martial arts. Should this practice be limited or encouraged? Why?

3. With the rising popularity of Chinese Kung Fu come an increasing number of fake Kung Fu masters. They cheat and hurt people, causing damages to the credit of Chinese Kung Fu. What should our government and Kung Fu practitioners do to stop it?

UNIT 6

Lesson 33
Traditional Chinese Medicine

Part A Conversation

Dialogue About Guasha

(G: Guide   T: Tourist   D: Doctor)

G: Are you feeling OK? You look tired and pale.

T: Nothing serious. My back is aching again. This is an old problem. I've been living with it for several years. Sometimes I can't even fall asleep at night.

G: That's too bad. Do you want to see a doctor about it?

T: Don't bother. I'll go to the nearby pharmacy for some plasters.

G: I know you guys might not trust Chinese medicines. But I do believe it is better to hear what a Chinese doctor has to say and then decide whether to buy the plasters or not.

T: Hmm, OK. Would you please go with me?

G: Of course.

(In the hospital, with T lying on the bed and D feeling his back.)

D: I can see you have had this back problem for quite some time.

T: Yes. But how do you know?

D: Your back muscles feel very tense and some parts are as hard as stones. For example, here.

T: Ouch! That really hurts! How can muscles harden?

D: There are many causes of it. But the hardening means stagnant qi and bad blood circulation. And you are also suffering hyperplasia, but not very serious. OK, you can get up now.

T: Then what now?

D: You need two sessions of Guasha treatment.

T: Guasha? It sounds so familiar. Oh, I remember, I once saw a movie by that title.

G: You have seen that movie?

T: Yes. But that's several years ago. It is about the misunderstanding of Guasha, a traditional Chinese medical treatment, is it?

G: Yes. Because Guasha treatment leaves red and even dark red marks on the patient, the American authorities regard the boy in the movie abused and take him away from his family.

T: Yes, yes, I remember now. But does Guasha hurt? The red marks on the boy look terrible as if he has been whipped.

D: It doesn't hurt at all. Some of my patients fall asleep during the treatment.

T: Really? Then how can it cure anything that way?

D: The small red spot caused by the treatment is called "sha". Raising "sha" removes blood stagnation, promoting normal circulation and metabolism.

T: It's still beyond me.

D: See this tool for Guasha? It's round-edged and so it won't hurt. When I scrape your back with it, it pushes a build-up of fluid ahead of it and after it passes, it leaves a vacuum behind and this vacuum draws toxic fluid out to the skin surface from deep within the tissues. When it floods to the surface it appears as small red or deep purple spots, that is "sha". "Sha" is a sign that toxins are being released.

T: I see. How will I feel when "sha" appears on my back?

D: Usually you will feel kind of hot where there is "sha".

T: Only this?

D: Only this.

T: Then will "sha" disappear?

D: Yes, in 3 to 5 days.

T: But I have had this back pain for quite some years, can Guasha really ...

G: Why not have a try? It's much better than taking medicine, anyway.

T: Yes, why not?

(D puts some Guasha oil on T's back.)

T: What's the liquid for?

D: Oh, this is Guasha oil. It contains some healing herbs and essential oil to help the extraction of the toxic waste.

G: Does it hurt you?

T: Not at all. Is there any "sha" appearing on my back?

G: It's so red after only several scrapes.

D: That means there is too much toxic waste in your body.

(Minutes later.)

D: OK. It's done. Get up and see how you feel now.

T: Amazing! I feel like a heavy burden taken off my back. So light, so relaxed. I can't believe it!

D: You have to come back for a follow-up treatment three days later.

T: Sure. Fortunately we'll stay here for another five days. By the way, doctor, is Guasha effective with other diseases?

D: Yes. Guasha can be used to treat almost any disease or disorder. It can even help relieve stress. The best thing is that it has no side effects at all.

T: Wonderful! I'll definitely spread the news to all my family and friends. Thank you so much, doctor.

D: It's my pleasure.

 Words and Expressions to Learn

pharmacy / 'fɑːməsɪ / *n.* 药房

plaster / 'plæstə / *n.* 膏药

ouch / aʊtʃ / *int.* 哎呀

stagnant / 'stægnənt / *a.* 不流动的，呆滞的

hyperplasia / ˌhaɪpə'pleɪzɪə / *n.* 增生

session / 'seʃən / *n.* 一段时间，时间段

abuse / ə'bjuːs / *v.* 虐待

fluid / 'fluːɪd / *n.* 流体，体液

vacuum / 'vækjʊəm / *n.* 真空

toxic / 'tɒksɪk / *a.* 有毒的，毒素的

extraction / ɪk'strækʃən / *n.* 抽出，拔出，导出

***   ***   ***   ***   ***   ***

live with sth. 长期忍受……

sth. be beyond sb. 某人无法理解某事

kind of 或多或少，有点

essential oil 精油

Traditional Chinese Medicine (TCM) is an integral part of Chinese culture. The main forms of modern TCM can be traced back 2,500 years.

The basic theories of traditional Chinese medicine arise through the concepts of yin, yang and qi. Yin and yang is a pair of complicated philosophical concepts. Yin literally translates as "in the shade", and is considered to represent darkness, the moon, coldness and passivity. Yang, "in the sunlight", on the other hand, represents brightness, the sun, heat and activity. A healthy body depends on the balance of yin and yang, and all diseases result from an imbalance of yin and yang. When these two forces are in balance, whether it occurs in a meal, in a person or in nature, harmony and equilibrium are achieved. From this comes the idea of a free-flowing energy of life — qi, which exists in living people but cannot (as yet!) be pinpointed in the laboratory. Blood, or xue in Chinese, is a term that refers to the material basis of qi or the body itself. Keep in mind this use of the word blood is different from the understanding of blood as it is used in modern medicine. From the interaction of these four ideas, yin, yang, qi and xue comes much of our understanding of health according to TCM.

TCM diagnoses are based on overall observation of symptoms. There are four types of TCM diagnostic methods: observe (望 wàng), hear and smell (闻 wén), ask about background (问 wèn) and feel the pulse (切 qiè). Then a diagnosis is made using a system to classify the symptoms. TCM requires skills in a range of diagnostic systems not commonly used outside of TCM. The diagnostic techniques include: palpation of the patient's radial artery pulse in six positions; observation of the patient's tongue; observation of the patient's face; palpation of the patient's body (especially the abdomen) for tenderness; listening to the patient's voice; observation of the surface of the ear; observation of the vein on the index finger of small children; comparisons of the relative warmth or coolness of different parts of the body and anything else that can be observed without instruments and without harming the patient.

As for the TCM treatment techniques, historically, they include eight branches:

tuina, the Chinese massage therapy, acupuncture and moxibustion, Chinese herbal medicine, Chinese food therapy, qigong and related breathing and meditation exercise, taiji and other Chinese martial arts, fengshui and Chinese astrology. Today, all methods except fengshui and Chinese astrology are routinely used as part of TCM treatments. Within each branch, specific treatment methods exist. For example, cupping and guasha come under the heading of tuina. Auriculotherapy comes under the heading of acupuncture and moxibustion.

Today both TCM and Western medicine are used in providing medical and health services in China. What is now TCM is an enormously rich resource, with literally thousands of years of experience, as refined by the intense thought, analysis and practice of some of the most intelligent human beings there have ever been.

 Words and Expressions to Learn ·······························

integral / ˈɪntɪɡrəl / *a.* 不可或缺的
arise / əˈraɪz / *v.* 出现，发生
equilibrium / ˌiːkwɪˈlɪbriəm / *n.* 平衡，均衡
pinpoint / ˈpɪnpɔɪnt / *v.* 为……准确定位，准确找出或描述
diagnostic / ˌdaɪəɡˈnɒstɪk / *a.* 诊断的，用于诊

断的
palpation / pælˈpeɪʃən / *n.* 触，摸
abdomen / ˈæbdəmən / *n.* 肚子，腹部
astrology / əˈstrɒlədʒɪ / *n.* 占星术
cupping / ˈkʌpɪŋ / *n.* 拔火罐
auriculotherapy / ɔːˌrɪkjʊləˈθerəpɪ / *n.* 耳烛疗法

***   ***   ***   ***   ***   ***

radial artery pulse 放射状的动脉脉搏
index finger 食指

acupuncture and moxibustion 针灸

Passage 2   Chinese Herbology

Herbology is one of the most important parts of Traditional Chinese Medicine. It is the art of combining medicinal herbs. Each herbal medicine prescription is a mixture of many herbs suited to the individual patient. One batch of herbs is typically decocted twice over the course of one hour. The practitioner usually designs a remedy using one or two main ingredients that target the illness. Then the practitioner adds many other ingredients to adjust the formula to the patient's yin yang conditions.

Sometimes, ingredients are needed to cancel out side effects of the main ingredients. Some herbs require the use of other ingredients as catalyst or else the prescription is ineffective. The latter steps require great experience and knowledge, and make the difference between a good Chinese herbal doctor and a common one. Unlike Western medications, the balance and interaction of all the ingredients are considered more important than the effect of individual ingredients. A key to success in TCM is the treatment of each patient as an individual.

Chinese herbology often includes ingredients from all parts of plants, leaf, stem, flower, root, and also ingredients from animals and minerals. The use of parts of endangered species has created controversy. Most herbal manufacturers have stopped the use of parts from rare animals.

Chinese herbs have been used for centuries. Legend has it that the first Chinese herbalist is Shennong, who is said to have tasted hundreds of herbs and passed his knowledge of medicinal and poisonous plants to the people. The first book on Chinese medicine, *the Shennongbencaojing*, lists some 365 medicines of which 252 are herbs, and dates back somewhere during early Han Dynasty. Later generations further developed this work, and the most important of these was said to be *The Compendium of Materia Medica* by Li Shizhen during Ming Dynasty, which is still used today for reference.

Chinese physicians use several different methods to classify traditional Chinese herbs:

The Four Natures. This relates to the degree of yin and yang, ranging from cold (extreme yin), cool, to warm and hot (extreme yang). The patient's internal balance of yin and yang is taken into account when the herbs are selected. For example, medicinal herbs of yang nature are used when the person is suffering from internal cold that requires to be purged, or when the patient has a general cold. Sometimes an ingredient is added to balance the extreme effect of one herb.

The Five Tastes. The five tastes are pungent, sweet, sour, bitter and salty, each of which has its own functions and characteristics. For example, pungent herbs are used to generate sweat and to direct and strengthen qi and the blood. Sweet-tasting herbs often harmonize bodily systems. Some sweet-tasting herbs also exhibit a bland taste, which helps drain dampness. Sour taste most often is astringent, while bitter taste dispels heat, purges the bowels and gets rid of dampness by drying them out. Salty taste softens hard masses as well as purges and opens the bowels.

The Meridians. The Meridians refer to which organs the herb acts upon. For example, menthol is pungent, cool and is linked with the lungs and the liver. Since the lungs are the organ which protects the body from invasion from cold and influenza, menthol can help purge coldness in the lungs and invading heat toxins caused by hot "wind".

 Words and Expressions to Learn

herbology / hɜːˈbɒlədʒɪ / *n.* 草药(学)

controversy / ˈkɒntrəvɜːsɪ / *n.* 非议,争议

purge / pɜːdʒ / *v.* 清除,清洗

pungent / ˈpʌndʒənt / *a.* 辛辣的,刺激性的

bland / blænd / *a.* 温和的,淡而无味的

astringent / əˈstrɪndʒənt / *a.* 收敛性的,止

血的

dispel / dɪˈspel / *v.* 驱散,消除

bowel / baʊəl / *n.* 肠道

meridian / məˈrɪdɪən / *n.* 经络

menthol / ˈmenθɒl / *n.* 薄荷脑,薄荷醇

influenza / ɪnfluˈenzɑː / *n.* 流感

***　　***　　***　　***　　***　　***

cancel out 抵消,中和,均衡

endangered species 濒危物种

Shennongbencaojing《神农本草经》

The Compendium of Materia Medica《本草纲目》

act upon 对……起作用,作用于……上

Passage 3　Acupuncture

Acupuncture, one of the main forms of therapy in traditional Chinese medicine (TCM), has been practiced for at least 2,500 years. In acupuncture, certain points on the body are stimulated by the insertion of fine needles. Unlike the hollow needles used to give injections or to draw blood, acupuncture needles are solid. The points can be needled between 15° and 90° relative to the skin's surface, depending on treatment.

Acupuncture is thought to restore health by removing energy imbalances and blockages in the body, raising or lowering the level of yin or yang in a specific part of the body in order to restore the energy balance.

Acupuncture was virtually unknown in the United States prior to the former President Richard Nixon's trip to China in 1972. But by 1995, there were about 10,000 acupuncturists practicing in the United States; as of the year 2000, there were 20,000.

Acupuncture's record of success has stimulated a number of research projects studying its efficacy. In 1997, the National Institutes of Health (NIH) of the US presented a report in which it described acupuncture as a sufficiently promising form of treatment which deserves further study. In 2000, the British Medical Association (BMA) suggested that acupuncture should be made more readily available, and that family doctors should be trained in some of its techniques.

The purpose of acupuncture in TCM is the rebalancing of opposing energy forces in different parts of the body. In Western terms, acupuncture is used most commonly as an adjunctive treatment for the relief of chronic or acute pain. In the United States, acupuncture is most widely used to treat pain associated with musculoskeletal disorders, but it has also been used in the treatment of headaches, vomiting and many other disorders. Acupuncture should not be used to treat traumatic injuries and other emergency conditions requiring immediate surgery. Also, while it appears to have benefits in relieving symptoms such as pain under certain circumstances, it has not been shown to alter the underlying course of a disease.

Why and how acupuncture works are still not known. Studies have shown a variety of effects such as release in the brain of various chemicals and hormones, changes in immune function, blood pressure, and body temperature.

In traditional Chinese practice, the needles are twirled as they are inserted. Many patients feel nothing at all during this procedure, while others experience a prickling or aching sensation, and still others a feeling of warmth or heaviness.

The practitioner may combine acupuncture with moxibustion to increase the effectiveness of the treatment. Moxibustion is a technique in which the acupuncturist lights a small piece of wormwood, called a moxa, above the acupuncture point. It is removed, when the patient begins to feel the warmth from the burning herb.

Words and Expressions to Learn

stimulate / ˈstɪmjʊleɪt / v. 刺激，激发

insertion / ɪnˈsɜːʃən / n. 插入，刺入

injection / ɪnˈdʒekʃən / n. 注射

blockage / ˈblɒkeɪdʒ / n. 堵塞

efficacy / ˈefɪkəsɪ / n. 效力，效能

adjunctive / ədˈdʒʌŋktɪv / a. 附属的，辅助的

musculoskeletal / ˌmʌskjʊləʊˈskelɪtəl / a. 肌肉
　　与骨骼的

vomiting / ˈvɒmɪtɪŋ / n. 呕吐

traumatic / trɔːˈmætɪk / a. 外伤的，损伤性的

hormone / ˈhɔːməʊn / n. 荷尔蒙，激素

twirl / twɜːl / v. 使快速旋转，转动

prickling / ˈprɪklɪŋ / a. 刺痛的

wormwood / ˈwɜːmwʊd / n. 艾蒿，洋艾

moxa / ˈmɒksə / n. 艾，艾蒿

***　　***　　***　　***　　***　　***

prior to 在……之前

President Richard Nixon 尼克松总统(美国
　　第36任总统)

as of 自……起

the National Institutes of Health (NIH)（美
　　国）全国卫生研究所

the British Medical Association (BMA) 英国
　　医学会

Part C Exercises

I. *Search and collect enough information about cupping and make up a dialogue between a guide and a tourist about it.*

II. *Answer the following questions according to Reading Passage 1.*

1. Explain the basic theories of Traditional Chinese Medicine in your own words.

2. What's the difference between the term "blood" in modern medicine and "xue" in TCM?

3. What is the main feature of TCM diagnoses?

4. Summarize the characteristics of the TCM diagnostic techniques.

5. Which sentence from the passage can best describe modern TCM?

III. *Decide whether the following statements are true or false about Chinese herbology.*

1. Each herbal medicine prescription can treat different patients suffering the same disease.

2. All the ingredients in a herbal medicine prescription work together on the disease until it is

cured.

3. The first book on Chinese medicine *Shennongbencaojing* was written by Shennong after tasting hundreds of herbs.

4. When prescribing herbal medicine, the doctor should consider the yin and yang nature of both the patient and the herbs.

5. Different tastes of the herbs have different medicinal functions.

6. Different herbs act upon different organs of the human body.

IV. *Complete the following summary of Reading Passage 3 with proper words and expressions from the passage.*

Acupuncture is one of the main forms of 1. _____ in TCM. It makes use of 2. _____ fine needles to 3. _____ certain nerve points so as to get rid of 4. _____ of energy and 5. _____ in the body. Acupuncture can be used to relieve various kinds of pains and aches, to treat vomiting and many 6. _____ , but it can't be used to treat 7. _____ which call for immediate 8. _____ . Though usually used as an 9. _____ treatment, acupuncture's record of success convincingly proved its 10. _____ .

V. *Translate the following Chinese passage into English and the English one into Chinese.*

1. 推拿在中国的使用已有2,000年的时间。它利用传统中医气在经络中运行的理论作为它的根本指导思想。推拿的目的是通过施以按摩和推拿(manipulation)技能来使气在身体系统中更和谐地运行流动,从而使身体能自然地自我康复。

2. In a typical cupping session, glass cups are warmed using a cotton ball or other flammable substance (可燃物), which is soaked in alcohol, lit, then placed inside the cup. Burning a substance inside the cup removes the air, which creates a vacuum. As the substance burns, the cup is turned upside down, placed over a specific area. The vacuum created by the lack of air anchors (固定) the cup to the skin and pulls it upward on the inside of the glass as the air inside the cup cools. Drawing up the skin is believed to open up the skin's pores (毛孔) which helps to stimulate the flow of blood, balances the flow of qi, breaks up obstructions (堵塞), and creates a channel for toxins to be drawn out of the body.

VI. *Topics for discussion.*

1. What do you think of the status quo (现状) of TCM in China now?

2. Which do you think is superior in terms of efficacy, TCM or Western medicine? Why? List the advantages and disadvantages of both TCM and Western medicine.

UNIT **6** Lesson 34
Chinese Customs and Etiquette

Part **A** *Conversation*

Dialogue   Getting Married the Chinese Way

(T: Tourist   G: Guide)

(In the hotel room.)

T: What's happening outside? There are so many people standing around the hotel entrance.

G: I'm not sure. They seem to be waiting for somebody. Let's wait and see.

T: Look! Some fancy cars are driving this way. Why are they all decorated with fresh flowers?

G: Oh, I see. It's a wedding ceremony. Block your ears because the firecrackers are coming.

(Minutes later.)

T: How did you know beforehand?

G: Every Chinese knows it. This is part of our marriage customs.

T: Do Chinese people get married in a hotel instead of a church?

G: It depends. Some people do get married in a church, but most young people in the cities nowadays hold their wedding ceremony in fancy hotels. In the rural area, however, the ceremony is still held in the groom's home.

T: I see. Do you Chinese still depend on matchmakers to find your better half, now?

G: Again, it depends. In the rural area, matchmakers still play an important role.

T: I see. Look, they are throwing colorful ribbons and confetti all over the new couple. This is the same in our country.

G: That is supposed to bring the new couple good luck and happiness.

T: Then, what will happen when they enter the hotel?

G: The ceremony will be presided over by a leader from either the bride's or the groom's work place, or sometimes a famous public figure. After some courtesies, the new couple will stand side by side to make the three bows.

T: Three bows? What are they?

G: A bow to heaven and the earth, a bow to the groom's parents and a bow to each other.

T: Is this a modern invention or an old tradition?

G: It's a new tradition. I mean, in ancient times, the new couple had to kneel down and kowtow three times instead of three bows. Then there will be a big banquet. The new couple has to walk around toasting and being toasted and collecting gifts, usually money in small red envelopes.

T: Are there any other changes?

G: Yes. Generally, the modern wedding ceremony is much simpler.

T: But I think when it becomes simpler, it will lose some of the solemness.

G: You are quite right. But life is changing, for better or for worse.

 Words and Expressions to Learn ·

firecracker / ˈfaɪəkrækə / n. 鞭炮，爆竹
rural / ˈrʊərəl / a. 农村的
groom / gruːm / n. 新郎
matchmaker / ˈmætʃˌmeɪkə / n. 媒人
confetti / kənˈfetɪ / n. 五彩纸屑

preside / prɪˈzaɪd / v. 主持，指挥
bride / braɪd / n. 新娘
courtesy / ˈkɜːtəsɪ / n. 礼貌，礼节
kowtow / ˈkaʊˈtaʊ / v. 磕头
solemness / ˈsɒləmnɪs / n. 庄重，庄严

***　　***　　***　　***　　***　　***

It depends. 说不准。/ 视情况而定。
bettler half 伴侣

kneel down 跪下

Part B Reading

Passage 1   Traditional Chinese Marriage Customs

Ever since ancient times, there has been a Chinese saying that the three most delightful moments in one's life come with success in the imperial examination, marriage and the birth of a son. From Qin Dynasty to Qing Dynasty, the feudal system lasted over two thousand years. During this period, the importance of marriage was far more than that a person found his better half. For the male side, it determined the prosperity and even the future fame of the family; while for the female side, it meant that parents lost the chance of seeing their daughter for a long time. Thus to choose an ideal partner was vital for both the individual and the family.

In feudal society, a marriage would be decided not by a young couple's love, but by their parents' desires. Only after a matchmaker's introduction and when parents considered the two family conditions were similar and could be matched would the marriage procedures go forward. Conditions that should be taken into consideration included wealth and social status. If a boy's family was rich, his parents would never permit him to marry a girl from a poor family. Essential to the marriage process were the "three letters and six procedures". The three letters were the betrothal letter, the gift letter with a gift list and the wedding letter used on the day the bridegroom met his bride at her home. Six procedures then led to the final wedding ceremony.

Proposing: when a boy's parents intended to make a match, they would invite a matchmaker to propose for them at the girl's home. According to tradition, at first the matchmaker could not be served tea in order not to "lighten the marriage". If the proposal was successful, however, the matchmaker (usually a woman) would be rewarded with profuse gifts and feasts to show the two families' gratitude. Many unmarried young people could not see and were unfamiliar with each other till their wedding day.

Birthday Matching: after knowing the girl's full name and birthday, the boy's parents would ask a fortune-teller to predict whether they could match their son's and whether there would be a happy marriage. The Chinese Zodiac would be surely taken into consideration.

Presenting Betrothal Gifts: if the match was predicted to be auspicious, the matchmaker would take gifts to the girl's parents and tell them that the process could continue.

Presenting Wedding Gifts: This was the grandest etiquette of the whole process. Prolific gifts were presented again to the girl's family, symbolizing respect and kindness towards the girl's family as well as the capability of providing a good life for the girl.

Selecting the Wedding Date: the boy's family asked the fortune-teller to choose a date according to the astrological book that would be proper to hold the wedding ceremony.

Wedding Ceremony: the wedding ceremony began with the groom and his party meeting the bride in her home. By this day the bride's dowry would have been sent to the boy's house. The dowry represented her social status and wealth, and would be displayed at the boy's house.

Before the meeting party's arrival, the bride would be helped by a respectable old woman to tie up her hair with colorful cotton threads. She would wear a red skirt as Chinese believed red stood for delight. When the party arrived, the bride, with a red head cover, would cry to show her reluctance to leave home. She would be led or carried by her elder brother to the sedan. The groom would meet a series of difficulties intentionally set in his path. Only after coping with these was he allowed to see his wife-to-be.

On the arrival of the sedan at the wedding place, there would be music and firecrackers. The bride would be led along a red carpet. The new couple would kowtow three times to heaven and the earth, parents and each other. Then the new couple would go to their bridal chamber and the guests would be treated to a feast.

On the night of the wedding day, there was a custom in some places for relatives or friends to banter the new couple. Though this seemed a little noisy, both of them could drop shyness and got familiar with each other sooner.

On the third day of the marriage, the new couple would go back to the bride's parents' home. They would be received with also a dinner party including relatives.

Of course, marriage customs differed in different regions, but these were the most common. They have been maintained for thousands of years, but in recent years (especially after the founding of modern China), people have tended to discard some of the details and advocate simplified marriage procedures and wedding ceremonies.

 Words and Expressions to Learn

betrothal / bɪ'trəʊðəl / *n.* 订婚

profuse / prə'fju:s / *a.* 慷慨的，大量的

astrological / əstrə'lɒdʒɪkəl / *a.* 占星术的

dowry / 'daʊərɪ / *n.* 嫁妆

banter / 'bæntə / *v.* 开玩笑，逗乐

***　　***　　***　　***　　***　　***

essential to 对……至关重要

Chinese Zodiac 属相

bridal chamber 洞房，婚房

Passage 2　Chinese Manners

China is known as a state of etiquette and ceremonies. Many customs and ceremonies have been passed down from generation to generation.

Chinese used to cup one hand in the other before the chest as a salute. This tradition has a history of more than 2,000 years but nowadays it is seldom used except during the Spring Festival. Now shaking hands is more popular and appropriate on some formal occasions. Bowing, as to convey respect to the higher level, is often used by subordinates, students, and attendants. But at present Chinese youngsters tend to simply nod as a greeting. To some extent this change reflects the ever-increasing paces of modern life.

It is common social practice to introduce the junior to the senior, or the familiar to the unfamiliar. When you start a talk with a stranger, the topics such as weather, food, or hobbies may be good choices to break the ice. To a man, a chat about current affairs, sports, stock market or his job can usually go on smoothly. Similar to Western customs, you should be careful about asking a woman private questions. However, relaxing talks about her job or family life will never put you into danger. She is usually glad to offer you some advice on how to cook Chinese food or get accustomed to local life. Things will be quite different when you've made friends with them. Implicit as Chinese are said to be, they are actually humorous enough to appreciate the exaggerated jokes of Westerners.

Gifts are considered as an important way to show courtesy. It is appropriate to give gifts on occasions like festival, birthday, wedding, or visiting a patient. If you are invited to a family party, small gifts like wine, tea, cigarettes, or candies are welcomed. Also fruit, pastries, and flowers are safe choices. As to other things, you should pay a little attention to the cultural differences. Contrary to westerners, odd numbers are thought to be unlucky. So wedding gifts and birthday gifts for the aged are always sent in pairs for the old saying goes that blessings come in pairs. Though four is an even number, it reads like death in Chinese and is thus avoided. So is pear for being a homonym of separation. And a gift of clock sounds like attending other's funeral so it is a taboo, too. As connected with death and sorrow, the colors black and white are also the last choice. Gift giving is unsuitable in public except for some souvenirs. Your good intentions or gratitude should be given priority to but not the value of the gifts. Otherwise the receiver may mistake it for a bribe.

As to proper manners in the business world, the following tips might be useful.

You can establish initial business contacts by phone, fax or email. More and more Chinese corporations have set up their own websites. After the first phase, an investigation to the company in person may show your sincerity to cooperate.

When negotiation is entered, the right of decision-making often depends on who are present at the meeting. In most cases, verbal communications are enough. Too many gestures may leave others an impression of arrogance. As to eye contact, when you speak, looking into others' eyes will do. And you'd better not take the Chinese nod for agreement; it's only a sign that they are listening attentively. Chinese prefer formal meetings, but after that there is usually a dinner together to show their hospitality. However some Westerners think it a waste at public expense. One piece of advice may be "Do as the Chinese do." When you become familiar with the Chinese partner, a private lunch meeting or dinner at home is a good opportunity to know each other better.

In China, many business women take up positions like director, general manager, president, etc. Generally speaking, career women demand no more respect than men.

But they will particularly appreciate the gentlemanly manners.

Chinese think punctuality is a virtue and try to practice it especially in the business world. Chinese tend to come a bit earlier to show their earnestness. And it would not be regarded as being late if you come within 10 minutes after the appointed time.

 Words and Expressions to Learn

salute / sə'lu:t / *n.* 行礼,致意

subordinate / sə'bɔ:dɪnət / *n.* 下属

implicit / ɪm'plɪsɪt / *a.* 含蓄的

pastry / 'peɪstrɪ / *n.* 点心,糕点

investigation / ɪnvestɪ'geɪʃən / *n.* 调查

negotiation / nɪgəʊʃɪ'eɪʃən / *n.* 谈判,协商

verbal / 'vɜ:bəl / *a.* 口头的,言语的

arrogance / 'ærəgəns / *n.* 傲慢,无礼

punctuality / ˌpʌŋktjʊ'ælɪtɪ / *n.* 准时,守时

***   ***   ***   ***   ***   ***

break the ice 打破僵局

contrary to 与······相反

odd number 奇数

give priority to 优先考虑

mistake ... for 把······误认为······

Part C Exercises

I. *Make up a dialogue between a guide and a tourist about birthday customs for the elderly after reading the following passage.*

Traditionally, Chinese people do not pay a lot of attention to birthdays until they are 60 years old. The 60th birthday is regarded as a very important point of life and therefore there is often a big celebration. After that, a birthday celebration is held every ten years, that is the 70th, the 80th, etc, until the person's death. Generally, the older the person is, the greater the celebration occasion is.

The Chinese traditional way to count the age is different from the Western way. In China, people take the first day of the Chinese New Year in lunar calendar as the starting point of a new age. No matter in which month a child is born, he is one year old, and one more year is added to his age as soon as he enters the New Year. So what may puzzle a Westerner is that a child is two years old when he is actually two days or two hours old. This is possible when the child is born on the last day or hour of the past year.

It is often the grown-up sons and daughters who celebrate their elderly parents' birthdays to show their respect for them and express their thanks for what they have done for their children. According to the traditional customs, the parents are offered foods with happy symbolic implications. On the birthday morning the father or mother will eat a bowl of "longevity noodles." In China long noodles symbolize a long life. Eggs are also among the best choices of food taken on the special occasion.

To make the occasion grand, other relatives and friends are invited to the celebration. In Chinese culture, 60 years makes a cycle of life and 61 is regarded as the beginning of a new life cycle. When one is 60 years old, he is expected to have a big family filled with children and grandchildren. It is an age to be proud of. That's why elderly people start to celebrate their birthdays at 60.

Regardless of the scale of the celebration, peaches and noodles, which are both signs of long life, are required. But interestingly the peaches are not real. They are actually steamed wheaten food with sweet stuff inside. They are called peaches just because they are made in the shape of peaches. When the noodles are cooked, they should not be cut short, for the shortened noodles can have a bad implication. Everyone at the celebration eats the two foods to extend their best wishes to the birthday person. The typical birthday presents are usually eggs, long noodles, artificial peaches, tonics, wine and money wrapped in red envelopes.

II. *Decide whether the following statements are true or false according to the passages.*

1. The three happiest moments according to traditional Chinese beliefs included success in the imperial examination, a happy marriage and longevity.
2. Marriage was more important for the male side since it determined the future of the family.
3. In ancient China, a marriage was decided by the young couple's love and their parents' desires.
4. Failure in any of the six procedures might lead to the failure of the whole process of the match making.
5. Bowing, shaking hands and cupping one hand in the other before the chest are the most popular ways to show respect in modern China.
6. Chinese women are not as sensitive to private questions as women in the West.
7. Chinese people don't have sense of humor but will try to understand the exaggerated jokes of Westerners.
8. When giving gifts to a Chinese friend, even numbers should be avoided, and so should the number "four".
9. When a Chinese nods his head, it does not necessarily mean he agrees with what is being said.
10. In China, punctuality is regarded as a virtue, especially in the business world.

III. Translate into Chinese the following sentences from the passages.

1. Only after a matchmaker's introduction and when parents considered the two family conditions were similar and could be matched would the marriage procedures go forward.

2. Prolific gifts were presented to the girl's family, symbolizing respect and kindness towards the girl's family as well as the capability of providing a good life for the girl.

3. But at present Chinese youngsters tend to simply nod as a greeting. To some extent this evolution reflects the ever-increasing paces of modern life.

4. As more and more foreign companies and individuals go to tap the Chinese market, it is better to know some Chinese practices in business contacts and negotiation beforehand.

5. Chinese think punctuality is a virtue and try to practice it especially in the business world. Chinese tend to come a bit earlier to show their earnestness. And it would not be regarded as being late if you come within 10 minutes after the appointed time.

IV. Complete the following passage by translating the Chinese into English.

1. _____ (中国经常被称为礼仪之邦). According to many Westerners, however, Chinese people often act in what appears to be a discourteous manner. The reason for this anomaly lies in the different cultural and historical views of social decorum. 2. _____ (为了避免在交际过程中不必要的错误和尴尬, 对中国礼节更好的理解至关重要).

Handshaking is considered formal greeting behavior in China. It is used to show respect, but only if the person is someone important, like a government official or a businessman. 3. _____ (握手时要坚定, 但又不能过于用力, 而且不能持续太久, 因为中国人和其他亚洲人一样, 更喜欢简短的握手). After shaking hands, you may exchange your name or the title of your company and then proceed to carry out the affairs.

Mianzi, commonly referred to as "face", is a reflection of a person's status in the eyes of his or her peers. Having "face" means you are viewed by your peers, superiors, and subordinates as one in harmony with the prevailing disposition of society. 4. _____ (它是一种不公开谈论的微妙的东西(subtlety), 却作为一种交际技巧而存在). Mianzi can best be understood as the avoidance of embarrassment in front of others. Otherwise, it can be considered impolite.

5. "Courtesy demands reciprocity," goes an old Chinese saying, and_____ _____ (这在私人和商业关系中都是十分重要的). The best choice for the initial meeting is a gift that expresses some unique aspect of your country. The gift packaging should be red or any other festive color. White and black should be avoided. It is not proper, and is even considered to be unfortunate, to take a clock as a gift or to choose one having to do with the number four, which sounds like death in Chinese. 6._____ (尽管偶数被认为是吉利的, 数字 "四" 却是个例外). Do not brag about your gift in front of the recipient, and you should use both hands when presenting it. Generally, the recipient may graciously refuse the present when first offered. In this case, you should correctly assess the situation and present it once again.

7. _____ (如果接收礼物的人没有马上打开你的礼物，这并不意味着他或她对你的礼物不感兴趣). It is polite to open it after you leave.

In China, a gift is also necessary when visiting a family. Usually, flowers, fruits and food are okay. During lunchtime, hosts will ask you to have more food or alcohol. If you do not want to disappoint them, you can have a little more according to your situation. 8. _____ (如果你真的吃饱了，最好直接拒绝，否则好客的主人会不停地在你的碗里盛满饭).

If you follow the usual rules of etiquette in China, you will extend the proper respect to the people. But there is no need to worry more about the cultural barriers, for the warm and friendly Chinese will try their best to respect your customs when communicating.

V. *Topics for discussion.*

1. Most traditional customs and ceremonies have been greatly simplified over the years. What do you think of this trend?
2. With the rapid changes in our social life, people tend to discard or despise many traditional virtues such as filial piety (孝), honesty and so on. Comment on the causes and ways of reviving the virtues in the younger generations.

UNIT 6 Lesson 35 Traditional Chinese Festivals

Part A *Conversation*

Dialogue   A Talk about the Spring Festival

(T: Tourist   G: Guide)

T: The Spring Festival is the most important festival in China, right? We celebrate Christmas as the birthday of Jesus Christ. What do you celebrate the Spring Festival for, then?

G: It takes a long story to answer your question.

T: Oh, I love stories. Go ahead and tell me the story.

G: Legend has it that there used to be an evil beast called Nian. It came out to eat people and spread destruction on the first day of the first lunar month. People suffered greatly but no one could defeat it. One year, an old man came up with a clever idea. He organized the people to dress themselves in bright red color and collected some dried bamboo and then waited for the arrival of Nian. As soon as Nian appeared, they set the bamboo on fire. It produced explosive noises when the bamboo cracked in the fire. Meanwhile, the people beat drums and shouted to make loud noises. The beast was frightened by the red color, the flame and the loud noises. It fled and never dared to come again. That's why we also call the Spring Festival "guonian".

T: "Guonian? " What does that mean?

G: It simply means passed or survived Nian.

T: Yes, I remember hearing people greeting each other in Chinatown "Guonianhao". I was puzzled, and now I know what it means.

G: From then on, we have been celebrating the victory with red color, festivities and firecrackers.

Now we call modern firecrackers "baozhu", which means "explosive bamboo".

T: That's interesting. Besides firecrackers, what else do you do to celebrate the Spring Festival?

G: Preparations begin a month earlier. We usually thoroughly clean and decorate our houses with paintings, papercuts, lanterns and so on, all in red, buy new clothes for each family member, and prepare enough food to last at least two weeks.

T: What is the highlight of the festival?

G: The New Year Eve's dinner. It's the grandest dinner party of the year both in terms of the number of people and the number of dishes. All family members and close relatives will gather together for this banquet to share their love to each other and their plans for the new year.

T: It sounds like our Thanksgiving dinner.

G: Yes, but we don't eat turkey. We have jiaozi, drink some wine or liquor, and eat delicious dishes.

T: Will all people eat jiaozi and drink wine?

G: I dare not say all, but most will do because jiaozi has the shape of ancient Chinese gold or silver ingot, and stands for wealth, while wine and liquor are called "jiu" in Chinese, which sounds like the Chinese word for longevity.

T: I see. I have another question. I once took my son to visit a Chinese friend during the Spring Festival. His wife gave my son a small red envelope with some money in it. He said it's your tradition, so we had to accept it. Is it really part of your tradition?

G: Yes, it is. We call that "hongbao", which means red packet. It is usually given to the younger generation by parents, grandparents, relatives and even close friends and neighbors.

T: Then if a child has a lot of close relatives, he will make a fortune during the Spring Festival.

G: It's no exaggeration. Actually, some college students can even raise enough funds for their tuition fees.

T: Wow, that's a lot. What else do you do after dinner?

G: People will put on their new clothes and go out to visit their relatives and friends. Wherever they go, there will be a banquet.

T: No wonder each family has to prepare so much food. Are there any public celebrations?

G: Sure. There will be numerous fun shows on TV. And in some places, there will be dragon and lion dances and folk performances of various kinds.

T: The Spring Festival is really a fun festival. I'll definitely go to Chinatown to have a feel of it next year.

 Words and Expressions to Learn

festivity / fes'tɪvɪtɪ / *n.* 欢庆，庆祝活动   turkey / 'tɜːkɪ / *n.* 火鸡

    ＊＊＊   ＊＊＊   ＊＊＊   ＊＊＊   ＊＊＊   ＊＊＊

Jesus Christ 耶稣基督   make a fortune 发财
let off 燃放   tuition fees 学费

Part **B** *Reading*

 The Mid-Autumn Festival

One of the most important Chinese festivals is the Mid-Autumn Festival. Ancient Chinese believed that the seventh, eighth, and ninth lunar months belonged to autumn. So the Mid-Autumn Festival falls on the 15th day of the eighth lunar month.

Mid-Autumn Festival celebrations date back more than 2,000 years. In feudal times, Chinese emperors prayed to Heaven for a prosperous year. They chose the morning of the 15th day of the second lunar month to worship the sun and the evening of the 15th day of the eighth lunar month to hold a ceremony in praise of the moon.

In Mid-Autumn, farmers have just finished gathering their crops and bringing in fruits from the orchards. They are filled with joy when they have a bumper harvest and at the same time, they feel quite relaxed after a year's hard work. So the 15th day of the eighth lunar month has gradually become a widely celebrated festival for ordinary people. Night falls. The land is bathed in silver moonlight. Families set up tables and sit together, chatting and sharing snacks under the moon. When enjoying the beauty of the night, they naturally remember the beautiful legends about the moon. The most popular one tells how a goddess named Chang'e ascended to the moon.

Long ago, a terrible drought hit the Earth. Ten suns burned fiercely in the sky, scorching the trees and grass. The land was cracked, and rivers ran dry. Many people died of hunger and thirst. The King of Heaven sent Houyi down to the Earth to help. When Houyi arrived, he took out his red bow and white arrows and shot down nine suns one after another. The weather immediately turned cooler. Heavy rains filled the rivers with fresh water and the grass and trees turned green. Life was restored and human race was saved.

One day, a charming young woman, Chang'e was on her way home when a young man came forward, asking for a drink. Chang'e recognized that he was Houyi. Inviting him to drink, Chang'e picked a beautiful flower and gave it to him to show her respect. Houyi, in return, selected a beautiful silver fox fur as a gift for her. This meeting kindled their love. And soon, they got married.

A mortal's life is limited, of course. So in order to enjoy his happy life with Chang'e forever, Houyi decided to look for elixir. He went to the West Heaven Queen Mother. Out of respect for the good deeds he had done, the West Heaven Queen Mother rewarded Houyi with some elixir. At the same time, she told him: If you and your wife share the elixir, you will both enjoy eternal life. But if only one of you takes it, that one will ascend to Heaven and become immortal.

Houyi returned home and told his wife everything and they decided to drink the elixir together on the 15th day of the eighth lunar month when the moon is full and bright. A wicked man heard about their plan. That day, when the full moon was rising, Houyi was on his way home from hunting. The evil man killed him. The murderer then ran to Chang'e for the elixir, Without hesitation, Chang'e picked up the elixir and drank it all.

Overcome with grief, Chang'e rushed to her dead husband's side, weeping bitterly. Soon the elixir began to have effect and Chang'e felt herself being lifted towards Heaven. Chang'e decided to live on the moon because it is nearest to the Earth. There she lives a simple and contented life.

For thousands of years, the Chinese people have related joy and sorrow, parting and reunion to the changes of the moon as it waxes and wanes. Because the full moon is round and symbolizes reunion, the Mid-Autumn Festival is also known as the festival of reunion. All family members try to get together on this special day. Those who can not return home will look at the bright full moon and feel deep longing for their loved ones.

Today, festivities centered about the Mid-Autumn Festival are more varied. After a family reunion dinner, many people like to go out to attend special performances in parks or on public squares.

People in different parts of China have different ways to celebrate the Mid-Autumn Festival. But one thing has definitely remained and is shared by all the Chinese. This is eating the festival specialty: cakes shaped like the moon.

Originally, mooncakes were a family tradition. But gradually they began to appear on markets and in stores. Mooncakes made in various parts of the country have very different fillings and flavors. So don't forget to taste all the delicious mooncakes at the Mid-Autumn Festival.

 Words and Expressions to Learn

ascend / ə'send / v. 上升
drought / draʊt / n. 旱灾,干旱
scorch / skɔːtʃ / v. 烤焦
restore / rɪ'stɔː / v. 恢复,复原

kindle / 'kɪndl / v. 点燃
elixir / ɪ'lɪksə / n. 长生不老药
wax / wæks / v. (月亮)盈,渐满
wane / weɪn / v. (月亮)亏,变得残缺

***   ***   ***   ***   ***   ***

a bumper harvest 大丰收
Chang'e 嫦娥

Houyi 后羿
West Heaven Queen Mother 西天王母

Passage 2 Chongyang Festival

The Chongyang Festival falls on the ninth day of the ninth month on the Chinese lunar calendar, so it is also known as the Double Ninth Festival.

The festival is based on the theory of yin and yang, the two opposing principles in nature. Yin is feminine, negative principle, while yang is masculine and positive.

The ancients believed that all natural phenomena could be explained by this theory. Numbers are related to this theory. Even numbers belong to yin and odd numbers to yang. The ninth day of the ninth lunar month is a day when two largest yang digits meet. So it is called Chongyang. Chong means double in Chinese. Chongyang has been an important festival since ancient times.

The festival is held in the golden season of autumn, at harvest-time. The bright clear weather and the joy of bringing in the harvest make for a happy atmosphere. The Double Ninth Festival is usually perfect for outdoor activities. Many people go hiking and mountain-climbing in the country, enjoying Mother Nature's final burst of color before she puts on her dull winter cloak. Some will carry a spray of dogwood.

It is hard to say when these customs started. But there are many stories about its origin. One of them goes like this: In ancient times, there lived a man named Huan Jing. He was learning magic arts from Fei Changfang, who had become an immortal after many years of practicing Taoism. One day, the two were climbing a mountain. Fei Changfang suddenly stopped and looked very upset. He told Huan Jing, "On the ninth day of the ninth month, disaster will come to your hometown. You must go home immediately. Remember to make a red bag for each one of your family members and put a spray of dogwood in every one. Then you must all tie your bags to your arms, leave home quickly and climb to the top of a mountain. Most importantly, you must all drink some chrysanthemum wine. Only by doing so can your family avoid the disaster."

On hearing this, Huan Jing rushed home and asked his family to do exactly what his teacher said. The whole family climbed a nearby mountain and did not return until evening. When they got back home, they found dead all their chickens, sheep, dogs and even the oxen. Later Huan Jing told his teacher, Fei Changfang, about this. Fei said the animals had died in place of Huan Jing's family, who escaped disaster by following his instructions. And so it happened that climbing a mountain, carrying a spray of dogwood and drinking chrysanthemum wine became the traditional activities of the Chongyang Festival.

The dogwood is a plant with a strong fragrance, and is often used as a Chinese herbal medicine. People in ancient times believed it could drive away evil spirits and prevent people from getting a chill in late autumn. But the custom of carrying a spray of dogwood during the Double Ninth Festival is slowly dying out and many people, especially young people in cities, do not even know what a dogwood spray looks like.

Even though the tradition of carrying sprays of dogwood has died out, that of climbing mountains is reaching new heights.

Early in West Han Dynasty, about 2,000 years ago, people used to climb a high platform outside the capital city of Chang'an on the occasion of the Chongyang Festival. For many, it was the last outing of the year before the onset of winter. The custom has developed into its present form, when people go climbing to get some exercise as well as enjoy the autumn scenery.

But what about those people who live in flat regions far from any mountain? The problem is solved by going for a picnic and eating cakes. The Chinese word for cake is "gao", a homonym of the Chinese word for "high". Mountains are high, so eating cake can, by a stretch of the imagination, take the place of going for a climb.

Since nine is the largest digit, people take two of them together to signify longevity. Therefore, the ninth day of the ninth month has become a special day for people to pay their respects to the elderly and a day for the elderly to enjoy themselves. It has also been declared China's Day for the Elderly.

 Words and Expressions to Learn

feminine / ˈfemɪnɪn / *a.* 阴性的，女子气的
masculine / ˈmæskjʊlɪn / *a.* 阳性的，有阳刚之
　气的
digit / ˈdɪdʒɪt / *n.* (个) 位数

cloak / kləʊk / *n.* 斗篷，披风
spray / spreɪ / *n.* 带花叶的小枝
dogwood / ˈdɒgwʊd / *n.* 山茱萸木
onset / ˈɒnset / *n.* 开始

***　　***　　***　　　***　　***　　***

make for 造成，有助于
Huan Jing 桓景

Fei Changfang 费长房
in place of 代替

Part  C Exercises

I. *Make up a dialogue between a guide and a tourist about the Dragon Boat Festival after reading the following passage.*

The Dragon Boat Festival (also called Duanwu) falls on the fifth day of the fifth month of the Chinese lunar calendar. For thousands of years, Duanwu has been marked by eating zongzi and dragon boat races.

There are many legends about the origin of the festival, the most popular of which is closely related to Qu Yuan. Qu Yuan was a minister of the State of Chu and one of China's earliest poets. In face of great pressure from the powerful Qin Kingdom, he warned the king against an increasingly corrupt government and suggested strengthening its military forces so as to fight against Qin. However, his warnings and suggestions were rejected, and later he was exiled by the king. During his exile, he still cared much for his country and people and composed many famous poems expressing his worries and concerns. In 278 B.C., he heard the news that Qin troops had finally conquered Chu, so he jumped into the Miluo River, clasping a large stone. This happened on the 5th day of the 5th month on the Chinese lunar calendar. After his death, the fishermen sailed their boats up and down the river to look for his body. People threw into the water zongzi and eggs to divert fish or shrimp from attacking his body. An old doctor poured a jug of realgar wine (雄黄酒) into the water, hoping to turn all aquatic (水生的) beasts drunk. That's why people later followed the customs such as dragon boat racing, eating zongzi and drinking realgar wine on that day.

The taste of zongzi varies greatly across China. Zongzi is often made of rice mixed with dates in North China, because dates are abundant in the area. East China's Jiaxing County is famous for its pork-stuffed zongzi. In the southern province Guangdong, people stuff zongzi with pork, ham, chestnuts and other ingredients, making them very rich in flavor. In Sichuan Province, zongzi is usually served with a sugar dressing. Most people still follow the tradition of eating zongzi on the day of Duanwu. But the special delicacy has become so popular that they are available all year round.

Dragon boat races are the most popular activity during the festival, especially in South China. A dragon boat is shaped like a dragon, and is brightly painted in red, white, yellow and black. Usually, a dragon boat is 20 to 40 meters long, and needs several dozen people to row it. Boatmen row the boat in cadence (节拍) with the drumbeats, as the captain standing in the bow of the boat waves a small flag to help coordinate the rowing. Dragon boat racing is quite a spectacle, with drums beating, colorful flags waving, and thousands of people cheering on both sides of the river. Nowadays, it has become a popular sport in South China.

Ancient Chinese believed realgar（雄黄）was an antidote（解毒剂）for all poisons, and therefore most effective to drive away evil spirits and kill insects. So everyone would drink some realgar wine during Duanwu, and children would have the Chinese character for King written on their foreheads with realgar wine.

II. *Answer the following questions according to the information in the dialogue and the passages.*

1. What does "guonian" in Chinese mean? And why is the Spring Festival called "guonian"?

2. Why are firecrackers also called "baozhu" in Chinese?

3. Why do most people eat jiaozi and drink some wine or liquor at the New Year Eve's dinner in China?

4. Retell the legend about how Chang'e ascended to the moon.

5. Why do Chinese people regard the Mid-Autumn Festival as a festival for family reunion?

6. Why is the Double Ninth Festival also called Chongyang Festival?

7. Why did Chinese people in ancient times carry a spray of dogwood, climb the mountains and drink chrysanthemum wine at Chongyang Festival?

8. Why is Chongyang Festival declared China's Day for the Elderly?

III. *Complete the following passage by translating the Chinese into English.*

The Lantern Festival (also called Yuanxiao Festival) is on the 15th day of the first Chinese lunar month. It is closely related to the Spring Festival. After the Lantern Festival, everything returns to normal. Yuan literally means first, while Xiao refers to night. 1. _____ (元宵节是我们在新的一年中第一次见到满月的日子). It is traditionally a time for family reunion.

The most important activity on this festival is watching lanterns. 2. _____ (各种形状和大小的灯笼挂满了街道，吸引着无数的参观者). Children will stroll in the streets with self-made or bought lanterns, extremely excited. "Guessing lantern riddles" is an essential part of the festival. 3. _____ (灯笼主人在纸上写上谜语，并把它们粘贴在灯笼上). If visitors have answers to the riddles, they can pull the paper down and go to the lantern owners to check their answers. If they have guessed right, they will get small gifts. The activity emerged during people's enjoyment of lanterns in the Song Dynasty. 4. _____ (因为猜灯谜既有趣又充满了智慧，所以它在全国各地的人们当中都很流行).

In the daytime of the festival, performances such as dragon lantern dance, lion dance, land boat dance, yang ko dance, walking on stilts and beating drums while dancing will be staged. 5. _____ (晚上，除了壮观的灯笼外，烟花形成另一道美丽的风景). Most families spare some fireworks from the Spring Festival and let them off on the Lantern Festival. Some local governments will even organize a fireworks party. 6. _____ (当新年的第一轮圆月缓缓升起，人们便深深陶醉于那银色的月光和美丽的烟火中).

Besides entertainment and beautiful lanterns, another important part of the Lantern Festival is eating yuanxiao. 7. _____ (元宵是用糯米粉做成的小球) with rose petals, sesame, bean paste, jujube paste, walnut meat, dried fruit, sugar and edible oil as fillings. Yuanxiao can be boiled, fried or steamed. It tastes sweet and delicious. Yuanxiao also has another name, tangyuan. 8. _____ (此外，汉语中"汤圆"与"团圆"（意思是团聚，重聚）有着相似的发音). So people eat them to pray for union, harmony and happiness for the family.

IV. Translate the following passage into Chinese.

Qingming, meaning clear and bright, is the day for mourning the dead. It falls on the 5th of April every year. It corresponds with the onset of warmer weather, the start of spring plowing, and of family outings. In ancient China, Qingming was by no means the only time when sacrifices were made to ancestors. In fact such ceremonies were held very frequently, about every two weeks, in addition to other important holidays and festivals. The formalities of these ceremonies were in general very elaborate and expensive in terms of time and money. In an effort to reduce this expense, Emperor Xuanzong of Tang Dynasty declared in 732 A.D. that respects would be formally paid at the tombs of ancestors only on the day of Qingming. This custom continues to date.

V. Topics for discussion.

1 There is one or more legends about each and every traditional Chinese festival. Share with your classmates your knowledge of such stories about any of our traditional festivals.

2 Nowadays, Western festivals are becoming increasingly popular among the young people in China, while they tend to be ignorant of our own traditional festivals. Comment on this phenomenon. And say something about some Western festivals.

UNIT 7
Departure

Lesson 36

Good-bye, China

UNIT 7 Lesson 36
Good-bye, China

Part A *Conversation*

Dialogue Here Is a Small Gift for You.

(G: Guide   T: Tourist)

G: Hmm, you all can't wait to go back home, huh?

T: You bet. We've been away from home for almost a month. I'm really missing my family and friends.

G: East and west, home is best. There is nowhere else sweeter than home.

T: You can say that again. And I am eager to show them the gifts I have chosen for them.

G: Wow, you've bought an extra bag!

T: Yes. And we really appreciate everything you have done for us during our trip. You are absolutely the best guide we've ever had.

G: It's very kind of you to say so. I have enjoyed every minute of being with you guys. You are all wonderful people, very active and cooperative. If you come to China again, I would be more than happy to be your guide.

T: We'll surely have you with us on our next trip. You have answered all our questions and given us excellent lectures on Chinese culture.

G: I'm much flattered. By the way, you have been to so many places in China, which one do you like best?

T: Oh, that is a hard question. Actually, our trip is full of highlights. Each and every place is special in some ways. I like the mountains, the rivers, the beaches, and I love the old buildings, the gardens, the handicrafts, the people and their customs. Everything has left impressions on my mind and they all make my understanding of

China fuller and my love for it deeper.

G: I am so glad to hear such a closing address. To show my thanks for your cooperation and tolerance for my lack of knowledge, I've prepared a small gift for each one of you. Here you are.

T: Oh, how nice! Thank you! What is it?

G: Post cards. Open it and take a look.

T: Wow, wonderful! They are the pictures of the places we've visited! That's the very thing I regretted not having bought! Thank you so much!

G: I am glad you like it.

T: I love it. You are really a considerate person. You know what, I also have a small gift for you.

G: A brooch! So delicate and beautiful!

T: It goes well with your sweater. Come here and let me put it on for you. There you go. Looks good.

G: Thank you very much.

T: You deserve it. And we do hope you can come to visit us in the United States.

G: I will if there is a chance.

T: Then we can be your guide and return all the kindness you've shown us.

G: Don't mention it. I have got a lot of fun traveling with you.

T: Me, too.

G: Oh, there is only half an hour left before take-off. Please get ready for the security check.

T: Then we have to say goodbye.

G: Yes, as the Chinese saying goes, "No good thing lasts forever." But this is a small world. Why should we feel sad about a temporary separation?

T: Well said. Good-bye, then. And we will stay in touch, won't we?

G: Of course. Bon voyage.

T: Good-bye.

Words and Expressions to Learn

tolerance / 'tɒlərəns / *n.* 容忍，忍耐

brooch / brəʊtʃ / *n.* 胸针

temporary / 'tempərəri / *a.* 暂时的，短暂的

***   ***   ***   ***   ***   ***

can't wait to do sth. 迫不及待地想做某事

You can say that again. 说得没错

be flattered 过奖

leave impression on 给……留下印象

closing address 闭幕词

Bon voyage. 一路顺风。/ 旅途愉快。

Part B Reading

Passage 1 Public Transportation in China

Transportation system in China has improved greatly since 1949. Now, a comprehensive transportation network of airports, railways, highways, subways, and waterways are making the daily lives of the Chinese people extremely convenient.

Airlines in China offer very good services. There are about 1,279 air routes in total, of which 1,035 are domestic lines, including routes to Hong Kong and Macau, and 244 are international. Most airlines and airports provide world-class facilities and services.

China has one of the biggest rail networks of the world, with a total length of 124,000 kilometers, of which 22,000 km are high speed railways. They cover almost every place in China, even remote mountainous areas, plateaus, and the seaside. The high speed train is the prime choice among all types of trains. Also called bullet train or CRH train, it travels at 250–300 km/h with high standard services. Facilities on these trains are similar to those on airplanes. The back of the seat can be adjusted to the desired angle; a small foldable table is available for each seat; and electrical sockets are available in each row or compartment. Besides, meals and snacks are provided at a cost.

China has numerous highways at all levels, connecting most cities, towns and countryside. Safety, quality, convenience and capacity of Chinese expressways have developed rapidly. The total length of highways in China amounts to 1.18 million km, including 68 national highways and more than 1,600 provincial ones. Now, all provincial capitals are centers of highway passenger transport. Shuttle buses run between provincial capitals and other cities, counties and towns. Outside main roads, traffic is also assured by minibuses and small vans.

China has 110,000 kilometers of navigable rivers, streams, lakes, and canals, more than any other country in the world. Passenger boats are still popular in some mountainous regions, where railways are few and road access is still inconvenient.

In urban areas of China, there are many convenient modes of transport. Public buses, metros, taxis, bicycles are the most common options. In big cities, the bus system works very well. Besides, trolleybuses provide a portion of the public transit service in 14 Chinese cities. The trolleybus service in Shanghai started in 1914 and still remains in operation, making it the longest-lived trolleybus system in the world.

Large cities in China have metro systems, ideal for transporting large numbers of people quickly over short distances, without causing traffic jams. Shanghai Metro, which opened in 1995, is the longest metro system in the world.

Taxis are everywhere at any time of the day. You have just to hail them at roadside or to book them by phone.

China used to be called the paradise of bikes. Though the number of cars is on the rise, bicycles, the easiest and most economic means of transportation, still remain the favorite of many Chinese people, at least in small and medium-sized cities. Bicycle paths follow main avenues. Nowadays, the Government provides public bicycle services in many cities to encourage low-carbon traveling. Public bikes can be found at specific places along the streets so that people can easily get one. As long as your cell phone has the function of Alipay or WeChat Payment, you can easily rent a public bicycle without applying for a permanent renting card.

  Words and Expressions to Learn ·······················

comprehensive / ˌkɒmprɪˈhensɪv / a. 综合的，全面的

domestic / dəʊˈmestɪk / a. 国内的，本国的

prime / praɪm / a. 首要的，主要的

assure / əˈʃʊə / v. 保障，保证

navigable / ˈnævɪgəbl / a. 适航的，可通航的

access / ˈækses / n. 通道，途径

metro / ˈmetrəʊ / n. 地铁

option / ˈɒpʃən / n. 选择

hail / heɪl / v. 招呼

economic / ˌiːkəˈnɒmɪk / a. 经济的，实惠的

avenue / ˈævɪnjuː / n. 干道，大路

adjust to 调节成为

foldable table 折叠桌

amount to 合计，总共达

provincial capital 省会城市

in operation 运行中，使用中

on the rise 上升，增长

low-carbon travelling 低碳出行

as long as 只要

Alipay 支付宝

Wechat Payment 微信支付

Passage 2　Shanghai Maglev

The 21st Century began with the development of rail transportation, with cooperation between Germany and China which points toward the development of the Eurasian Land-Bridges. One of two 31-kilometer (20-mile) tracks of the world's first magnetic levitation railroad lines, between Shanghai's Longyang Subway Station and Pudong International Airport, was officially inaugurated on Dec. 31 at 10:10 a.m. local time. The launching ceremony was attended by the former Chinese Prime Minister Zhu Rongji, the former German Chancellor Gerhard Schröder, numerous Cabinet ministers from either side, and leading industry and scientific representatives from China and Germany.

The maiden voyage of the "maglev" proved that with this first commercial maglev route in the world, China has achieved the number-one rank of the world's nations in, not only land transportation investment, but also 21st century railroad technology.

Indeed, the Maglev is faster than any train we've known, though it has no wings, no wheels or engine, either. Magnets are the attraction. First, powerful magnets lift the entire train about 10 milimeters above the special track, called a guideway, since it mainly directs the passage of the train. Other magnets provide propulsion, and braking, and the speeds — up to 500 kph in test runs — are reached largely due to the reduction of friction.

Is there a need for such speed? Certainly not for such a short distance, barely 30 kilometers from the subway station in Pudong to the Pudong International Airport. And not at the cost, insist critics.

Still, critics miss the point. And the excitement. The Maglev isn't about taking us from point A to B in Pudong. Rather, it's the ride, a glorious glide, from the past to the future, from the ordinary motion of today to the hyper-speeds of Tomorrowland.

The Maglev technology is actually rather old. Germany inventors patented the basic system way back before World War II . In the following seven decades, magnetic levitation trains haven't moved much closer to reality. And that's another point of critics.

A test track in northern Germany was built nearly 20 years ago, but even the Germans have shied away from building a maglev line because of the cost.

"The huge investment just doesn't make sense in a country like Germany, with a well-developed rail system," says Dr. Wolfgang Rohr, German Consul General in Shanghai. "But for countries like China — or the United States or Australia — they could jump to this new technology which has huge potential." He points out that the Maglev is pollution-free, with no exhaust. Besides, the maglev's energy consumption is only about one-fourth that of aircraft for similar capacity and even speed.

"In Germany, we've been having endless discussions about this," says a German tourist riding the Shanghai Maglev over the holidays. "Here, in China, they just do it!"

"They built this all in less than two years. Amazing! In two years in Germany, we'd just have a plan for the evacuation of the birds along the way." Adds his friend.

Meanwhile, in the United States, a pilot project has settled on a 47-mile Pittsburgh system and a 40-mile track linking Baltimore and Washington, D.C. On the other side of the country, Maglev-backers are lobbying congress to fund a 92-mile circuit between three Southern California airports that could be expanded to a 273-mile web to relieve the region's gridlock. And the US projects would all make use of American Maglev technology.

All that is a big if, though. For now, Shanghai is the first out of the tracks, and early-riders give the train-plane two thumbs-up.

 Words and Expressions to Learn

inaugurate / ɪˈnɔːɡjʊreɪt / v. 举行落成典礼   friction / ˈfrɪkʃən / n. 摩擦力

propulsion / prəˈpʌlʃən / n. 推进力   patent / ˈpeɪtənt / v. 取得……的专利

potential / pəʊˈtenʃəl / *n.* 潜能,潜力

exhaust / ɪgˈzɔːst / *n.* 废气,尾气

pilot / ˈpaɪlət / *a.* 试验性的

lobby / ˈlɒbɪ / *v.* 游说,说服

circuit / ˈsɜːkɪt / *n.* 环线

gridlock / ˈgrɪdlɒk / *n.* 交通全面堵塞

***　***　***　***　***　***

the Eurasian Land-Bridge 欧亚大陆桥

magnetic levitation railroad 磁悬浮铁路

German Chancellor Gerhard Schröder（前）
德国总理施罗德

maiden voyage 首航,处女航

miss the point 未击中要害,未抓住要点

shy away from 回避,退缩

Consul General 总领事

Pittsburgh（美国城市）匹兹堡

Baltimore（美国城市）巴尔的摩

out of the tracks 打破常规

give ... two thumbs-up 翘起两手拇指表示
称赞,叫好

Part  Exercises

I. *Make up a dialogue between a guide and a tourist about the developments of the public transportation system in China according to Reading Passage 1.*

II. *Decide whether the following statements are true or false according to Reading Passage 2.*

1. Though the maglev technology comes from Germany, Shanghai has the first and only maglev track in the whole world.

2. Germany has not built any commercial maglev line with its own technology only because it already has the best rail system in the world.

3. Besides being fast, another advantage of maglev is that it causes no pollution of any kind.

4. The US will soon build maglev lines to relieve the traffic jams in some regions.

5. The author thinks maglev is worth building regardless of the cost.

III. *Fill in the blanks with a suitable preposition or the proper form of the given word in the brackets.*

The Qinghai-Tibet railway extends 1,956 kilometers from Xining to Lhasa. About 960 kilometers of the line is more than 4,000 meters 1. _____ sea level and the highest point is 5,072 meters.

About 550 kilometers of the track is laid 2. _____ frozen earth, the 3. _____ (long) distance anywhere in the world. Tanggula Station which is 5,068 meters above sea level, is the highest station in the world. Fenghuoshan Tunnel, 4,905 meters above sea level is the world's most elevated tunnel 4. _____ (build) on frozen earth. Kunlun Mountain Tunnel, 5. _____ (run) 1,686 meters is the world's longest plateau tunnel built on frozen earth.

The train is designed to operate 6. _____ a speed of 100 kilometers per hour 7. _____ the frozen earth areas and 120 kilometers per hour on non-frozen earth.

The Qinghai-Tibet Railway has greatly improved the local transportation conditions and investment environment in Tibet. Moreover, it is playing a key role 8. _____ facilitating the economic growth, enhancing communication 9. _____ the inland area and Tibet, promoting 10. _____ (culture) exchanges between Tibetan nationality and other ethnic groups, accelerating national unity, and benefiting residents nearby the railway.

IV. Translate the following passage into Chinese.

Train travel is suitable for tourists who like to kill time leisurely on their journey. Self-driving tour may sound free and convenient, but train travel also has its own advantages. In the first place, when traveling by train, you can meet many new friends who will share with you their experience on the train, so you will not feel lonely or bored. In the second place, it is a visual enjoyment to appreciate the sceneries along the way through the train windows. Then, you can have plenty of time to think about what you care about, or you are interested in. Last but not least, train travel is more relaxing than self-driving tour since you do not have to worry about whether there is traffic jam on the way or sufficient gasoline in the tank.

V. Topics for discussion.

1. Do you think it worthwhile to build more maglev lines in our country when the cost is 310 million *yuan* (38 million U.S. dollars) per kilometer? Why?
2. More and more people are buying cars. Comment on the advantages and disadvantages of owning private cars.
3. It is said tour guides sometimes receive tips from tourists especially those from abroad. Comment on this phenomenon.
4. Some guides get commissions when they take their groups to shop in certain places. What do you think of it?

Key to the Exercises

Lesson 1

II

— Good afternoon, Miss.

— Good afternoon. I'd like to book a package tour for my parents.

— OK. We have a lot of packages suitable for middle-aged people and seniors. You can have a look at our catalogue to see which package you are interested in.

— It seems most of the tours are headed to the famous rivers and mountains. My parents are advanced in years. Is there any one that goes to somewhere near Shanghai and does not involve mountain climbing?

— What about Suzhou? They can visit the famous gardens.

— They have been there several times. They are indeed interested in history and ancient architectures.

— I have the right thing. Let them go to the Hong Village in Anhui Province. It is six and a half hours' ride from Shanghai, and they can appreciate the ancient buildings by the Hui tradesmen in history. This is one of the hottest routes this year.

— Sounds good. I will take it.

— OK. Please fill out this form.

III 1. regardless of 2. in case of 3. By and large 4. ended up 5. is subject to 6. is stocked with 7. Keep in mind 8. be immune to

IV 1. D 2. C 3. A 4. B 5. D

Lesson 2

II 1. I'd like to book fifteen tickets to Qingdao, please. 2. Ten round-trip and five one-way tickets. 3. If it is under the age of 12, you only pay the children discount fare. 4. You only need to pay 10% of the full adult fare for it. 5. Do you have a discount for the adult fare since we are buying so many tickets? 6. I will give you 30% off. Is that OK? 7. Can it be any lower? 8. OK, then. When will you send the tickets over? 9. I need the names and ID numbers of you all. 10. I will fax them to you, OK?

III 1. F 2. F 3. F 4. T 5. T 6. F 7. T 8. F 9. F 10. T

IV 1. You will go through extra security checks at the customs and some airlines may refuse to carry you. For international flights, they will take your full name and ask for a contact name and telephone number. 2. When they cannot make clear what is in a bag, they will usually hand search it. 3. Because the security staff may ask them to open the box or bag to check what is in it. 4. Because the plane may experience turbulence after it has taken off. 5. In the pocket at the back of the seat in front of each passenger. 6. (In the last several paragraphs of Reading Passage 1.)

Lesson 3

II

— Good afternoon. May I have a look at your passport, please?

— Sure. Here you are.

— Are you coming to China for traveling?

— Yes. I will wait in Shanghai for my tour group. They are now in Beijing.

— Uh huh. Your visa is valid for one month. How long will your travel in China last?

— About twenty days.

— Would you please open this bag? We have to do a routine check.

— Okay. Only some clothes and daily necessities. Absolutely no weapons or narcotics.

— Anything to declare?

— No.

— Fine. You are through. And wish you a nice stay in China.

— Thank you. Good-bye.

III 1. C 2. A 3. C 4. D 5. C

Lesson 4

II 1. Can I help you? 2. What kind of room do you want, Sir? 3. Do you prefer a room with shower or with bath? 4. How much is the room per night? 5. That is a bit too high. 6. That is the cheapest/least expensive room 7. May I have your name, please? 8. How are you going to pay, please? 9. May I have the card number, please? 10. What else can I do for you?

III 1. Do you want a single room or a double room? 2. Do you prefer a room with bath or a room with shower? 3. I need a double room with twin beds facing the garden. 4. This is the least expensive deluxe suite left for tomorrow. 5. What time can I check in tomorrow?

IV

1. Three-star hotels are usually large enough to offer greater quality facilities and services than the lower star hotels.

2. (In the last paragraph of Reading Passage 1.)

3. Among criteria used in making such assessments are size of rooms, decor/furnishings, public

areas, hospitality services, staff attitudes, housekeeping, sanitary standards.

4. Your best course of action is to focus on what you want from a hotel when you are traveling.

5. Internationally, classifications tend to be similar around the world, but different meanings may apply to the same words. If you use a travel agent, ask what the classification used for hotels in your itinerary really mean.You can also contact the tourist office of your destination to learn more about the rating system and a certain hotel.

6. It implies if you don't know the exact meaning of hotel classification terms, you will end up paying more for different hotels of similar ratings.

Lesson 5

I

— Good evening. What can I do for you?

— Good evening. We've just arrived from Shanghai. Do you have rooms available for a night?

— How many people are in your party?

— Eight.

— What kind of rooms do you want?

— We need six single rooms and a double one.

— I'm afraid we don't have so many single rooms left. Will suites do?

— How much do you charge for a suite?

— RMB 880 *yuan*.

— Oh, that's too high. Is there anything less expensive?

— They are the least expensive suites we have now. If you take two suites, we can offer you a 10% discount.

— OK, then. We'll take two.

— Please fill out the form here, please.

— Sure. Here you are.

— These are your keys. The suites and the double room are on the 12th floor and the single rooms are on the 9th. Room numbers are on the key cards.

— Thanks. Good night.

— Good night.

II

1. Because the way you answer your company's phone will form your customer's first impression of your business.

2. Because by so doing, your customers don't have to ask if they've reached such and such a business.

3. Keep your voice volume moderate, and speak slowly and clearly when answering the phone.

4. Speaker phones give the caller the impression that you're not fully concentrating on his call, and make him think that his call can be heard by everybody in your office.

5. Check on how your business' phone is being answered by calling in and seeing if the phone is being answered in a professional manner.

6. In so doing, the customers will know that they are welcome at the hotel, and whenever they are back in town it can count on them staying in the hotel!

7. It means different people have different needs and one type of customer service is not suitable for all your customers.

8. It means the silent complainers usually walk out of your shop without saying a word, and never come again. These silent complainers have friends. And their friends have friends.They will pass on negative comment on your shop.

9. It will strengthen customers' trust in a business so that, in the future, the customers will often come to the business for real savings.

10. It means if you don't pay attention to your customers' needs, they will go to do business with your competitors.

III 1. put you through to   2. in the long run   3. sheds light on   4. count on   5. qualify for   6. kiss ... goodbye   7. concentrate on   8. needless to say

Lesson 6

II 1. k   2. g   3. c   4. i   5. j   6. b   7. f   8. d   9. h   10. e   11. a

III 1. 酒店经理们和他们的助手广泛使用电脑来记录客人的账单，房间的预定和分配情况以及会议和特殊事件。此外电脑也被用来订购食品、饮料及供应品，向酒店拥有者和最高级别经理提交报告。酒店经理和电脑专家合作确保酒店的电脑系统正常运转。一旦酒店的电脑系统瘫痪，经理们必须能够继续满足客人和员工的要求。

2. Hotel front desk clerks deal directly with the public, so professional appearance and pleasant personality are important. Clear speaking voice and fluency are also essential, because these employees talk directly with hotel guests and the public and frequently use telephones or public-address systems. Good spelling and computer literacy are needed, because most of their work involves the use of a computer. In addition, speaking a foreign language fluently is increasingly helpful, because of the growing number of international guests in many hotels.

Lesson 7

I 1. Have you got a table for two, please?   2. Do you have a reservation?   3. Can we have a table by the window in the non-smoking area?   We want to enjoy the night view of Shanghai. 4. This way, please. Here's the menu.   5. Excuse me . Are you ready to order, now?   6. But this is our first time to come to your city. What do you recommend?   7. We'd like to try the specialty of your hotel.   8. We cook the beef in a special way here in our hotel. I'm sure you'll certainly be quite satisfied with it.   9. How do you want the beef — rare, medium, or well done?   10. Can I have the bill, please?

II 1. T   2. F   3. T   4. T   5. T   6. F   7. T   8. T

Ⅲ 中餐更加健康美味。大多数中国菜都是用肉和蔬菜一起烹制而成，因此，比西方菜肴所含的热量和油脂更低。中国人在菜汁或者少量水中高温快炒使蔬菜保持色泽鲜亮，口感清脆。这种方法也在最大程度上保留了菜肴中的维他命和矿物质。

Lesson 8

Ⅱ 1. T 2. F 3. T 4. T 5. F

Ⅲ 1. Steaming 2. Roasting 3. Red cooking 4. Stewing 5. Stir-frying 6. Shallow frying
7. Deep-frying 8. Paper-wrapped deep-frying

Ⅳ 筷子在中国饮食文化中扮演着重要角色。筷子在古时候叫作"箸"。中国人把筷子作为一种主要的餐具已有三千多年的历史了。专家认为木制和竹制筷子的历史比象牙筷子早大约一千年。西周时发明了青铜筷子。在马王堆汉墓中曾发现过西汉时代的漆器筷子。金银筷子在唐朝时候非常流行。人们相信银筷可以探测食物是否有毒。筷子可以根据制造材料划分为五大类：即木制、金属、骨制、石制及合成材料制成的筷子。竹筷和木筷在中国家庭中最为常用。使用筷子时应避免几点。中国人吃饭时通常不用筷子击打饭碗，因为这是过去乞丐常有的行为。也不要把筷子竖着插在饭碗里，因为只有在祭祀时人们才会这样做。

Ⅴ 1. Some people say that it is a pity to leave China without doing three things — visiting the Great Wall, eating Roast Beijing Duck and drinking Maotai. 2. For experienced cooks, true artists that they are, recipes are merely reference points. They often make adjustments as they go along, depending on the number of people they need to serve, the ingredients they have available and their personal taste. 3. Some cooks seldom use recipes, preferring instead to depend on their intuition as they add a pinch of this and a dash of that to create just the right flavors. 4. Cooking is a language everyone understands. Good chefs in China are "fluent" in several cooking "dialects". 5. The art of cooking in China places great stress on color, aroma, taste, form and sound of a dish. 6. "Light south, salty north, sweet east, and spicy west" accurately describes the features of Chinese cuisine.

Lesson 9

Ⅱ 1. It looks very much like the roast turkey we have on Thanksgiving Day in America. 2. Could you please show me how to eat this dish? 3. First, hold a pancake in your left hand and use a selection of scallion as a brush to paint a little splashes of bean sauce on the pancake. Next, place the scallion in the middle of the pancake and with chopsticks add a few pieces of duck meat. Finally, roll the pancake up and enjoy. 4. Its skin is so crisp and its meat so tender! I've never tasted any roast duck like this. 5. When the skin turns crisp and golden brown, the duck is done.

Ⅲ 1. T 2. F 3. T 4. T 5. T 6. T 7. F 8. F 9. T 10. T

Ⅳ 1. About ten thousand years ago, our ancestors invented the three-legged and four-legged pottery Ding to boil food above fire. 2. At that time, people threw all the edible food into Ding and heated it until the food was cooked. People called this kind of food "geng". 3. Using a hot pot to make instant-boiled mutton is believed to date back to Kublai, the founding emperor of the Yuan Dynasty.　4. The mutton hot pot originated in North China and has a history of more than one thousand years.　5. Flame under the pot can keep water boiling.　6. Dip the boiled mutton slices in the mixture of condiments and relishes, and you can enjoy them.　7. Beggar's chicken is our specialty.　8. Jiaozi looks like gold and silver ingots so when people eat it during festivals they really hope it could bring fortune and good luck to them.

Lesson 10

Ⅱ 1. Brick tea is quite popular here.　2. Most of them come in tea bags.　3. I want some jasmine tea. I heard Chinese people like flower scented tea.　4. Flower-scented tea is especially popular in North China.　5. Which brand of green tea is good?　6. We have an excellent selection of Chinese green tea. Take your pick. You'll find a whole bunch of them on the shelf.

Ⅲ 1. F　2. T　3. T　4. F　5. T　6. T　7. F　8. F　9. T　10. T

Ⅳ 1. for　2. commonly　3. as　4. tasty　5. boiling　6. mixture　7. to　8. With　9. out　10. to　11. absorption　12. conductivity　13. among　14. beautifully　15. artistic

Ⅴ 根据一个很流行的传说，五千多年前中国人传说中的皇帝神农（农业和中医药的创始人）外出旅行。神农以其智慧而闻名天下，他相信最安全的饮水方法是将水煮沸。一天，他发现几片叶子落进沸腾的水里。好奇而又喜欢追根究底的皇帝喝了一口，惊喜地发现此汤味道香醇而且具有恢复健康和体力的作用。传说的另一个版本说神农在自己身上试验各种草药的药性，有的有毒，而茶具有解毒的功效。最早关于茶的著作——陆羽的《茶经》中也提到过神农。

Lesson 11

Ⅱ 1. It's a dormant volcano.　2. On many occasions it is common for sunshine and rain to occur at the same time. It may rain very hard one minute, but you may soon find the sun shining warmly the next minute. Sometimes, you can even watch it rain in the west and shine in the east. Besides, it is reported there are lake monsters in it.　3. It is the highest volcanic waterfall in the world.　4. September. Because it is very rainy in July and August, and visitors cannot watch the Heavenly Lake clearly at that time. And generally, it snows from October.　5. Part of the fun is guessing the nationality of the team, based on their sculpture's artistic style, before reading the signs.　6. The only differences are that the temperature is about a hundred degrees lower than that of the typical Disney park, and all the structures are made out of ice rather than plastic — and slipping and falling here doesn't result in lawsuits.　7. All the ice comes from the Songhua River nearby, which provides a limitless supply.　8. The snow festival is mostly a display of art; the ice festival is mostly a display of architecture.

Ⅲ

1. 近年来，哈尔滨郊区的老年人为了娱乐和健身的目的自发组成许多秧歌队。在农村，大秧歌队组织起来参与婚礼庆典，生日宴会等。在农忙季节，队员们参加地里的劳动。但是当农历新年来到时，他们便穿上演出服到私人家里表演秧歌，庆祝新年，传承这种古老的传统。

2. 狩猎仍然是大多数鄂伦春族人主要的生存手段。一些鄂温克族人依赖饲养驯鹿，偶尔打猎贴补家用。而其他的人进行季节性狩猎。达斡尔族人中一小部分仍然靠打猎谋生。这些民族代代相传的狩猎与农牧结合的生活方式形成了我国北方的狩猎文化圈。

Lesson 12

II 1. It is the crystallization of the industry and wisdom of the Chinese people and also a symbol of ancient Chinese culture.   2. Hall of Supreme Harmony (Taihedian). The emperors executed their rule over the whole country there.   3. It was built for emperors to worship heaven and to pray for a good harvest.   4. You will see a lot of people there performing their morning exercises in different ways.

III

— Look, this is the place I've told you.

— So many hutongs. Where shall we go first?

— As the saying goes, in Beijing, hutongs with names are about three thousand six hundred and hutongs without names are more than bull hairs.

— More than bull hairs?

— Of course. This way please. Look, these are all courtyards.

— Let's go closer. Oh, are these stone blocks?

— Yes. Different stone blocks have different meanings. From them we can have a general idea about the job of the host.

— I see. Is it true that four families shared a courtyard?

— Not necessarily. A rich family in the past might have several courtyards while several poor families might share a single one.

— Are the courtyards here still the same as before?

— No. They have changed a lot. The setup of most courtyards has changed.

— Look, air conditioners. Life in the courtyards has been modernized.

— In my opinion, courtyards are the most important symbol of life in Beijing no matter how they have changed.

Lesson 13

II 1. To achieve a friendly relationship between Western Han and Xiongnu.   2. Besides peace for sixty years, she also spread Han culture and knowledge to the Xiongnu people.   3. It is said that each year when it turns cold, grass and leaves on other trees become yellow, the plants on this tomb remain green and so it got the name.   4. To enjoy the beautiful grasslands.   5. You may try activities such as Mongolian wrestling, horse & camel riding, archery, visiting traditional families, and trips to the aobaos.   6. Pingyao.   7. It reflected people's wish for the town to last forever since tortoise is a symbol of longevity in ancient China.

III 1. blind to   2. the same case with   3. round up   4. had been at war with   5. on the decline   6. make sense   7. If only

IV

1. — I heard that people in Shanxi are crazy about vinegar.

   — Yes. Shanxi has a long history of vinegar production. It is said that three thousand years ago, a village in Shanxi began to make vinegar with a mysterious recipe. In the Song Dynasty, every household had a vinegar jar and everyone was good at making vinegar.

   — Is the process of making vinegar complicated?

   — Yes. It requires a lot of procedures and various ingredients.

   — It seems that people in Shanxi can't live without vinegar.

   — Exactly. This is not only because they like the taste of vinegar, but also because they believe that eating vinegar constantly can prolong people's life.

   — Really?

   — I'm not sure. But vinegar can help to bring down blood pressure, and therefore it does good to our health. Oh, there is a vinegar museum. Want a visit, then?

   — Where is it?

   — In Qingxu County. Not far from downtown of Taiyuan.

   — Let's have a visit, then.

   — OK. Then we'll know what tools and ingredients people used to make vinegar in the past.

2. 说起内蒙古的美丽,没有领略过它的风光的人很难想象。且不说那雄伟的大青山,巍巍贺兰山,滔滔黄河水;也不说那莽莽苍苍的林海,烟波浩渺的湖泊,浩瀚无垠的沙漠;只看看那无边无际的草原,就足以让你感叹不已,流连忘返了。如果你在夏天来到草原,展现在你面前的将是一泻千里的绿野。田野是绿的,溪水是绿的,线条柔美的小丘也是绿的,眼睛所到处全是翠色横流,直至遥远的天边。在那苍翠的原野上,点缀着一些野花,姹紫嫣红,把千里草原打扮得更加迷人。而那星星点点散布在草原上的雪白的蒙古包及那缕缕炊烟,彩云般流动着的马群、羊群、牛群,远处飘来的牧羊姑娘的阵阵歌声,又给这幅美丽的画面增添了无限的生机。放眼远眺,天空是那么蔚蓝,那么高远,大地是那么碧绿,那么壮阔。置身于这样的境界,怎么能不让人陶醉,让人心旷神怡?

Lesson 14

II 1. T 2. F 3. T 4. F 5. F 6. T 7. F

III 1. legendary 2. imitating 3. musical 4. created 5. married 6. reproduction

   7. Chinese 8. carved

IV 青海湖距离西宁市180公里,海拔3,200米,是中国最大的咸水湖。鸟岛是青海湖中最迷人的景致。鸟岛位于青海湖西岸,现在已经成了一个半岛。虽然面积不足1,000平方米,每年春天和夏天却能吸引大量的候鸟。对这成千上万只候鸟来说,这个小岛已成为它们重要的家园。数目众多的不同种类的鸟儿在岛上栖息。鸟儿的歌声可以传到很远。对这些鸟和观鸟者来说,这个岛是个真正的天堂。

Lesson 15

II 1. They sell terracotta warrior replicas. 2. The real terracotta warriors are life size and truly magnificent. 3. They are really like an army. 4. They actually are an army buried with Qin

Shi Huang.   5. It is said there are totally about 7 or 8 thousand. I am not sure.   6. Besides the terracotta warriors, there are copper chariots and copper horses and so on.   7. Three pits of the whole mausoleum have been excavated .   8. A farmer discovered it when he was digging a well in the fields.   9. Maybe we could discover something, too.

Ⅲ 1. F   2. T   3. F   4. F   5. T   6. T   7. F   8. F   9. T   10. T

Ⅳ 华山以其险峻的悬崖而闻名。沿着通往山顶的12公里长的蜿蜒小路到处是令人生畏的悬崖峭壁，探头向下看一看就足以使人倒吸冷气。在华山五峰中，东峰（朝阳峰），西峰（莲花峰），和南峰（落雁峰）相对较高。站在东峰顶上，人们可以在清晨时分欣赏日出。西峰状如莲花，是华山最秀美的峰。此外还有中峰（玉女峰）和北峰（云台峰）。中锋因相传曾有玉女乘白马入山间而得名。北峰峰顶平坦，如云中之台，著名的"智取华山"的故事就发生在这里。

Lesson 16

Ⅱ 1. The red rock glows and hot air goes up like smoke as though it were on fire under the blazing sun.   2. The Gaochang Ancient Town and the Bizaklik Thousand-Buddha Caves.   3. Grapes and Hami melons.   4. In the beginning of the last century, a Swedish explorer discovered it by accident.   5. It is important to protect our environment.

Ⅲ 1. Known   2. attractions   3. Surrounded   4. geologically   5. majestic   6. reflected 7. making   8. extending   9. floating   10. endless

Ⅳ 天山字面意思是天国里的山脉。位于新疆地区中心附近，天山山脉从东到西连绵2,500公里，其中1,700公里位于新疆维吾尔自治区。从北到南宽250到300公里。北部山麓稠密的森林遮天蔽日。天山山脉拥有丰富的冰川水资源以及肥沃的盆地来支持富足的农业和兴旺的畜牧业。游客会发现美丽富饶的天山山脉最迷人的地方是广袤的草原和优美的牧场。巴音布鲁克草原是天山中部附近最大的牧场，位于海拔2,500米的一个盆地中。一望无际的草原，巨大的湖泊、河流、漫游着的牛羊群还有圆形的蒙古包共同形成一幅醉人的风景。

Lesson 17

Ⅱ

1. Many famous people in Chinese history have climbed it.

2. Once Qin Shi Huang came to Mount Tai to offer sacrifice to heaven. There was a sudden downpour. He took shelter under the five pines and didn't get wet. So he gave them the title of Dafu in gratitude.

3. A group of grand buildings built in traditional Chinese style: Patterned after a royal palace, it is divided into nine courtyards. The main buildings run along a north to south axis, with the other buildings symmetrically in line. The whole group includes three halls, one pavilion, one altar, and three ancestral temples. Altogether there are 466 rooms and 54 gateways covering an area of 218,000 square meters. The yellow tiles and red walls are all covered with beautiful decorations. 2,100 pieces of steles from various dynasties make a fine exhibition of calligraphy and stone sculpture.

4. Confucius is respected as a sage, and Confucianism has become the backbone of Chinese culture.

5. The cemetery has already lasted 2,340 years. At the time Confucius was buried there, the cemetery was about 66,700 square meters. It was continually expanded to over 2,000,000 square meters in the following dynasties. The walls around the cemetery are 7 kilometers long surrounding more than 10,000 tombs.

6. Yes. Nanjing is now the capital of Jiangsu Province, the home to several high ranking universities, a major economic center and a popular place with tourists.

7. Because many famous historical figures were buried there.

8. Because the tablet features Wu Daozi's painting, Li Bai's poem and Yan Zhenqing's calligraphy.

9. It's famous for the countless local snacks and delicacies.

10. We can go to visit the Forbidden City in Beijing, because Zhu Yuanzhang's grandson copied the layout of the Palace when he moved the capital to Beijing.

III 1. in 2. to 3. during 4. From 5. than 6. along 7. as 8. on

IV

— Yes, this is just like the pavilion I saw on postcards.

— Out of all Suzhou's gardens, this is the largest pavilion. The furniture is all made of cedar, so this is also called the Cedar Hall.

— These two rooms are completely different; I can't even take it all in!

— This is called the Mandarin Duck Hall.

— "Mandarin duck" refers to a bird though, right? What could a bird have to do with this pavilion?

— "Mandarin duck" does refer to a bird, but here, it conjures up the idea of "a pair". Look, this is the men's side, used for receiving male guests; and that is the women's side, which, of course, is for receiving female guests.

— I got it.

V 趵突泉是济南的标志。它不仅是济南72泉之首，而且被誉为"天下第一泉"。对它的描述最早见于《春秋》，所以趵突泉至今已有2,600年的历史了。它水质清纯，口感醇厚，可以直接饮用。当水从三个泉眼喷薄而出时，会发出雷鸣般的响声，水柱向上喷涌，就像滚动的车轮。水温终年保持在18摄氏度。冬天，一层薄雾升腾在泉池上方，清澈的泉水倒映着周围雕梁画栋，廊檐上翻的古式建筑，为游客展现一幅人间仙境的美丽图画。趵突泉及周边区域已被建成一座同名公园并成为济南三大主要景点之一。

Lesson 18

II

1. In ancient times Huangdi, the ancestor of the Chinese nation, made pills of immortality here, so the mountain got the name.

2. Pine trees, grotesque rocks in different shapes, the sea of clouds, and the hot spring.

3. No. Because the sea of clouds appears only when the weather conditions are just right.

4. Because in Shanghai's development, it has formed its own unique city scene and colorful culture. A lot of cultural relics beginning in Tang and Song Dynasties are well preserved till this day.

5. The Bund is dotted with buildings of Western styles dating back to the early 20th century, So the Bund is also reputed as "an international exhibition of architecture".

6. Yes. People can cross the Huangpu River through a 646.7-meter-long sightseeing tunnel, connecting the Bund to the Oriental Pearl TV Tower,

9. 13。

10. The west Lake, the Solitary Hill, the Botanical Garden, the Peak Flown From Afar, and the Running Tiger Spring.

Ⅲ 1. running   2. encircled   3. economically   4. leading   5. surging   6. caused   7. rotation   8. marvelous   9. Annually   10. height   11. generates   12. Various

Ⅳ 1. 太平湖位于黄山南麓,九华山的东南方,面积大约88平方公里,水深40米。它是安徽省最大的人工湖。湖中有各种形状的小岛十多个。风格简朴的房子及它们的彩墙和茶树一起倒映在镜子一样的湖水中。湖面上点缀着渔船的白矾和竹筏。太平湖是许多诸如鹿、野兔等野生动物的家园。最近湖中又建了许多新景点,包括鹿岛、猴岛、白鹭洲、蛇塘、鳄鱼塘等。太平湖距黄山北入口40公里,距九华山90公里。1996年12月太平湖大桥正式通车,给旅游提供了更大的方便。

2. Mount Putuo, the lowest of China's sacred mountains, is located on a small island of only twelve square kilometers, five kilometers east of Zhoushan island in Zhejiang Province. The peak of Mount Putuo is 291 meters above sea level and is reached by a stone staircase with 1,060 steps. A holy place before the arrival of Buddhism, the island is full of mystic caves, tranquil valleys, overhanging cliffs and golden beaches. Besides the many temples, the island is also lush in vegetation and a profusion of forests because of its warm and humid climate. Amidst such an environment, a stroll around the mountain or an immobile day at the beach is equally comfortable. On top of all this, Mount Putuo has some of China's greatest seafood on offer. Sampling fresh seafood dishes has become an indispensable part of any trip to Mount Putuo.

Lesson 19

Ⅱ 1. 人间四月芳菲尽,山寺桃花始盛开。   2. 不识庐山真面目,只缘身在此山中。   3. Because it offers a mild climate and a habitat rich in aquatic plants and fish with no industrial pollution. 4. Black sleeve cranes.   5. It got its present name from the huge reef surrounding it. When the tide comes in, the waves hit the reef and it sounds like the beating of a drum. Gu in Chinese means drum, and lang waves.   6. Only electricity-powered vehicles are allowed on the island, so the environment is free from noise and gas pollution.   7. Visitors can see many works left by poets in history, the Memorial Hall of Zheng Chenggong and Shuzhuang Garden on Gulangyu Island.

IV 1. Located 2. professional 3. covering 4. collection 5. historical 6. paintings 7. variety
    8. exhibition 9. tourists 10. composed

V 1. Mt. Jinggang is one of the sacred places for the Chinese revolution. 2. On August 1, 1927, the
   Communist Party of China led the famous Nanchang Uprising in Nanchang, the capital city of
   Jiangxi Province. 3. The Cloud-and-Fog Tea from Mt. Lushan was a tribute to the royal court in
   the Song Dynasty. 4. Jingdezhen, known as "the capital of china", began to produce porcelain in
   as early as Tang Dynasty. 5. Jiangxi Province, known as "the land of fish and rice", is also famous
   for tea, sugar canes, fruits and so on.

Lesson 20

II 1. F 2. F 3. T 4. T 5. T 6. F

III 1. In 2. with 3. with 4. on 5. to 6. and 7. as 8. from 9. for 10. as

IV

— Do you have any plan for this May Day vacation?

— I want to travel to Henan.

— Really? There are a lot of places of interest in Henan, such as the Yin Ruins, Longmen Grottoes,
    Shaolin Temple and so on.

— Besides places of interest, Luoyang peony is also famous.

— Yes. We have the saying "The peony in Luoyang is the most beautiful under heaven". Since
    1983, Henan has held Luoyang Peony Festival every year.

— I will definitely go to see "the King of Flowers". Oh, do you know some specialties in Henan? I
    want to buy some for my family and friends.

— There are many. When I went to Henan last year, I bought some cracked mushrooms grown in
    Biyang County in Henan. They are great.

V 龙门石窟位于洛阳市南八英里处。公元494年，北魏的一位皇帝从今天的山西大同迁都到洛阳后，工
   匠们开始在此修建佛窟。因此这里的佛窟是大同云冈石窟的延伸。龙门石窟的修建持续了几个朝
   代。在1,300个洞里，有40座小佛塔，大约100,000尊佛像，这些佛像大到57英尺，小到1英寸不等。
   这些洞窟和石像与云冈石窟、敦煌石窟在中国佛教文化中具有同样的历史意义。

Lesson 21

II 1. It is as light as mist and as fine as gossamer. 2. Because its drawing technique is very
    advanced and the place marks are very similar to those on a modern map. 3. Because the
    body of this tomb's owner and other articles buried with the dead were perfectly preserved for
    more than 2,000 years. 4. It is the best preserved painting of its kind from the Han Dynasty
    with the highest artistic value in China. 5. Because of its marvelous natural scenery, rare plants
    and animals and famous legends such as the mysterious "Wild Man" said to be found in the
    mountains. 6. It was named after Shennong, one of the two ancestors of Chinese people who
    invented crockery and discovered herbal medicine. 7. Many are white animals. 8. The mystery

of the Wild Man.

Ⅲ 1. Seen　2. flight　3. glowing　4. reflections　5. carved　6. providing　7. generally
8. renamed　9. rebuilt　10. inspiration

Ⅳ Legend has it that in Wuchang, there used to be a wine shop opened by a young man named Xin (辛). One day, a Taoist priest, in gratitude for free wine, drew a magic crane on the wall of the shop with orange peel and ordered it to dance whenever it heard clapping. Thousands of people came to see the spectacle and the wine shop was always full of guests. 10 years later, the Taoist priest revisited the wine shop. He played the flute and the crane came down from the wall and then he rode on the crane and flew away. In memory of the supernatural encounter, the Xins built a tower and named it Yellow Crane Tower.Destroyed many times in history, the tower was rebuilt time and again until 100 years ago when it was, for the last time, reduced to ashes. The present tower is a complete reconstruction and is the result of four years of work beginning in 1981. The new Yellow Crane Tower is regarded as the symbol of Wuhan city.

Lesson 22

Ⅱ 1. The 56 ethnic groups of China live in different parts of China and it is difficult to experience each ethnic group's architecture, their festivals and taste their snacks during one single visit. But the Chinese Folk Cultural Village in Shenzhen will help solve this problem.　2. Because of their nomadic living habits, Mongols live in yurts which are not only cool in summer and warm in winter but easy to set up or take apart.　3. The construction of the Ling Canal.　4. The symbolic landscape in Guilin is a water buffalo leisurely working in the rice paddies, with buffalo boys on their back against the misty but graceful green mountains as background.　5. The colorful village life, the unique customs and festivals of the different minority peoples.

Ⅲ 1. Different from (Unlike)　2. lacks the grandness of the Great Wall　3. natural beauty　4. at home and abroad　5. "the Oriental Hawaii"　6. in the southernmost part of China　7. 35,000 square kilometers　8. is regarded as　9. a return to nature　10. ethnic minorities

Ⅳ 1. to　2. around　3. to　4. of　5. As　6. into　7. into　8. into　9. to　10. on

Ⅴ 1. 西街是阳朔最古老的街道,有1400多年的历史。西街位于阳朔县的中心,自20世纪80年代以来,西街已成为一扇中西文化之窗,每年吸引大约十万名外国游客来感受它独特的文化融合。有时候,西街的外国人比中国人的数量还要多,因此西街也被称作"洋人街"或"地球村"。除了阳朔方言,英语已经成了人们的日常用语。来西街的中国人会以为他们在国外,而外国游客却来此寻求中国的古代文明。然而,无论你是中国人还是外国人,西街都是个绝好的地方来放松自己的身心。西街将驱走你所有的压力和负担,让你平静地看待生活。不同的时间西街会呈现不同的面貌:早晨时分平静安宁;傍晚时分时髦新潮。去西街旅游是任何游客都不应错过的经历。

2. With a pleasant average temperature of 25.5℃ all year round, Yalong Bay is situated in the southernmost part of Hainan Province, 25 kilometers away from the tropical seaside tourist city, Sanya. The scenery is amazing, with endless rolling hills, serene gulfs, clear blue sea and

silvery sand beaches — three times as long as any in Hawaii. With several well-preserved coral reefs, tropical fish of varied kinds, colors and shapes live here. The ocean is crystal clear, allowing visitors to view underwater sights up to 10 meters deep from the surface.

Lesson 23

II 1. The former got its name because legend has it that nine dragons were trapped in the cave; the latter got its name because according to the legend the nine dragons quarreled bitterly about the ownership of the cave, and the people came to the bank of the stream to scold them for disturbing them.   2. The figures describe the cave's length, height, width, the height of the tallest stalagmite and the area of the third hall in the cave.   3. The Multi-Color Lake. The water in the lake shows different colors.   4. It never overflows in rainy summer and fall, and never dries up in winter and spring.   5. It's well known for its colorful lakes, snow mountains, valleys and virgin forests.   6. Because in sunlight the water of the numerous colorful ponds along the valley has a shining golden color and it looks like a golden dragon rushing out of the forest.   7. Because many people have recovered from diseases after drinking or bathing in its water.

III

1. 黄果树瀑布群由18个瀑布组成。大瀑布是亚洲最大的瀑布,约高74米,宽81米。隐藏在大瀑布后面的是134米长的水帘洞,洞中遍布神奇的钟乳石。水帘洞由5个洞厅,6个洞窗,3股洞泉和6个通道组成。雨季降雨充足时,大瀑布以万马奔腾的气势倾泻进犀牛潭。从水帘洞看出去,瀑布像一幅巨大的帘子挂在洞前。有人说,那就像银河从天而降,震得悬崖瑟瑟发抖。从洞窗伸出手,你可以触摸到几泻而下的溪水。而在干季时,溪水会分成几条细流沿悬崖峭壁落下,犹如仙女柔软的头发,迷人而优雅。透过六个洞窗,你可以从不同的角度观赏瀑布。天气晴好时,景色尤为动人:一条彩虹跨在瀑布上方,蒙蒙的雾气慢慢飘荡在山谷上空。在瀑布对面的山上有一处凉亭,游客们可以从那里观赏大瀑布飞流直下的壮丽全景。

2. In normal situations, a giant panda is always very tender and tame, just like a shy lady. When it meets strangers, it often covers its face with a palm, or lowers its head to hide its face. Therefore, the giant panda is also called "miss panda". It seldom has the initiative (主动) to attack other animals or human beings. If it happens to encounter a human in the wildness, it always tries to avoid direct contact. However, it's another case when the panda becomes a mother. A mother panda is very easy to get irritated (激怒), using her teeth and claws to protect her little baby, even when some visitors are just trying to see her baby for care purposes. Sometimes the panda likes dressing itself, or doing things to make itself comfortable. For example, the panda often relaxes itself by stretching its belly and then arching (使成拱形) its back, just like a cat. Besides, the panda will stretch its front limbs and yawn after waking up. If the panda is soaked with water, or after it wades across a river, it will shake water off its body like a dog.

Lesson 24

Ⅱ 1. F 2. F 3. T 4. F 5. F 6. F 7. T 8. T

Ⅲ 1. about 2. like 3. with 4. off 5. from 6. into 7. for 8. of 9. in 10. from

Ⅳ 1. traveling 2. was built 3. to drive 4. finished 5. connecting 6. hovers 7. tallest 8. central 9. were 10. convenience

Ⅴ 1. which is located at the foot of Western Hill to the southwest of Kunming 2. covering an area of more than 300 square kilometers 3. the sixth largest fresh water lake in China 4. Dianchi Lake is a favorite attraction for visitors 5. just like thousands of silver fish swimming and playing 6. Dianchi Lake lies in silence and breathes in peace as if asleep. 7. Stretching along the west bank of the lake 8. Legend has it that 9. that they became Dianchi Lake 10. Western Hill is a pleasant place for a stroll beside the picturesque lake

Ⅵ 喝青稞酒时,应保持上身挺直,双手端酒碗,直视前方,听主人家唱一支歌。歌罢,你说几句客气话,用右手拿着碗,将左手第三指在酒中蘸三次,然后向空中弹三次酒,作为对佛的奉献,然后将剩余的酒倒掉。如果主人家请你三口喝完一杯酒你应该先呷两口,第三次将杯中的酒一饮而尽。如果你不想再喝了,在向空中弹酒三次后,就舔一下你的手指,主人家就会明白你的意思。如果客人不能喝太多或者喝多了感到不适,就应该向主人家解释清楚。西藏高原氧气稀薄,不建议大家过量饮酒。

Lesson 25

Ⅱ 1. T 2. T 3. T 4. F 5. F 6. T 7. F 8. F

Ⅲ 1. Andy Lau is a famous movie star in Hong Kong. 2. To be frank, I don't like going traveling in my holidays. 3. In recent years, the development in the coastal areas is very exciting. 4. How do you usually kill time at your weekends? 5. They began to sing loudly in celebration of the victory of their soccer team.

Ⅳ 台湾岛富含110多种矿产资源,其中主要矿产有煤炭、石油、天然气、金、银、铜、硫。此外,台湾地热资源丰富,植物种类繁多,森林面积占全岛陆地面积的52%,在中国排第一位。台湾水资源也很丰富。台湾的珊瑚产量占世界总产量的80%,所以赢得了"珊瑚王国"的美誉,台湾还是世界上主要的蝴蝶出口地区之一。

Lesson 26

Ⅱ 1. In the year 2009. 2. Flood control. 3. By generating cleaner hydropower. 4. Because with the help of the reservoir behind the Dam, the upper reaches waterway will be suitable for large ships and low water level seasons won't affect shipping any more. 5. The largest hydroelectric project and the largest construction project in the world. 6. It is the only magnificent yellow waterfall. 7. The river suddenly narrows and drops into a pond like water being poured from a kettle. 8. Because of the lucrative trade of silk along the road. 9. Paper making and printing technologies. 10. Because it was mainly used for transporting spices.

Ⅲ 1. F 2. F 3. F 4. F 5. F 6. T 7. T 8. F

IV 1. Generally 2. Running 3. through 4. nurturing 5. mighty 6. like 7. into 8. engineering 9. for 10. irrigation 11. generating 12. ending 13. excessive 14. over/above 15. surrounding

V 1. that are often capped by fog or clouds 2. are flanked by continuous rows of strange peaks, many of them rising into the clouds 3. that resembles a sculpture of a graceful girl looking down at the boats in the river 4. about ten meters high and six meters round 5. guiding sailing boats through the gorge and easing the Yangtze River's infamous floods 6. At dawn and dusk, Goddess Peak is often immersed in glowing clouds

Lesson 27

II 1. In its ingredients and in the process by which it is produced. 2. First, Chinese decorators separate each color with a dark outline, but European artists blend colors together with no separating line. Second, Europeans use decorations purely for their artistic value, but Chinese decorations are symbolic too. 3. Because it involves so many skills. 4. The inside painting. 5. Glass.

III 1. T 2. F 3. F 4. F 5. T

IV

— Welcome to our store. What can I do for you?

— Could you please tell me why there are so many pots with flowers, roots and small stones in them?

— Oh, they are called potted landscapes. In China, a potted landscape is often compared to a 3-dimensional picture.

— You mean it can form a picture from any angle?

— Yes. Please look at this one. The tree collected from the mountains is centuries-old. The gardener put its root into this pot and spent three years shaping it into the present form.

— Amazing! Look! It has so many branches and so many beautiful flowers!

— Chinese people believe a person's temperament will be influenced when he is enjoying the beauty of a potted landscape.

— Really? I will buy one as a birthday present for my wife. I'm sure she will love it.

V 中国瓷器的出口比通常认为的要久远得多。瓷器诞生于商朝(公元前17世纪—公元前1046年),并且一直是中国特有的一种手工艺品。陶瓷工艺在唐代达到鼎盛时期,瓷器也开始被销往亚洲其他国家和欧洲各国。它曾经是丝绸之路上最受欢迎的贸易品之一,深受欧洲贵族阶层的喜爱。慢慢的,用来泛指陶瓷制品的 "china" 一词被用来命名最早制造最优质瓷器的古老国度——中国。

Lesson 28

II 1. The Yin Dynasty. 2. Because the earliest seals bear the curly script which is called zhuan. 3. Shoushan stones from Shoushan County, Fuzhou City and "chicken's blood" stones from Zhejiang Province. 4. Free hand brushwork (xieyi) and detailed brushwork (gongbi).

5. Landscapes, figures and birds-and-flowers.

Ⅲ 1. Most of them are children picking fruits, representing good harvest in the coming new year.   2. It's a kind of hope that good luck will be brought home, right?   3. tell folk tales or legends by drawing paintings   4. Which ones do you prefer?   5. Please wrap them for me.

Ⅳ 1. To practice calligraphy, the four treasures of the study are required.   2. Seal engraving is a traditional Chinese art.   3. We have a veteran seal engraver here who can engrave the seal for you.   4. A main difference between oil painting and Chinese painting is that the former is created by colors while the latter by lines.   5. The realism in Chinese paintings is a subjective expression.

Ⅴ 中国书法和国画是紧密联系在一起的,因为二者都用到线条。中国人把简单的线条变成了一种高度发达的艺术形式。线条不光用来勾勒轮廓,也用来表达艺术家的思想和情感。他们用各种不同的线条来表达不同的主题,达到不同的目的。这些线条或直或弯,或刚或柔,或粗或细,或浅或深,墨汁可稠,也可稀。线条的使用是使国画独具一格的因素之一。

Lesson 29

Ⅱ 1. Su Embroidery, Shu Embroidery, Xiang Embroidery and Yue Embroidery.   2. Its uniqueness is that it is patterned after a painting draft, but is not limited by it.   3. Hundreds of Birds Worshiping the Phoenix.   4. 25 to 28 days.   5. During the Warring States Period.

Ⅲ 1. This is a famous brand with a history of hundreds of years.   2. They are all hand-made.
3. Do these shoes come in size eight and a half?   4. These shoes sell well. We sell as many as we get in.   5. We don't bargain at our store.   6. Court officials in the past liked shoes of this brand.
7. sounds like many successive promotions.   8. Let's have a look at these embroidered shoes over there. I'm sure you'll find them very Chinese.   9. Do embroidered shoes have to be worn with Chinese style clothes to look good?   10. I think they look good with jeans, too.

Ⅳ

1. Shu Brocade made in Sichuan originated from Han Dynasty and reached its heyday in Wei, Jin, Sui and Tang Dynasties. Red is the predominate color of Shu Brocade. Yun Brocade appeared in Jiankang (today's Nanjing) in the Northern and Southern Dynasties and was greatly developed during Yuan Dynasty. The wide use of gold and silver threads gained the brocade the name of Yun. In Yuan, Ming and Qing Dynasties Yun Brocade was a royal tribute. Zhuang Brocade is the creation of the Zhuang nationality in Guangxi. It features rich colors. The phoenix, the symbol of auspiciousness, takes a dominant role in these designs.

2. "春蚕到死丝方尽,蜡炬成灰泪始干。"这首唐诗精确地描述了蚕的特点。尽管科技已有了很大的发展,一只蚕在它二十八天的生命里只能吐1,000米(3,280英尺)长的蚕丝。原材料的稀缺这一因素决定了蚕丝的价值和神秘色彩。

Lesson 30

Ⅱ 1. Qipao usually is made of delicate materials with a high and tight fitting collar; qipao generally has two big slits at either side of the lower hem. Nearly all colors can be used. Often qipao gets a certain pattern, such as dragons, flowers, butterflies or other typical Chinese icons for prosperity and wealth.

2. The collar of qipao is high and tight fitting, not just for preventing coldness but also for beauty. The collar of qipao generally takes the shape of a semicircle, its right and left sides being symmetrical, making the soft and slender neck of a woman more attractive.

3. Because people believed in the power of jadeware to give people a long life. They thought they would live forever if they had jadeware. Therefore, the practice of burying the dead with jadeware became common.

4. The jadeware technique peaked in Qing Dynasty.

5. Bats and gourds were often used as a basis for more than 100 patterns.

6. The value of a jade object depends on the skills and reputation of craftsmen, the dates of carving, peculiar modeling and the owner's status.

III 1. with Chinese characters on them   2. What size would you like   3. How about trying it on for size   4. Black ones only come in medium   5. what a pity   6. I think it suits you too   7. It must be very comfortable to wear   8. You have a good eye

IV 蜡染布料可以做成衣服、围巾、背包、台布、床罩、窗帘和其他的装饰物品。不过，由于蜡染的原料是纯棉布，保存时要小心防止潮湿和腐蚀。倘若是买来收藏的，需要定期晒晒太阳。蜡染可以随时用水洗，但切记不要漂白，也不可以机洗以免损坏布沿。洗后可以熨烫。蜡染织物应该保存于干净整洁的环境中。如果使用和保存恰当，蜡染织物会使你的住所和办公室独特而怡人。

V Legend has it that in the Spring and Autumn Period, a man named Bian He from the State of Chu had obtained a piece of jade at Mount Jing in present-day Hubei Province and presented it to King Li. However, it was regarded as a stone by the king's artisans. Feeling insulted, King Li had Bian He's left foot cut off and drove him away. When King Wu succeeded the throne, Bian He presented the jade to the throne again. The same thing happened, and this time he lost his right foot. Then King Wen was enthroned. Bian He, with the jade in his arms, was seen at the foot of Mount Jing with bleeding eyes after crying bitterly for three days and nights. Hearing about him, King Wen was curious and sent someone to ask him, "There are many people who have lost their feet, but why is that only you are so sorrowful? " The man sighed, "I am sad not because I have lost my feet, but because my jade has been mistaken for a stone, a loyal subject for a mean one." King Wen had the jade cut in public, and a precious piece of jade appeared. It was named Heshibi — He Family's Jade. Over four centuries later, the jade was very popular and then obtained by the ruler of the State of Zhao. When the ruler of Qin heard about it, he offered to trade 15 of his walled towns for the jade. The ruler of Zhao then sent a minister Lin Xiangru to take the jade over to Qin which was stronger than the State of Zhao. When the minister found that the ruler of Qin was not really serious about the trade, the minister managed to bring the jade back to Zhao, relying on his resourcefulness and bravery. This is the origin of the idioms "jiazhiliancheng"(meaning as valuable as walled towns) and "wanbiguizhao" (meaning to return the Jade intact to the State of Zhao).

Lesson 31

II 1. Why do the performers sing in such piercing voices? 2. This has something to do with its origin. 3. I guess the bright colors of their costumes are also used to attract the audience's attention. 4. The sharply contrasting colors made it easier for the audience to see the performance clearly. 5. Different facial paintings represent different personalities of the characters. 6. In a word, the makeup in the opera reveals the characters voicelessly. 7. I noticed different characters sang and acted differently. 8. They are some special terms for different role types. 9. Each type has its own makeup and fixed singing and acting styles. 10. It's a term we Chinese use to mean the non-professional Beijing Opera singers and performers.

III 1. F 2. F 3. F 4. T 5. F 6. F 7. T

IV 1. 1—d 2—c 3—a 4—b 5—e 6—h 7—f 8—g
2. 1—h 2—a 3—c 4—b 5—i 6—l 7—f 8—k 9—d 10—j 11—e 12—g

V 昆剧，也叫昆山腔或昆曲，起源于江苏省昆山地区。它是中国古典戏曲之一，有着500多年的历史。昆曲拥有一套完整的表演体系以及自己独特的旋律。它众多的演出曲目中有许多精美优雅的曲子。乐队由传统乐器组成，包括笛子，箫，笙和琵琶。笛子是一种横向吹奏的竹制管乐器，演奏主旋律；箫是一种竖笛。笙是一种用来吹奏的风琴。琵琶是一种弹拨弦乐器。许多中国戏剧都深受昆曲旋律和表演风格的影响。

Lesson 32

II 1. Generally speaking, they can be divided into two basic groups: those using internal energy or Qi as the primary source of power for movement and those using external energy i.e. muscle power.

2. It emphasizes basic external training of hands, eyes, body, stances, steps and coordination as well as internal training of energy, spirit, breath and strength.

3. A person needs a strong will and persistence to learn Kung Fu well.

4. No. Kung Fu should be learnt systematically. After acquiring a solid foundation of the basic skills, one can choose a sect or routine.

5. Kung Fu artists advocate virtue and peace, not aggression or violence.

6. People now practice Tai Chi for both its defense function and its health benefits.

7. Meeting yang with yin in combat, or in other aspects of our life, is a primary goal of Tai Chi training.

8. Tai Chi makes you focus on the movements of your limbs and the flow of your breath and energy inside your body. This brings about mental calm and clarity and improves people's overall health.

9. Force in Tai Chi lies in coordination and relaxation, rather than muscular tension and it is used to neutralize, yield or initiate attacks.

10. It has spread to more than 150 countries and regions among a population of more than 2 billion.

III 1. to   2. with   3. as   4. to   5. in   6. of   7. of   8. by   9. for   10. by

IV 自然界的任何一方面都存在着两个对立面。当这两个对立面处于平衡时，自然界就处于完美的和谐状态。在中国文化中，阴阳理论常常被用来描述这种现象。每个积极面都对应着一个消极面；有热必然有冷，有暗自会有明，有善就会有恶。当然这样解释气功过于简单化了。气功的深度和错综复杂足以写成几本书，仅凭研读来理解气功，学者们也许要花几个世纪时间。因此，气功绝对是一种应该尝试而不是仅仅通过研读来了解的东西。

Lesson 33

II

1. (Students have to summarize paragraph 2 of Reading Passage 1)

2. Blood, or xue in TCM, is a term that refers to the material basis of qi or the body itself. In modern medicine, blood refers to the fluid that circulates in the body carrying oxygen and nutrition to different parts of the body.

3. TCM diagnoses are based on overall observation of human symptoms.

4. TCM diagnose on the basis of observation without instruments and without harming the patient.

5. What is now TCM is an enormously rich resource, with literally thousands of years of experience, as refined by the intense thought, analysis and practice of some of the most intelligent human beings there have ever been.

III 1. F   2. F   3. F   4. T   5. T   6. T

IV 1. therapy   2. solid   3. stimulate   4. imbalances   5. blockages   6. disorders   7. traumatic injuries   8. surgery   9. adjunctive   10. efficacy

V

1. Tuina has been used in China for 2,000 years. It makes use of the traditional Chinese medical theory of the flow of qi through the meridians as its basic guideline. Through the application of massage and manipulation techniques, tuina seeks to establish a more harmonious flow of qi through the system, allowing the body to naturally heal itself.

2. 在典型的拔罐治疗中，医生将棉团或其他可燃物浸入酒精，点燃后放进玻璃拔罐器中使之受热。在拔罐中燃烧物质清除了罐中的空气，从而产生真空。在可燃物燃烧时，拔罐器被翻转过来放在患者身体特定部位上。因缺少空气而产生的真空将拔罐器固定在患者皮肤上并随着罐中空气冷却将皮肤向上抽拉。据说使皮肤向上拱起会使毛孔打开，这一结果将促使血液循环，平衡身体里气的流动，打通堵塞之处，并形成一种通道使体内毒素被吸出体外。

Lesson 34

II 1. F   2. T   3. F   4. T   5. F   6. F   7. F   8. F   9. T   10. T

III 1. 只有经过媒人的介绍，而且双方父母认为两个家庭情况相似、门当户对时，婚姻程序才有可能继续下去。   2. 男方赠送大量的礼物给女方家以表示对女方的尊敬和善意，同时显示有能力为女孩提供优越的生活。   3. 但是现在中国的年轻人往往点点头就表示问候。从某种程度上说，这种变化反映了现代日益加快的生活节奏。 4. 随着越来越多的外资公司和个人来开发中国市场，人们最好事先了解一下中国人在商务接洽及谈判时的习惯做法。 5. 中国人认为守时是一种美德并会尽量做到守时，在商界尤其如此。中国人通常会提前一点到达以显示其诚意。如果你在约定时间后十分钟之内到达，也不会被认为是迟到。

IV 1. China has often been referred to as a nation of etiquette. 2. In order to avoid unnecessary mistakes and embarrassment in communications, a better understanding of Chinese etiquette is essential. 3. The grip should be firm, but not overly strong, and should not be prolonged because Chinese, like other Asians, prefer a brief handshake. 4. It is a subtlety that is not openly discussed in Chinese society, but exists as a communicative skill nevertheless. 5. it is important to both private and business relationships. 6. Though even numbers are considered lucky, the number four is an exception. 7. If the recipient does not open your gift right away, it does not mean that he or she is not interested in it. 8. If you are truly full, you had better refuse directly; otherwise, the hospitable hosts will continue to refill your bowl.

Lesson 35

II 1. It simply means passed or survived Nian. Legend has it that there used to be an evil beast called Nian. It came out to eat people and spread destruction on the first day of the first lunar month. People suffered greatly but no one could defeat it. One year, an old man came up with a clever idea. He organized the people to dress themselves in bright red color and collected some dried bamboo and then waited for the arrival of Nian. As soon as Nian appeared, they set the bamboo on fire, which produced explosive noises when the bamboo cracked in the fire. Meanwhile, the people beat drums and shouted to make louder noises. The beast was frightened by the red color, the flame and the loud noises. It fled and never dared to come again. That's why we also call the Spring Festival "guonian".

2. Originally, people burnt dried bamboo to make cracking noises so we call modern firecrackers "baozhu", which means "explosive bamboo".

3. Because jiaozi has the shape of ancient Chinese gold or silver ingot, and stands for wealth, while wine and liquor are called "jiu" in Chinese, which sounds like the Chinese word for longevity.

4. The story is in Reading Passage 1.

5. Because the full moon is round and symbolizes reunion, the Mid-Autumn Festival is also known as the festival of reunion.

6. The festival is based on the theory of yin and yang, the two opposing principles in nature. Numbers are related to this theory. Even numbers belong to yin and odd numbers to yang. The ninth day of the ninth lunar month is a day when two largest yang digits meet. So it is called Chongyang. Chong means double in Chinese.

7. The key lies in the story in Reading Passage 2.

8. Since nine is the largest digit, people take two of them together to signify longevity. Therefore,

the ninth day of the ninth month has become a special day for people to pay their respects to the elderly and a day for the elderly to enjoy themselves. It has also been declared China's Day for the Elderly.

Ⅲ 1. Yuanxiao Festival is the first time when we see the full moon in the New Year.   2. Lanterns of various shapes and sizes are hung in the streets, attracting countless visitors.   3. Lantern owners write riddles on pieces of paper and paste them on the lanterns.   4. As riddle guessing is interesting and full of wisdom, it is popular among people all over the country.   5. At night, in addition to the magnificent lanterns, fireworks form another beautiful scene.   6. When the first full moon of the New Year climbs up slowly, people become really fascinated by the silvery moonlight and the beautiful fireworks.   7. Yuanxiao is small balls made of glutinous rice flour.   8. What's more, tangyuan in Chinese has a similar pronunciation with "tuanyuan", meaning reunion.

Ⅳ 清明，即清澈、明亮，是哀悼死者的日子。清明节是每年的四月五日，正好是天气回暖、春播及举家出游的开始之时。古代中国，清明绝对不是祭奠祖先唯一的日子。事实上，祭祀仪式举行得很频繁，除了重要的节假日之外，大约每两个星期就有一次。总的说来，祭祀仪式复杂多样，耗费大量时间和金钱。为了削减这种支出，唐玄宗于公元732年宣布只有在清明节这一天才能到祖先坟前进行正式的祭祀仪式。这一传统一直延续至今。

Lesson 36

Ⅱ 1. F   2. F   3. T   4. F   5. T

Ⅲ 1. above   2. on   3. longest   4. built   5. running   6. at   7. in   8. in   9. between   10. cultural

Ⅳ 乘火车旅行适合那些喜欢在旅途中消磨时光的游客。自驾游听起来可能更自由更方便，但乘火车旅行也有其自己的优势。首先，乘火车旅行时，你会在火车上遇到许多新朋友，与你分享他们的经历，这样你就不会感到寂寞和无聊。其次，透过火车窗户欣赏沿途的风景也是一种视觉上的享受。 此外，你可以有足够的时间来思考你关心或感兴趣的事情。最后同样重要的一点是，乘火车旅行比自驾游更轻松，因为你不必担心路上是否会有交通拥堵或者油箱里是否有足够的汽油。